I0003458

Emacs Writing Studio

Emacs Writing Studio

A Practical Guide to Plain Text Writing and Publishing

Peter Prevos

Third
Hemisphere
Publishing

Kangaroo Flat, Australia

ⓒ Peter Prevos (2025)

Kangaroo Flat, Australia
peterprevos.com

ISBN 978-0-9875669-9-7 (Paperback)

This work is licensed under a Creative Commons *Attribution-Share Alike 3.0 Australia* license. You are free to share—to copy, distribute, and transmit the work under the following conditions:

ⓘ *Attribution*: You must attribute the work in the manner specified by the author (but not in any way that suggests that they endorse you or your use of the work).

ⓢ *Share Alike*: If you alter, transform, or build upon this work, you may distribute the resulting work only under the same or similar license to this one.

Written in Emacs Org Mode. Typeset in LaTeX.

Contents

vi

Foreword

With *Emacs Writing Studio* you have what you need to get started with writing. The book and the concomitant configuration for Emacs provide a solid foundation for you to organise your ideas, capture information, and elucidate your thoughts.

This book provides an overview of Emacs' capabilities for writers. It does it in a way that is approachable. You get the essentials and are then guided through the various facets of the workflow.

Consider *Emacs Writing Studio* a companion on a long journey. It helps you get started with Emacs and will be there for you as a valuable reference when you need to do something a little bit more advanced but forgot how to proceed.

What you get at the outset is a curated experience. This is exactly what you need to get on with the task of writing: it minimises distractions. Though do not think of it as a constraint: you are still using Emacs — a powerful tool that can be reprogrammed or extended to do more with text and related patterns of interaction.

The *Emacs Writing Studio* setup consists of sensible defaults. You will not be locked in to a bespoke system. This is the standard Emacs experience and you are free to modify it to your liking.

You can always find more resources to address whatever issue you may have. Beside the official manual of Emacs, you will discover a rich corpus of knowledge produced by the community. There are blog posts, drawings, and video demonstrations. They will all apply to what you have here.

No configuration can be a replacement for the work you put in. This is true for your time using Emacs but also for writing in general. Do not come with the expectation that *Emacs Writing Studio* will do miracles for you: it will not make you an Emacs expert overnight and it will not boost your creativity without you doing anything.

This is a tool that has been tested and proven to work well. Like every tool, it must be used properly by someone who has the requisite skills or is willing to acquire them through continuous practice. As a beginner, you will not know much: the book is here to ensure that you find the information you need to keep going.

The expectation you can have is that *Emacs Writing Studio* will deliver on its promise of giving you a set of tools for authoring your next works. It will do it in a reliable way. The rest is up to you: conduct the research and start creating.

Beside the technicalities, this book will make you think about matters of method. It does it indirectly through the functions it describes. You then have to consider how each of those will fit in to your workflow.

Piecing together a set of tools or procedures is part of the process of discovery that authors must go through. Through trial and error, you figure out what works for you. You may then stick with it and strongly prefer it over alternative approaches. Whether your methods are appropriate for others does not really matter: you know that one size does not fit all.

Emacs is the perfect tool for those who want to be particular with their writing. It is highly configurable and will grow with you as a user to always match your current level. If you do ever get the chance to learn some Emacs Lisp, you will realise that there is so much you can do to tweak every little thing exactly how you want it to be.

The key to learning your way around Emacs is to be patient and methodical. Try one thing at a time, learn how to use it, and then move on to the next one. This is why *Emacs Writing Studio* is helpful: it lets you experiment at your own pace while giving you something that works well out-of-the-box.

Remember that you are just getting started and you will be here long-term. Good luck!

Protesilaos "Prot" Stavrou

Preface

My writing journey started in the early 1990s with paper diaries to record my random thoughts and as a travel diary. Paper notebooks are great, and I still use them today as the primary place to gather thoughts. The only disadvantage of paper notebooks is finding old information and linking bits and pieces together takes a lot of work. Besides my notebooks, I also amassed a paper archive, a library and a collection of photographs. Being a computing enthusiast, I have ever since searched for the ultimate digital tool to combine all these pieces of information into the ultimate personal knowledge management system.

Over the years, I have tried a multitude of computer applications to achieve this ideal state. I wanted something that stores information in an enduring format that does not rely on a brand of software. Ideally, it had to be searchable and a single application to undertake different tasks. I used to hop from application to application, jump from the action list to my schedule, and move on to the word processor, spreadsheet, PDF reader, etc. I managed a complex web of software tools to deliver a single project. Wouldn't it be nice if there was one program that could help you with all your tasks?

My online research always pointed towards Emacs. I tried to use it in the early 2000s but quickly gave up due to the steep learning curve. About eight years ago, I tried again, and this time, I was helped by a steady flow of websites and instructional videos to get me started. Over the following years, I studied Emacs and configured it to write and publish articles and books. As I further explored the capabilities of Emacs, I discovered not only a powerful writing tool but a vibrant community of enthusiasts and developers who continually contribute to its evolution. This sense of belonging has enriched my experience, inspiring me to push the boundaries of what I can achieve with Emacs. Emacs is to me like being in Willy Wonka's Chocolate Factory where almost everything is possible.

I developed *Emacs Writing Studio* (EWS) to meet my specific needs for writing this book and other projects. My commitment to crafting the EWS configuration, the website online videos and this book is driven by a desire to share the benefits of my journey with other authors. EWS is not just a tool, but a culmination of years of learning and experimentation. My aim is to write the book that I would have loved to read when I first came in contact with Emacs.

This book, which is both a guide to EWS and a product of its capabilities, has been rigorously tested and refined to ensure it meets the needs of large writing projects.

Emacs is known for its steep learning curve. Don't let it's reputation discourage you from giving the system a go. The main purpose of this book is to flatten the learning curve by providing a configured system as a starting point. Entrepreneur and author Seth Godin recently wrote on his blog:

> We've adopted the mindset of 'too busy to learn'. As a result, we prefer tools that give us quick results, not the ones that are worth learning.

Acknowledgements

The development and maintenance of a complex system like Emacs is a testament to the power of community. I am deeply grateful to the countless volunteers who have contributed to its core system's code and the abundance of packages. Their collective effort is what makes Emacs a thriving ecosystem.

My motivation for writing this book came from the inspiring work of people like Protesilaos (Prot) Stavrou, David Wilson from *System Crafters* and many others who helped me flatten the learning curve of my Emacs journey through their blogs and online videos.

Mastodon and Emacs users Harold Kirsch, Thomas Montfort, Ben Finney, Antonio Simón (Quijote Libre), Bob Irving and Frédéric Vachon have reviewed early versions of the book. Their feedback has helped to make this book both easier to read and more comprehensive, which is a fine balance to achieve. Erin's in-depth questions have helped me improve the explanations in this book.

Thanks to Oliver Roman, Stefan Kangas, Fredrik Salomonsson and Tomasz Hołubowicz for correcting typos.

Peter Prevos
Kangaroo Flat, 2025

Chapter I

Introduction

Over thousands of years, writing has moved from clay tablets and chiselling in stone to paper, computers, and, most recently, artificial intelligence. Before the advent of electronic writing, all an author needed was a notebook, a pen, and a typewriter. Being an author in the digital age is, in many ways, more complex than in the days of clay, stone, or paper.

Contemporary writers are often overwhelmed by the multitude of electronic tools, each serving a specific function. The information is scattered across various platforms and stored in incompatible formats, leading to a complex and time-consuming writing process. The relief from this complexity is one of the key benefits of Emacs.

Unfortunately, the previous paragraph describes how many students, authors, researchers and other writers manage their workflows. What if you could do this differently and use the same program to create written works from ideation to publication? This book introduces Emacs, a powerful tool that can assist with everything from sparking your initial ideas to publishing your finished article, book or website. Emacs lets you ditch the software juggling act and focus on your writing.

This book is for writers who want to break free from the constraints of conventional writing tools and embrace a more flexible, powerful, and customisable environment.

Whether you're a novelist weaving intricate tales of fiction or a researcher crafting detailed non-fiction, *Emacs Writing Studio* (EWS) offers a comprehensive guide to transforming your writing process.

1.1 Fiction writers

As a fiction writer, your imagination is your most valuable asset. You need a tool that can keep up with the fluidity of your ideas, allowing you to focus on crafting rich characters, intricate plots, and vivid worlds without distraction. With Emacs, you can maintain organised notes, drafts, and character sketches within a single environment.

The powerful search and replace functions, combined with customisable templates, let you easily manage consistency in character names, locations, and other critical details across your manuscript. When inspiration strikes, Emacs' minimalist interface enables you to dive straight into writing without the distraction of unnecessary graphical elements.

Neal Stephenson, an American writer of speculative fiction, refers to Emacs as a "thermonuclear word processor" (Stephenson, 1999), not in a way that destroys your writing in a ball of fire, but in its immense power compared to conventional writing tools.

1.2 Non-fiction writers

Non-fiction writing demands precision, organisation, and meticulous research. Whether you're working on a dissertation, a technical report, or a historical biography, Emacs provides you with the tools to effectively manage massive amounts of information. You can efficiently structure your research notes, manage bibliographies, and outline your work.

Emacs allows you to seamlessly integrate these elements into one application, ensuring that all your research is at your fingertips as you draft your work. The ability to export your manuscript to a range of formats, such as PDF or HTML, ensures that your work is ready for publication or sharing with peers without the hassle of format conversions.

1.3   Multitasking writers

In today's fast-paced world, many writers manage multiple projects. Emacs is the perfect tool for managing a diverse writing portfolio.

You can effortlessly switch between different projects, be it a short story, a research paper, or even your daily journal. Emacs' powerful task management features help you keep track of deadlines and tasks and track progress across all your writing endeavours.

1.4   Distracted writers

If you find yourself easily distracted by the features of modern writing software, Emacs offers a refreshing change. With its focus on plain text and keyboard-driven commands, Emacs provides a genuinely distraction-free environment where the only thing that matters is your words, allowing you to focus on your writing without interruptions.

Writing in Emacs brings you back to the days when the typewriter stood between the writer and the written words. But Emacs also has powerful editing capabilities, so there is no need for correction fluid.

1.5   Curious writers

Finally, this book is for those who are not just looking for a tool but for an opportunity to learn and grow as technology users. Emacs is not just software; it is a way of life. As you learn to use its powerful features, you develop new skills that enhance your writing process and overall productivity, inspiring you to explore new possibilities in your writing journey.

Emacs was initially conceived for software developers, but you don't need to be a computer wiz to use it as an author. This book flattens the steep learning curve, helping you unlock the full potential of Emacs as your ultimate writing companion.

Chapter 2

Why Emacs?

The official tagline of Emacs is that it is an "extensible self-documenting text editor". These somewhat opaque words barely do justice to Emacs because they focus on its original purpose as a software development tool. Emacs is a multi-purpose computing environment that can help you manage your information, track projects, write and publish articles, books, websites and any other text-based activity. Emacs is not a productivity hack; it is a productivity hacking system. Emacs is the Swiss army chainsaw of productivity tools.

The development of Emacs (short for "editor macros") systems started in the 1970s. Software that is so old might seem obsolete, but a vibrant community of developers continually improves the system. Emacs being extensible means that users configure it to their personal needs. An Emacs configuration instructs the system to behave the way you want it to, such as keyboard shortcuts and additional functionality. Emacs is also extensible through the thousands of freely available packages. An Emacs package is a plugin that adds new capabilities to the system or enhances existing ones, like an app on your phone.

Many versions of Emacs have existed over the decades. The currently most widely used version is GNU Emacs, first released by Richard Stallman in 1984 (Johnson, 2022;

Stallman, 1981b). GNU Emacs (further referred to as Emacs) is free software released by the Free Software Foundation. Free software is sometimes called 'libre software' to emphasise the freedom aspect over monetary value. The foundation loosely defines free software as:

> "Free software" means software that respects users' freedom and community. Roughly, it means that the users have the freedom to run, copy, distribute, study, change and improve the software. Thus, "free software" is a matter of liberty, not price. To understand the concept, you should think of "free" as in "free speech", not as in "free beer".

Emacs is a officially text editor, but this does not make sense to authors. From an author's perspective, Emacs is a text *processor* because editing is only one step in the writing process. A text editor is a tool for software developers to write code, and a text processor is a tool for authors to write prose. EWS is a bespoke configuration that transforms Emacs into a tool for researchers and authors.

2.1 Why use Emacs?

When working on a writing project, authors need a collection of tools to get the job done. They jot down notes in a research tool and meticulously build bibliographies in a database. Then, they write in a familiar word processor. To stay on top of their deadlines, they juggle a productivity tool for managing projects. Finally, after hours of focused work, the researcher might unwind with a quick game of Tetris to take a well-deserved break from the application circus.

The problem with this all to familiar workflow is that each program requires you to learn a new set of skills, navigate a different internal logic, and bend to its preordained workflow. Most software is inflexible, forcing you to adapt to the developer's vision of how you should work, besides some configuration options provided as a screen of tick boxes.

Emacs offers a revolutionary approach. You can write research notes, manage a bibliography, and, yes, even play Tetris — all within a single, unified environment. Imagine the convenience of mastering one set of commands instead of grappling with multiple programs. Emacs empowers you to configure and customise it to your preferences, transforming it from a mere writing tool into an extension of your personal workflow. Ditch the software juggling act and focus on what truly matters: your writing.

This statement may be misleading because Emacs requires the assistance of other software to function as a writing studio. Emacs is also an interface to other free software. You will thus need to install additional software so that Emacs can read and export to binary file formats such as PDF and audio or video files. Emacs also relies on external software for spell checking, advanced searching and generating diagrams.

While Emacs appears different from the eye candy of modern graphical software, there is a method to its apparent lack of sophistication. Don't be fooled by its austere façade. Beneath the surface lies a robust and meticulously crafted contemporary computing environment that you can bend into a distraction-free writing tool.

Another advantage is the longevity of this tool. How you use Emacs now will also be the way you use Emacs in decades to come. Reading the 1981 Emacs manual is almost like reading the most recent version, as the underlying basic functionality has changed only slightly (Stallman, 1981a).

Many writers have lamented the constraints of commercial word processors when tackling large documents. Working with this software can be a frustrating experience. These programs were first developed when paper memos and reports ruled the world and have changed little since. Graphical software emulates printed pieces of paper even though most people write for electronic mediums. Emacs breaks free from this paradigm by separating the content from the design. This liberating approach allows you to focus on crafting your ideas without getting bogged down in the design of the end product. As an added benefit, Emacs can transform the same text file effortlessly into a print-ready PDF, a website, or an e-book.

2.2 Malleable software

Emacs is a 'malleable software' platform, meaning you are free to change and enhance how it works. The first principle of malleable software is that it is easy to change. Advanced Emacs users can build bespoke applications using the Emacs version of the LISP language, also called Elisp (Monnier & Sperber, 2020). This task might sound daunting, but it is about the possibility. New Emacs users can configure almost everything in the system without knowledge of Elisp.

This book presents a no-code version of using Emacs. The last chapter and the appendix provide some guidance on how to start using Elisp, but you can use Emacs as an author without writing any code.

You will need to learn Emacs Lisp for more advanced applications. This knowledge requirement might seem like a hurdle, but knowing how to use it will give you nearly unlimited power over how you use your computer. Software should adjust to the user, not vice versa. Most Emacs users share what they have developed, so you can freely copy their work. You can also extend and configure Emacs with any of the thousands of freely available packages. EWS is a curated collection of such packages to meet the needs of authors.

The advantage of this approach is that you have complete freedom when using this software. You can instruct it to do almost anything you like and configure it to your specific needs, as long as you can do it with text. The disadvantage is that it requires a different approach than contemporary software. Using Emacs throws you back to the original intent of using a computer and genuine user-friendliness. Are you ready to change the way you use your computer? To paraphrase a famous scene from The Matrix:

> If you take the blue Microsoft pill, the story ends, and everything stays the same. If you take the purple Emacs pill, you stay in Wonderland, and I show you how deep the rabbit hole goes.

2.3 Redefining user-friendliness

Emacs' lack of a slick graphical interface might discourage new users. Unfortunately, most people confuse user-friendliness with a smooth design and using a mouse. However, the graphical approach is not user-friendly at all because it restricts freedom. Graphically driven software is a gilded cage. It might be pleasant to work in, but it is still a cage.

Emacs is a plain text processor that focuses on the semantic meaning of characters on the screen instead of how they will eventually appear on a page or screen. Plain text is not the same as plain English; it refers to the way information is stored. Plain text is the opposite of rich text, which hides the definitions for font sizes, colours and other attributes.

Plain text most commonly has a `.txt` extension and does not have any formatting such as bold text. Windows users might be familiar with the venerable Notepad software. However, there are other plain text formats, such as HTML, Markdown, LaTeX, and Org, that include an extensive range of capabilities to turn plain text into a work of art.

Plain text can be read across all computer systems, so you never have to worry about locking your writing into a proprietary format or being stuck using a particular software package. Anything you write in Emacs can be read with NotePad, TextEdit or any other such software. The only difference is that other programs don't have the versatility of Emacs. Plain text is not a niche application. This format has basically remained unchanged for decades and is unlikely to fade away in the future.

Text modes can also display 'graphics'. When at primary school in the 1970s, our teacher proudly showed us some computer art. The artwork consisted of printed alphanumeric characters that resembled an image, such as this kitten (source: asciiart.eu).

```
  /\_/\
 ( o o )
 ==_Y_==
   ‘_’
```

Some people still create ASCII art, as it is called to adorn computer code. However, there is no need to resort to these ancient techniques as Emacs can also display images in standard formats such as PNG and JPG.

Graphical interfaces simulate the physical world by making objects on the screen look like pieces of paper and folders on a desk. You point, click, and drag documents into folders; documents appear as they would on paper and when done, they are sent to the rubbish bin. Graphical interfaces are a magic trick that makes you believe you are doing something physical (Tognazzini, 1993). This approach might be convenient, but it prevents people from understanding how computers work. In word processors, the screen looks like a printed page. While this might be aesthetically pleasing, it distracts the writer from creating content and instead motivates them to fiddle with formatting.

Graphical software adheres to the *What You See is What You Get* (WYSIWYG). This means that the screen displays a document that resembles a paper page. This technique is only relevant when writing documents intended for printing. However, these days only a tiny part of electronic text is written for print, so the WYSIWYG approach does not make much sense in the digital age.

The graphical approach distracts the mind from the content. It lures the user into editing for style instead of writing text. Text in WYSIWYG software is referred to as rich text, as it encompasses both content and design. The formatting instructions in rich text are invisible to the user, which can cause issues in obtaining the final result to look how you want it to. Office workers around the globe waste oceans of time trying to format and typeset documents in graphical environments.

Plain text uses the *What You See is What You Mean* (WYSIWYM) approach. Instead of focusing on the design of the document, a WYSIWYM editor preserves the intended meaning of each element. Sections, paragraphs, illustrations, and other document elements are labelled as such using various conventions (Khalili & Auer, 2015). In plain text, the content and semantics are directly visible and changeable by the user.

Regular plain text files are the most rudimentary format and don't contain any semantics. Other plain text formats, such as HTML, LaTeX (pronounced *la-tech*, derived from the Greek word), Markdown, and Org, include instruction sets to define the final result (the markup). Table 2.1 shows how to denote *italic text* in four popular plain text formats.

Table 2.1: Italic text in common plain text formats.

Format	Italic semantics
HTML	`<i>Italic Text</i>`
LaTeX	`\emph{Italic Text}`
Markdown	`_Italic Text_`
Org mode	`/Italic Text/`

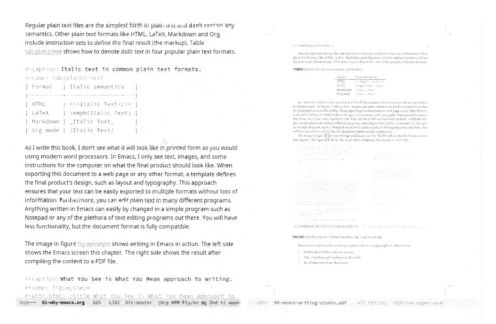

Figure 2.1: What You See is What You Mean approach to writing.

Using plain text helps you become more productive by not worrying about the document's design until you complete the content. The main benefit of using plain text over rich text is that it provides a distraction-free writing environment. As I write this book, I don't see what it will look like in printed form as you would using modern word processors. Emacs only displays text, images, and some instructions on what the design of the final product. When exporting this document to a web page or any other format, a template defines the final product's layout and typography. This approach ensures that your text can be easily exported to multiple formats. The image in figure 2.1 shows writing in Emacs in action. The left side shows the Emacs screen for part of this chapter. The right side shows the result after compiling the content to PDF.

The plain text indicators for tables, captions, references and so on are converted to the appropriate format, as defined by a template. This approach lets you focus on content. Once you have define a template, all typesetting and formatting will be done by the export function. Similar results can be achieved with HTML documents (including e-books) and word processor formats.

In summary, the benefits of writing in plain text over using graphical software are:

1. Independent of the software you use.

2. Text, metadata and markup are visible.

3. No distractions on the screen.

4. Ability to export to any format.

2.4   The learning curve

Emacs has a steep learning curve due to its vast universe of possible configurations. To make Emacs work for you, you must learn the basic principles and some of the associated add-on packages. Emacs is more complex than other plain text processors, but it also is much more potent than any other tool. However, with this great power comes great responsibility, so you must learn some new skills to use it as your writing tool.

The purpose of EWS is to flatten the learning curve. The best attitude is to be overwhelmed by the multitudinous possibilities and master only those functions that you need for the task at hand. Even without any configuration, Emacs can accomplish a great deal.

Emacs' methods and vocabulary seem foreign compared to other contemporary software. The main reason for these differences is that development started in the 1970s, a time when computing was notably different to our current experience. The Emacs vocabulary is vestigial, a remnant of an earlier epoch in the evolution of computing. For example, opening a file is 'visiting a file'. Pasting a text is 'yanking', and cutting it is the same as 'killing'. Emacs terminology is more poetic than craft terms such as cutting, pasting, and moving files between folders as if they were pieces of paper. These differences are not only part of Emacs' charm but also of its power. You will find that the Emacs equivalents of these familiar tasks are more potent that what is common in modern software. But this steep learning curve is worth its weight in gold, my personal mantra is that:

> The steeper the learning curve, the bigger the reward.

2.5   Advantages and limitations of Emacs

In summary, these are some of the significant advantages of using Emacs to create written content:

1. One piece of software to undertake most of your computing activities makes you more productive because you only need to master one system.

2. You store all your information in plain text files. You will never have any problems with esoteric file formats.

3. You can modify almost everything in the software to suit your workflow.

4. Emacs runs on all major operating systems: GNU/Linux, Windows, Chrome, and macOS.

5. Emacs is free (libre) software supported by a large community willing to help.

After singing the praises of this multi-functional editor, you would almost think that Emacs is the omnipotent god of software. Some people have even established the *Church of Emacs* as a mock religion to express their admiration for this supremely malleable software environment. Notwithstanding this admiration, Emacs has some limitations.

Emacs can display images and integrate them with text, but it has limited functionality in creating or modifying graphical files. If you need to create or edit pictures, consider using GIMP (GNU Image Manipulation Program). Video content is unsupported other than hyperlinks to a file or website. These limitations are excusable given that Emacs' core capability is processing text.

The second disadvantage is that Emacs does not include a fully operational web browser. You can surf the web within Emacs, but only within the limitations of a plain text interface. Reading websites in plain text also has some advantages by providing a distraction-free and secure browsing experience.

Lastly, Emacs risks becoming a productivity sink. Just because you can configure everything does not mean that you should. Don't spend too much time *on* your workflow. Spend this time *in* your workflow and write. Most productivity hacks do not materially impact your output because you write with your mind, not the keyboard.

2.6 The *Emacs Writing Studio* workflow

This book follows the typical workflow that researchers and authors use when preparing, writing and publishing a manuscript. The process of writing in real life is more often than not complex and chaotic, as it involves successive iterative cycles. An orderly pattern emerges when we step back from the details of the daily grind. We read literature and draw inspiration, develop new ideas, create new works, and publish the results. Even though reality is never as linear as this list suggests, it serves as a helpful guide to organise the content of this book (figure 2.2).

The basic principle of this workflow is that authors collect information from literature, the web, movies, and other sources (*inspiration*), which they process in a note-

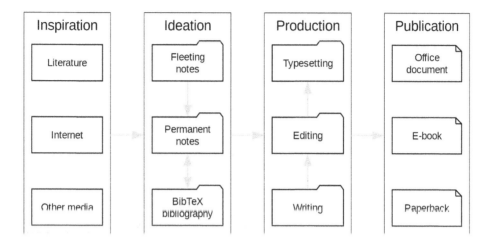

Figure 2.2: Emacs Writing Studio workflow.

taking system. These notes are the central repository of information and inspiration and can link to a bibliography (*ideation*). These ideas and notes form the foundation of the writing process (*production*). The author finally publishes the manuscript in its final format (*publication*).

These are the four productive phases of a typical writing project, but there is also some overhead to incur. At the end of a long day of writing and editing, authors must also perform some *Administration* to manage projects.

Inspiration

Ideas don't pop into minds out of thin air. Our thoughts, plans, and inspirations derive from our lived experiences and what we read, hear, or watch.

Emacs has extensive facilities to read any plain text format imaginable and display PDF files, e-books and images. However, as a text editor it has no facilities to directly work with these formats, so Emacs acts as an interface to other free software. Listening to a podcast or watching a video is impossible within Emacs, but it can provide an interface to integrate with multimedia applications.

You can also maintain a bibliography to organise and access your collection of electronic literature. Emacs can also browse the internet in plain text.

Chapter 5 discusses how to read e-books, surf the internet, and consume multimedia files with Emacs.

Ideation

Ingesting all these new ideas is only worthwhile if you keep a record of your new-found inspirations. Hence, maintaining notes is essential to facilitate the ideation process. A note can be a fleeting idea or a permanent thought worth archiving.

Emacs is an ideal tool for storing notes in plain text. Several packages are available to manage your digital brain. This step in the EWS workflow revolves around the Denote package by Protesilaos (Prot) Stavrou.

You don't need to follow any specific note-taking methods such as *Zettelklasten* or *Bullet Journal*. My personal collection of notes is a primordial soup of ideas, categorised using organically grown tags and opportunistically linking files. Besides digital musings, you can add anything worth keeping to Denote, including binary files such as PDFs or photographs.

Chapter 6 discusses how to use Org and the Denote package to develop a personal knowledge management system.

Production

Once you have gathered your thoughts, it is time to start writing. Org is ideal for writing articles and books or developing websites. Emacs developers have also published numerous additional utilities to assist with the writing process, including auto-completion, grammar checking, a dictionary, a thesaurus, and other indispensable tools. During production you also might want to collaborate with other authors, which requires some control over different versions.

Chapter 7 describes how to use Org to write articles, websites and books, and manage large projects.

Publication

The glorious moment has arrived when you can publish the fruits of your labour. Org has powerful capabilities to export the text to various formats, most importantly word processor documents for sharing, PDF files for physical books, ePub for e-books, HTML for websites and ODT for corporate documents.

Org exports files to print-ready PDF files through the LaTeX document preparation system, which is popular among technical authors and publishers but can be used for any physical book. The benefit of using Org over other LaTeX editors is that you don't need to know any LaTeX syntax to get started.

Chapter 8 discusses how to use Org to convert your plain text document to an electronic or physical publication to share with the world.

Administration

Working through a writing project is a fantastic journey of creative expression, but is also involves some overhead in managing your projects. Emacs interfaces with other GNU software to help you manage your files using the powerful directory editor (Dired). You can also use Emacs to organise photographs and images with the built-in Image-Dired package.

Lastly, working on a big project means tracking a multitude of tasks. Org has a fully functional task management system to help you keep track of your projects. You can implement your personal workflow or use a Getting Things Done (GTD) approach.

Chapter 9 discusses how to manage files and projects to keep you own track in your writing projects.

2.7   How to read this book

This book is not a technical Emacs manual but a guided tour for authors. It describes typical use cases for researching, writing and publishing and how to implement these using Emacs. Each chapter contains references to the comprehensive built-in help system for the intrepid reader to explore the content in more detail. The knowledge in this book is enough to get you started on your writing project, and Emacs itself contains all the documentation you need to become a keyboard ninja.

The next chapter explains the principles of using an unconfigured GNU Emacs system to get you started on the learning curve. However, no Emacs user uses the software in its unconfigured state. The EWS configuration alters the appearance and functionality of Emacs, introducing enhancements to facilitate the discovery of relevant information. EWS also deploys some Emacs packages (plugins) to assist authors, such as the Citar for accessing bibliographies and Denote for taking notes. Chapter 4 explains the principles of the EWS configuration.

Chapters five to eight describe a typical workflow for a writing project: from research to writing and to publication. These chapters show you how to read articles, books and websites (chapter 5) and convert Emacs into a personal knowledge management system (chapter 6). These chapters also explain how to prepare manuscripts for publication (chapter 7) and export them to various formats (chapter 8).

Chapter 9 covers administrative tasks, including project and file management. The Org mode package offers powerful capabilities to help you manage your calendar and action lists, enabling you to stay productive. The final part of this chapter demonstrates how to Emacs can manage files. Working on large projects undoubtedly means that you copy, paste, rename, and perform other tasks with your computer files. The Dired (Directory Editor) package provides everything you need to achieve this.

The final chapter 10 provides some advice on how to become an Emacs Ninja by providing some tips on how to deepen your knowledge, including a short introduction to Emacs Lisp.

The appendix to this book provides the annotated EWS configuration along with guidance on how to interpret and modify the code to your specific needs.

The best way to read this book is by sitting in front of your computer and trying things out as you read about them. Experiment with different options, create some files and play around.

Chapter 3

Getting Started with Emacs

Start your engines; it is time to use Emacs. This chapter introduces using Emacs without any configuration, also known as vanilla Emacs. These basic skills will be helpful when introducing the more advanced functionality in the remainder of the book.

The installation process for Emacs depends on your operating system. The GNU Emacs website (`emacs.org`) contains instructions on how to install Emacs on the most common operating systems. Please note that you will need the latest release of Emacs, which at the time of writing is version 30. Installing Emacs and all the required software is more involved on Windows than it is on Linux or macOS. The Emacs Writing Studio website provides guidance on installing the additional software on this operating system.

Once you have installed the software, it's time to open Emacs and explore its features. The first thing that appears is a splash screen with links to help files and other information (figure 3.1). Click on any of the links to read the tutorial or press the q button to close ('kill' in Emacs-speak) the screen. Pressing q is the standard method to kill read-only screens.

When the splash screen closes, you enter the 'Scratch Buffer', which you can use for temporary notes. In Emacs terminology, a buffer is an area in the memory of your computer that holds content that can link to a file. A buffer is a dynamic version of a document, whereas the file remains unchanged until you save the buffer to its associated file. Emacs does not save the content of the Scratch Buffer when you exit the program, so don't start writing your dissertation just yet.

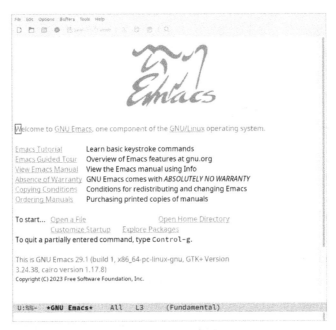

Figure 3.1: Emacs 29.1 splash screen.

3.1 Emacs quickstart guide

You don't need to know much about Emacs to start using it. It works more intuitively than some people suggest. Let's start by creating an Org document and exporting it to a webpage to get a feel for Emacs.

In the menu bar, select *File > Visit New File*, select the directory, and type the filename with a .org extension, for example: test.org. Visiting a file is a term in Emacs that refers to reading a file into a buffer. This file will be in Org mode, a special type of plain text file. Now, start typing as you usually do in any other text software.

You can also use Org syntax to add structure and metadata to the document. For example, add #+title: Hello World as the first line to define the title. To insert a heading, start a line with a single asterisk, such as * Chapter. Using two or more asterisks renders subheadings.

```
#+title: Hello World

* Chapter One
Dolor sit amet, consectetur adipiscing elit nulla varius.

** Section
Nullam ut consequat lacus. Praesent porttitor urna eget semper.
```

You'll notice that these two lines are of a different colour than the regular text. These colours are not the actual colours of the text in the final product but are semantic hints to indicate the document structure. These colours facilitate quick scanning of the document. Now, add some regular text below the heading. Lastly, save the results with *File > Save*. You have now created your first written document in Emacs.

If you find that Emacs doesn't wrap your long sentences at the screen boundary, don't worry. You can easily change this default behaviour by going to the menu bar and selecting *Options > Line Wrapping in This Buffer > Word Wrap (Visual Line Mode)*. Now, Emacs behaves more like the writing software you're used to. However, when you open a new file, you will have to enable this again. When we start configuring Emacs, it will be set so that visual line mode is enabled for all text files.

Next, we export this simple example to a webpage. Org is a *What You See is What You Mean* system, so the way the text is presented on the screen is not necessarily how it will appear in our final published result. Org mode translates the syntax to the desired typographical design when exporting the document using a template, which, in the case of a webpage, is a Cascading Style Sheet (CSS).

So any text in the #+title: line is the document's title (the <title> tag), and any line started with one or more asterisks becomes a heading (<h1>, <h2> and so on). The export module converts these keywords to the relevant output. Later chapters introduce additional syntax to add images, tables, formulas and other artefacts.

The last step is to create the webpage. In the *Org* menu, select *Export/Publish* and type the h and o keys. Org translates your document to an HTML file and opens your default browser to display the results.

Presto, this is the basic workflow for writing and publishing a document in Emacs Org mode. There is obviously a lot more to this, and Emacs has a myriad of plugins and fine-tuning options to create a document just as you like it.

3.2   Working with the keyboard

Emacs is, for the most part, a keyboard-driven application. You can use the mouse and the menu bar for occasional tasks, as shown in the previous section, but there is no need to use this peripheral. Although there is no formal agreement on whether using a keyboard or a mouse is most efficient (Omanson, Miller, Young, & Schwantes, 2010; Tognazzini, 1992), most Emacs users prefer to keep their hands on the keys.

It might seem that clicking on an icon in a menu bar requires less mental effort than remembering sequences of keystrokes. However, the practical problem with icon bars is that there is insufficient space to cover all available functionality. Keyboard shortcuts are easy to remember as they quickly become part of your muscle memory.

Using keyboard shortcuts instead of the mouse prevents you from having to regularly move your hands between the two input devices. For example, when misspelling a word in a standard word processor, you move your hand from the keyboard to the mouse, move the cursor to the offending word, click the mouse and select the desired spelling. In Emacs, you use one keystroke to change the typo to the most likely correct version and keep writing.

The most important thing to remember in the keyboard versus mouse debate is that writing is more about thinking than smashing thousands of keys per minute, so using a mouse is not a sin. You can use a mouse in Emacs for some tasks, like selecting text or moving the cursor. The main advantage of the menu system is that it helps discover functionality in Emacs. You don't need a mouse to access the menu. Press F10 and use the arrow keys to navigate the drop-down menu to discover Emacs' functionality.

As Emacs was developed before the standardisation of computer interfaces, the way it interacts with the keyboard is slightly different from what you are used to. Let's start with the basics. A standard computer keyboard has five types of keys:

1. Alphanumeric: Letters, numbers and punctuation.

2. Editing: such as arrow keys and backspace

3. Function and multimedia

4. Escape

5. Modifier keys: Shift, Control, Alt, Windows/Command

Pressing an alphanumeric key adds the character to the computer's memory and displays it on the screen. This is a complex way of saying that they add characters to the screen. Editing keys, such as arrow keys, page up and down, delete, and backspace, do what their labels indicate. Function and multimedia keys perform more complex tasks. For example, pressing F3 in Emacs records a macro. Multimedia keys are usually defined by the operating system and activate tasks such as increasing the screen brightness or playing music. The escape key is the most potent member of the keyboard. Like Dorothy's Ruby Slippers in the *Wizard of Oz*, pressing it three times gets you out of trouble when you are stuck.

These are the only keys you ever need to write prose, but we want to do more than insert and edit text. Computer keyboards also have modifier keys, which are special keys that temporarily modify the standard action of another key when pressed together.

The modifier keys on modern PC and Apple keyboards are Shift, Control, Alt / Option, and Command / Windows. Chromebook computers have the same modifier keys, but there is no equivalent to the Windows / Command key. Some smaller keyboards also have additional modifier keys, such as Fn, to expand the available options. Modifier keys have no effect when pressed by themselves. As the name suggests, these keys modify other keys when pressed simultaneously.

Some of the Emacs terminology for these keys stems from a time when the current standard keyboard layout did not yet exist. What we now call the Alt key used to be the *Meta* key. The Windows key on PC keyboards or Command on Apple systems maps to the former *Super* key. Your operating system uses the Windows or Command key for assorted tasks, so Emacs does not use it by default. Older keyboards also featured the 'Hyper' key, which Emacs can still recognise but is no longer available on modern computers. Advanced computer users can assign this key to another modifier.

Emacs documentation abbreviates key sequences using a convention. When you use the menu bar, as described in the previous section, some items include an abbreviated keyboard shortcut in their descriptions.

For example, C-a stands for pressing the Control and a key at the same time. The dash indicates that the first key modifies the second key. In contrast, a space between keys indicates that they are typed consecutively. The space bar and other named keys are indicated between angled brackets like this <spc> or <Tab>. Without angled brackets, indicates that you type the letters 'spc' or 'tab'.

Each modifier key has an abbreviation, as shown in table 3.1. You can combine modifier keys, which can lead to awkward combinations, such as C-M-S-a (Control, Alt and Shift a), requiring the nimble fingers of a sleight-of-hand artist to execute smoothly. The shift modifier is usually not indicated because C-M-A is the same as C-M-S-a. The escape key can also act as a modifier key. Pressing escape once is the same as holding the meta key: <esc>-x is the same as M-x.

The most critical keyboard shortcut to know about is C-g, which cancels a partially typed command. Unlike the triple escape key, this command can also quit running functions.

All keystrokes in Emacs execute a function, which means they perform a task. The c-g key mentioned above executes the `keyboard-quit` command. A *command* is a function that can be invoked interactively, typically through keybindings, menu selections or with m-x. A *function* performs a specific task and is called from other functions or commands but not directly by the user. All commands are functions, but not all functions are commands, and this book uses these words interchangeably.

Table 3.1: Emacs modifier keys.

Modifier	Example	Function
Shift	S-8	* sign on US keyboard
Control	C-e	End of line
Alt / Option	M-d	Delete (kill) word
Windows / Command	s	Used by the operating system
Hyper	H	Not mapped to regular keys

Most technical books display the names of functions in `typewriter-font` to distinguish them from standard text. Emacs functions are most commonly written with dashes instead of spaces between words, which hackers refer to as 'kebab-case'. Not all functions have a keyboard shortcut; however, when a shortcut is available, it is also displayed in typewriter text. Knowing the names of functions and their corresponding keyboard shortcuts helps to better understand how Emacs works. You also need to know the function name because keyboard shortcuts can change as they are fully configurable.

But wait, there is more. Emacs also uses prefix keys. When you press these, the system will wait for further input. For example, C-x C-f means that you first press Control and x and then Control and f, the default sequence for finding (opening or creating) a file with the `find-file` command.

After pressing a prefix key, Emacs displays it at the bottom of the screen (the echo area), awaiting further input. When you enter the next key, it is either another prefix, or you have completed the key chord. The length of key sequences is theoretically unlimited, but are usually not more than three or four keys in practice. The standard prefix keys are:

- `C-x`: Used for built-in Emacs commands

- `C-c`: Used by Emacs packages

- `C-h`: Help functions

- `M-x`: Execute commands

If you like to know what shortcuts are available after a prefix key, then use `C-h` after the prefix. For example, `C-c C-h` opens a new buffer with a list of all available shortcuts that start with `C-c`. The names of the commands can be cryptic. Click on the function name to view its help file. In Emacs, help is always around the corner.

Figure 3.2: Cover of the 1981 version of the Emacs manual.

Due to Emacs's ancient roots, it does not comply with the Common User Access (CUA) standard for user interfaces (Berry, 1988). This standard defines the familiar keyboard shortcuts such as `C-c` and `C-x` to copy or cut something to the clipboard. Emacs uses these keys as prefixes or different functionality. You can configure Emacs to recognise these common keyboard shortcuts, but EWS sticks to the default behaviour.

One more prefix key needs mentioning. Some commands have alternative states, meaning the same function can have different outcomes. You activate an alternative state by adding C-u (the universal argument) before the regular key sequence. Emacs repeats the action four times when a function does not have an alternative state for the universal argument. So, using C-u <up> moves the cursor up four lines. Using a double universal argument makes it sixteen, and so on. When typing C-u C-u C-u #, Emacs inserts 64 (4^3) hashtag symbols. You can also repeat keystrokes by adding a number after Control or Alt repeats the next keystroke. For example, M-80 - adds eighty dashes to your text.

This detailed description of how Emacs uses the keyboard might dazzle you. The cover of the 1981 version of the Emacs manual even suggested that Emacs is best used by aliens with unearthly nimble fingers (Figure 3.2). Don't worry; by the time you complete this book, you will play your keyboard like a piano virtuoso.

3.3 Issuing commands

The modifier and prefix keys provide an abundance of shortcuts to issue commands to Emacs, but the number of keys is not unlimited, so some commands don't have a shortcut. When a command is without a keybinding, you can provide your own; just be careful not to create conflicts with existing shortcuts, as explained in the Appendix. This book always displays both the default or EWS keyboard shortcut and the command name.

Functions without a keybinding need to be called by name. The standard way to execute commands is to use M-x and then type the command name and the Return/Enter key (<Ret>). When you type M-x, the bottom of the screen (the minibuffer) shows M-x, waiting for further instructions. The minibuffer is where you enter input and instructions. For example, type M-x tetris <Ret> to play Tetris. Don't get too distracted; simply press q a few times to exit the game and return to your work. Experimental research suggests that prolonged Tetris play can affect your dreams (Stickgold, Malia, Maguire, Roddenberry, & O'Connor, 2000).

Typing the full function name every time is too much work for those who seek ultimate efficiency. The minibuffer completion system helps you find the commands you seek. When typing a partial function or file name, you can hit the Tab key. Emacs will display completion candidates in the minibuffer. For example, to implement line-wrapping in a text file you execute the `visual-line-mode` function by typing M-x visu <Tab>.

To see how this completion works, use the Tab key after each letter you type into the minibuffer. You will notice that Emacs narrows the completion candidates as you get closer to your desired selection until there is only one option. This principle also works with variable names and filenames. The Tab key is your secret weapon to help you remember and discover functions, variables, file names, buffer names and other selection candidates. You can access the menu and toolbars using the mouse, but they only contain a limited selection of the available functionality, as the screen is not large enough to accommodate all of them.

The remainder of this book only mentions the names of commands without adding the M-x and <Ret> parts. When the text suggests using a function or command called `example-command`, you do so with M-x `example-command` <Ret>. Any available keyboard shortcuts are also indicated, in which case you can use the short way to access the function.

3.4 Major and minor modes

Emacs is a versatile tool that accomplishes specialised tasks through editing modes that alter the basic behaviour. An editing mode can be a major or minor mode. A major mode is like opening an app within the Emacs environment, just like you open an app on your phone. The most popular major mode is Org, which provides a writing and publication system. Org is the major mode discussed throughout this book.

A more quirky Emacs mode is Artist mode. This tool enables you to create plain text drawings using the mouse and keyboard. Go ahead and try, issue the `artist-mode` command, and start drawing with the mouse. You can find out more about how to use the Artist package through the built-in help system with `C-h P artist`.

All major modes share the same underlying Emacs functionality, such as copying and pasting (killing and yanking) and opening files, but they add specialised tasks, for example exporting to a webpage. A major mode determines the core functionality for an open buffer. A buffer is the part of the memory that holds the text you are working on or other content. Each buffer has one major mode, and each major mode has its own distinct functionality, including specific key bindings and drop-down menus.

Minor modes provide further functionality, such as spell-checking, text completion or displaying line numbers. A minor mode is an auxiliary program that enhances the functionality of a major mode. While each buffer has only one major mode, a buffer can have several minor modes.

In many cases, Emacs recognises the major mode based on the file extension. All Org files end in `.org`, so Emacs automatically enables Org mode when opening such a file. The name of the major mode is displayed in the line below the window. Minor modes must be explicitly enabled, either for a specific buffer, globally for all buffers, or hooked to a major mode.

As an exercise to understand these principles, open the `test.org` file created in the first section of this chapter using `C-x C-f`. You will note that the title and headings are marked in a different colour and that a new option is available in the menu bar. Now save this file under a new name (`test.txt`) with `C-x C-w` (`write-file`). The buffer is no longer an Org file but a plain text file. The buffer changes as the title and headings are no longer coloured. Additionally, the Org option in the menu bar is unavailable, and the line below the open buffer now displays 'text' instead of 'Org'. To go back to Org, you issue the `org-mode` command.

The available keyboard shortcuts (the keymaps) and drop-down menus depend on the major and minor modes that are active at the time. Some keymaps are global and apply to the whole of Emacs. Other maps are specific to a mode. Unless a mode overrides it, some shortcuts remain the same for all modes. Packages can modify or add shortcuts, depending on the required functionality. A shortcut like C-c C-c is used by different modes for different actions, depending on the context in which it is used.

3.5   Opening and saving files

Opening files in Emacs is called 'visiting a file' and uses the find-file function (C-x C-f). So effectively, finding, opening and visiting a file have the same effect. Emacs opens the file and displays its contents in the buffer, ready for writing and editing. When you type a name that does not yet exist, Emacs creates a new file. If you open a directory, Emacs displays the contents of that folder in the Emacs file manager (The Directory Editor or 'Dired' (see chapter 9). Alternatively, you can open a file with the toolbar icon or through the menu bar.

Emacs asks you to select a file or folder in the minibuffer. Typing the complete path to the file you seek would be tedious, so Emacs assists with auto-completion, explained in section 3.3. Please note that file paths in Emacs use forward slashes and not backslashes, as is the case in Windows (C:/Users/Freud/ and not C:\Users\Freud\).

When finding a file, Emacs starts in the folder of the currently active buffer. You can remove the text before the cursor to move to higher levels in the directory tree. You don't have to remove all subdirectories. To find a file in your home directory, ignore the current text in the minibuffer and type a tilde followed by forward slash (~/) and <Tab>. To start searching in the root folder of your drive, type two forward slashes (//). On a Windows computer, the best method is to type the drive letter, followed by a colon and a slash (c:/). When you hit the Tab key twice, all the available files and folders appear in the minibuffer.

Please create a new file (C-x C-f) to get some practice and start writing into the buffer. After you have added some text, you should save your work to the file. The contents of the file stays the same until you save the buffer. After you complete your edits, C-x C-s saves the buffer to its associated file. To save a buffer under a new name, you can use C-x C-w (table 3.2). You can see whether a buffer is different from the associated file in the mode line. If it contains two asterisks at the start, then your file needs saving. Two dashes indicate that the content of the file is identical to the buffer.

Table 3.2: Most commonly used file functions.

Keystroke	Function	Description
C-x C-f	find-file	Find (open or create) a file
C-x C-s	save-buffer	Save the current buffer
C-x C-w	write-file	Write current buffer (Save as)

3.6 Buffers, frames and windows

When opening Emacs, the software runs within a frame (figure 3.3). This might sound confusing because a frame is often referred to as a window in most operating systems. To confuse matters further, you can divide an Emacs frame into windows. You can also open multiple frames on a desktop, for example, one on each monitor.

The default Emacs screen features a menu bar at the top and a toolbar with icons immediately below it. The windows start below the toolbar. Each window contains a buffer, which includes text, a user interface or output from functions. The mode line below each window displays the name of the buffer or its associated file, as well as other metadata. Each frame has an echo area at the bottom, where Emacs displays feedback. Echo is a computer science term referring to the display of information, such as error messages and other feedback. The bottom of the screen also contains the minibuffer, an expandable section where Emacs seeks your input when, for example, selecting a buffer or a file.

Like any writing software, you are working on the version in memory (the buffer), and the previous version is on disk (the file). You can have multiple buffers open simultaneously, allowing you to easily switch between them. The active buffer is the one you are currently working on. The names of special buffers, such as *Messages*, are surrounded by asterisks. These types of buffers are not linked to a file.

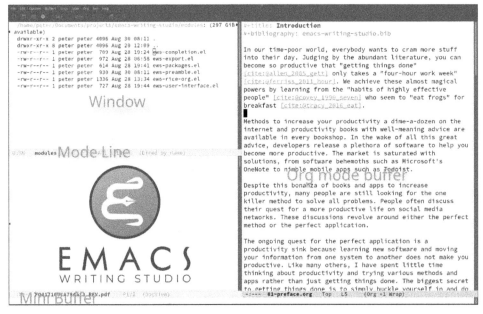

Figure 3.3: Emacs frame with three windows, a Dired buffer, image buffer and Org buffer.

Emacs is highly stable, and some users have hundreds of open buffers because they rarely need to restart the program. The C-x b shortcut (switch-to-buffer) selects another buffer as the active one. With the C-x left and C-x right key sequences (previous-buffer and next-buffer), you can move between buffers in chronological activation order.

By default, a frame has one window. You can split the current window horizontally (split-window-below) or vertically (split-window-right) by pressing C-x 2 or C-x 3. The C-x 0 shortcut (delete-window) removes your current window, but the buffer stays in memory, and C-x 1 removes all windows except the one the cursor is currently in (delete-other-windows), so the current buffer encompasses the whole frame. To move between windows, use the C-x o shortcut (other-window). This function cycles through the available windows.

When splitting a window vertically, the same buffer appears twice. Each window can have its own cursor position so you can easily refer to other parts of your writing without jumping around and losing focus. Activating `follow-mode` flows the text of the buffer so windows that hold this buffer become columns of the same document. When the cursor moves below the bottom of the left window, it appears again in the right window, so all windows share one cursor. To deactivate follow mode, rerun the same function.

Table 3.3: Buffer and window functions.

Keystroke	Function	Description
C-x b	switch-to-buffer	Select another buffer
C-x <left>	previous-buffer	Move to the previous active buffer
C-x <right>	next-buffer	Move to the next active buffer
C-x 0	delete-window	Delete the current window
C-x 1	delete-other-windows	Delete all other windows
C-x 2	split-window-below	Split current window horizontally
C-x 3	split-window-right	Split current window vertically
C-x o	other-window	Move to next window
	follow-mode	Show buffer over multiple windows

3.7 Finding help

Emacs has an extensive built-in help system with different ways to access information, accessible with the C-h prefix key. The complete Emacs manual is available with C-h r (`info-emacs-manual`). This manual opens in Info mode, which is a specialised mode for manuals. The full Emacs manual is not bedtime reading but rather a pool of knowledge to dip into when the need arises. The g key lets you jump to a chapter or section of the text (`Info-goto-node`), using minibuffer completion discussed earlier. For example, C-h r g help <Ret> takes you to the part of the manual about the help system.

When reading a manual in the info system, the space bar scrolls the screen up, so you can walk through the manual page by page (`Info-scroll-up`). The backspace button or S-<spc> returns you to the previous screen (`Info-scroll-down`). The manual contains hyperlinks in the table of contents and sprinkled throughout the text. You can click on these with the mouse or press the Enter key when the cursor is on the link. To jump to the previous or the next chapter, you can use `Info-up` and `Info-down` functions bound to u and d. If you are looking for something specific, then `Info-search` (s) lets you find specific terms. As always, q quits the screen.

Some packages in Emacs have their own manuals. You can view a list of the available manuals with `C-h R` (`info-display-manual`). Additionally, you can use minibuffer completion to find a manual here. You can read these manuals the same way as described in the previous paragraph.

Not all Emacs packages have an extensive manual. Another method for finding information about a package is the `describe-package` function (`C-h P`), which extracts information from the source code that describes the package.

The help system also has other commands to find more specific descriptions. If you want to find out which command binds a particular shortcut, use `C-h k` and enter the key sequence. Emacs displays a message at the bottom of the screen when you enter a key sequence that has no associated function, e.g., "C-c k is undefined". To find out more about a variable, use `C-h v` (`describe-variable`) and type its name. And to learn more about a command, use `C-h x` (`describe-command`). A popup window describes the relevant variable or command, which you can close with q.

The remainder of the book provides regular references to the relevant parts of the Emacs help system for readers who would like to know more details about the system. You don't need to read the manuals end-to-end because this book contains everything you need to know to get started as an Emacs author. The references to Emacs documentation are for people interested in learning more details about how the software works.

3.8   Writing in Emacs

You now know enough to start writing more complex documents. Either visit an existing plain text file or create a new one and start typing. To be fully productive, you need to understand some of the basic principles of Text mode, the foundational major mode for writing prose. The Emacs documentation describes text mode as the mode for writing text for humans, in contrast to Prog mode, which is for writing code that computers read. Text mode forms the foundation for all other prose formats, such as Org, Markdown or Fountain. This means that all major modes for authors use the same basic functionality for writing. When you enable Org, text mode is also automatically enabled.

This section summarises the most common commands for writing text. The Emacs manual provides a detailed description of all functionality relevant to writing human languages, which you can read with C-h r g basic and C-h r g text.

Moving around a buffer

Emacs documentation sometimes refers to the cursor as 'point'. The cursor is the character displayed on the screen (a line or a box), and the point indicates where the next typed character will appear. Point is more critical when you write Emacs functions, so this book focuses on the cursor, as that is where the writing action happens.

In addition to the standard methods for moving around a buffer, Emacs provides additional functionality to help you navigate your manuscript. For example, typing C-p (previous-line) does the same as the <up> key (table 3.4). Some people prefer these keys so their hands stay in the default position for fast touch-typing.

Table 3.4: Moving around a buffer in Emacs.

Keystroke	Function	Direction
C-b, <left>	left-char	Left
C-f, <right>	right-char	Right
C-p, <up>	previous-line	Up
C-n, <down>	next-line	Down
M-b, C-<left>	backward-word	Previous word
M-f, C-<right>	forward-word	Next word
C-v, <pagedown	scroll-down-command	Scroll down
M-v, <pageup>	scroll-up-command	Scroll up
C-a, <home>	move-beginning-of-line	Start of line
C-e, <end>	move-end-of-line	End of line
M-<, C-<home>	beginning-of-buffer	Start of buffer
M->, C-<end>	end-of-buffer	End of buffer

Getting lost in a sea of words on your screen is easy. Some simple keystrokes can help you focus your eyes quickly. Keying C-l (`recenter-top-bottom`) moves the line that your cursor is on to the centre of the screen. If you repeat this keystroke, the cursor will move to the top of the screen. If you perform this action three times consecutively, the cursor will move to the bottom of the screen.

You will occasionally need to move from one part of a document to another and then want to jump back to where you came from but lose your place. You can do this more efficiently by setting a mark.

A mark is a bookmark for a position (point) within your text. Setting a mark is like dropping a pin on a map. You can set a mark to remember a place you want to jump to, which is incredibly handy when editing large files. You set a mark with C-<spc> C-<spc> (`set-mark-command`), which stores the cursor's current location in the mark ring. The mark ring is the sequence of marks for the current buffer. You can now move to another part of your document and edit or read what you need. You jump back to the previous mark with C-u C-<spc>. While C-<spc> (`set-mark`) stores the current location in the mark ring, adding a universal argument extracts that position and jumps the cursor to it. Repeatedly pressing C-u C-<spc> moves through all the marks stored in the ring. If you reach the first stored value, you return to the last one, hence the name "mark ring".

Search and replace

While jumping around the text with arrow keys and other functionality is excellent, sometimes you know exactly what you need. The search and replace functionality in Emacs is powerful, and this section only scratches the surface of its capabilities.

Emacs' most common search method is incremental search (`isearch-forward`). An incremental search (C-s) begins as soon as you type the first character of the search term. As you type the search query, Emacs shows you where it finds this sequence of characters. Repeatedly pressing C-s steps through the matches in the buffer. When you identify the place you want, you can terminate the search with C-g, and the cursor returns to its original location. The Enter or Return key stops the cursor at its current location, allowing you to edit the text.

The C-s shortcut searches incrementally from the cursor. You cycle through the search results by repeatedly pressing C-s. Using C-r (isearch-backward) searches the text before the cursor. Emacs saves search terms in the search ring. Typing C-s C-s recycles the previous search term. Using M-p and M-n lets you scroll through previous search terms in the ring.

To search and replace text in a buffer, use M-% (query-replace). This function highlights all instances of the text to be replaced and provides a range of options at each instance. Type space or y to replace the marked match and delete or n to skip to the next one. The exclamation mark replaces all instances without further confirmation. If something goes wrong, use u to undo the most recent change or U to undo all changes made in this search. The enter key or q quits the replacement process. More options are available, which you can glean by hitting the question mark.

Copy and paste text

Writing is fun, but sometimes it is more efficient to copy something you wrote previously or copy text from somebody else (referenced, of course), or perhaps even text generated with a language model. The system for copying and pasting text works differently from modern systems but with significantly more power.

To select (mark in Emacs speak) a piece of text, you first set a mark with C-<spc> and then move the cursor to highlight the desired section. To select a complete paragraph, use the M-h key. In a plain text context, a paragraph is a line of text separated by blank lines. Repeatedly pressing M-h selects subsequent sections. Using C-x h selects all text in a buffer, and C-g nullifies any selection. Once the text is marked, you can act on it by deleting, copying, or moving it. In some modes, you can select with the shift and arrow keys, but this functionality is disabled in Org because these keys activate other features.

The modern craft analogues of copy, cut and paste were coined by Harry Tesler in 1974 (Tesler, 2012). Emacs terminology is more prosaic. Copying a text is the same as saving it to the 'kill-ring' and yanking a text retrieves it from that seemingly bleak location.

While the clipboard in most systems only retains the last entry, the kill ring provides access to your 'killing spree'. In other words, Emacs stores a history of all text you copy and cut from a buffer to the kill ring. The default length of this history is sixty entries. Once the kill ring is full, the oldest item vanishes.

The kill commands copy or move text to the kill ring. The two yank commands copy an entry from the kill ring to the current buffer. The yank-pop (M-y) command cycles through the contents of the kill ring so you can access the history. Table 3.5 lists the keyboard shortcuts for copying and moving text from and to the kill ring.

Table 3.5: Copying and pasting in Emacs.

Keystroke	Function	Description
M-w	kill-ring-save	Copy selection to the kill ring
C-w	kill-region	Move selection to the kill ring
C-y	yank	Insert the most recent kill ring entry to the buffer
M-y	yank-pop	Replace yanked text with kill ring entry

Correcting mistakes

An ancient Roman proverb tells us that it is human to make mistakes (*Errare humanum est*), but to keep making them is diabolical. Emacs does not care about these sensibilities and provides ample options to let you correct your digressions. The most convenient aspect of electronic writing is that it is easy to change your mind or correct a mistake without resorting to correction fluids or other archaic methods. A series of editing commands are available to modify text and fix your typos (table 3.6). Commands that start with kill- store the deleted text on the kill ring so you can yank the deleted text back into the buffer if needed.

Besides removing unwanted characters and words, you can also swap their positions. When you accidentally reverse two letters in a word, you can switch their order with the

Table 3.6: Emacs deletion commands.

Keystroke	Function	Action
C-d, <delete>	delete-char	Delete character after point
<backspace>	delete-backward-char	Delete character before point
C-x C-o	delete-blank-lines	Remove blank lines below point
M-d, C-<delete>	kill-word	Delete the next word
C-k	kill-line	Delete to the end of line

transpose-char command with the cursor between them (C-t). Swapping words is quickly done with the transpose-words (M-t) command.

Emacs can assist you if you make a mistake when capitalising a word. The three commands below change the word under the cursor. If you are in the middle of a word, move first to the start. Adding a negative argument (M--, Alt / Option and the minus key) before these commands modify the letters before the cursor. This addition is valuable when you have just finished typing a word and realise it needs to start with a capital letter. Typing M-- M-c fixes it for you without jumping around the text or grabbing a mouse.

- M-l: Convert following word to lower case (downcase-word).

- M-u: Convert following word to upper case (upcase-word).

- M-c: Capitalise the following word (capitalize-word).

When you mark a region and would like to change the letter type, then use C-x C-l to convert the selected text to lower case (downcase-region) and C-x C-u for upper case (upcase-region). When using these commands for the first time, Emacs warns you because, apparently, they are confusing to new users. Just confirm and save this for future sessions.

The Emacs undo command is mapped to C-/. If you need to undo the step, use C-? (undo-redo). Emacs behaves differently from other software concerning undoing and redoing edits, which requires some explanation. In standard word processors, previous undo texts are lost if you undo something, make some changes, but then change your mind.

For example, type "Socrates", erase it with C-<backspace>, change it to "Plato", and then undo this edit to revert back to Socrates and add some more text. In standard word processors, you cannot return to the state where the text mentioned Plato (State B in Figure 3.4). In Emacs, all previous states are available. You can return to any prior state with consecutive undo commands in Emacs. Subsequent undo and redo commands follow the chain in figure 3.4, never losing anything you typed. This behaviour can be confusing, but you will love it after using it for a while because you never lose any edits.

Figure 3.4: Emacs undo states.

Another feature of the Emacs undo system is that it can apply only to a selected region. Let's say that you have just completed the first chapter and have started writing the next one. You then realise that you need to undo some of the edits in chapter one. If you use the undo function, it will first undo all your work on chapter two before changing the first chapter. You can solve this problem by selecting the relevant region of text in chapter one and then issuing the undo command over just that region.

Languages other than English

For the majority of the world, English is not the first language. When you set the keyboard settings in your operating system to another language, Emacs can get confused when using modifier keys. Typing M-x on a Ukrainian computer results in the Cyrillic letter Che instead of an x, which Emacs cannot compute.

Emacs supports an extensive range of input methods for typing the wide variety of languages spoken worldwide. To see an overview of the various languages that Emacs supports, run view-hello-file (C-h h). An input method either converts keyboard characters directly or converts a sequence of letters into one character. For example, using one of the methods to type Chinese, you start keying, and a menu appears in the minibuffer, from where you can select the desired character.

To choose an input method for the current buffer, use the `set-input-method` command with `C-x <Ret> C-\`, which lets you select the preferred method in the minibuffer. The start of the mode line indicates the current input method in use. You can temporarily disable the chosen method with `C-\`. Using this key again returns you to the previously selected input method.

For more specific information on how to use your keyboard to write another language, use `C-h I`, which runs the `describe-input-method` function. To view a list of all available input methods, run the `list-input-methods` command, and a new buffer pops up with a long list of the languages of the world. The Emacs manual provides detailed information on the various input methods with `C-h r g input`.

Modifying the display

The appearance of the buffer on the screen depends on the major mode, theme, configuration, and active packages. You do have some interactive control over the size of the text. To temporarily increase the height of the text in the current buffer, type `C-x C-+`. To decrease the size, type `C-x C--` (`text-scale-adjust`). To restore the default (global) font height, type `C-x C-0`.

The default Text mode in Emacs does not truncate lines like a regular word processor but keeps going until you hit enter. In Emacs, a logical line is a sequence of characters that finishes with a return. A visual line relates to how it is displayed in Emacs. The default setting is that logical lines continue beyond the screen boundary. While this may be useful for writing code, it can be confusing when writing prose.

Emacs has several line-wrapping functions, of which Visual Line Mode is the most useful for writing long-form text. To activate this mode, execute `visual-line-mode`. Doing this whenever working on a buffer can be tedious, and this is where configuration comes in. We need to configure the system to enable line wrapping for all text modes by default.

3.9   Configuring Emacs

The previous sections explained how to use Emacs in its bare, unconfigured state, more commonly referred to as vanilla Emacs. The software can do anything you need to be an author without any configuration, but that is not ideal.

As a malleable system, Emacs is almost infinitely configurable, so you can make it behave how you see fit. Additionally, Emacs users have shared their configurations and published thousands of packages to enhance functionality. This chapter discusses the principles of configuring Emacs.

While using commercial software is like renting a furnished house, using Emacs is more like owning a house. However, your digital home needs some updates, including fresh paint, new carpets, and furniture, to make it feel like home.

Some systems, such as Doom Emacs, Spacemacs, and SciMax, provide useful starter kits. While these configurations are helpful, they sometimes offer everything but the proverbial kitchen sink. On the other side of the spectrum, you configure your system from scratch, which can become a productivity sink, wading through the myriad of options.

The EWS configuration is a minimal starter kit for authors. EWS provides building blocks that can be modified to suit your preferences. But before installing the EWS configuration, let's first introduce the principles of configuring Emacs.

The initialisation file

When you start Emacs, it loads the initialisation file, also known as the init file. This file contains Lisp code that loads additional packages and configurations when Emacs starts. You can run Emacs without an init file, but you will undoubtedly want to modify the defaults.

The first time you start Emacs, it will create a configuration folder where the init file resides. This folder also contains the packages you need to personalise your system. Emacs looks for a file called `.emacs`, `.emacs.el` or `init.el`. The dot in front of the file name indicates that it is hidden from view, preventing clutter in your directories.

Emacs packages

The Emacs base system provides extensive functionality, but you can enhance its capability with any of the thousands of packages. Many people develop and share software in Emacs Lisp to enhance or extend the system's capabilities. Developers of these packages mainly distribute them through a public package repository, which are websites that let you easily download and install packages. The two most important ones are:

- ELPA: GNU Emacs Lisp Package Archive — default archive (`elpa.gnu.org`).

- MELPA: Milkypostman's Emacs Lisp Package Archive (`melpa.org`).

The primary difference between these two repositories lies in who holds the copyright. The Free Software Foundation holds the copyright for all packages in ELPA. For MELPA packages, the copyright remains with the author. The end result for the user is the same as all packages are licensed as free software. You can explore the list of packages with the `list-packages` command.

Packages are constantly updated by their developers. To ensure you get the latest version, use the `package-upgrade-all` function. This naming convention might seem counterintuitive, as using `upgrade-all-packages` is linguistically clearer. However, the convention for naming Emacs Lisp functions is that the first word is the package name, which in this case is `package`. This naming convention makes it easy to group functions by package.

Customising Emacs

Besides crafting your personal configuration in Emacs Lisp or using a starter kit, Emacs has a customisation menu to configure the system without writing code. Let's assume you want to remove the toolbar from view because you only use the keyboard to issue commands.

Type M-x customise-variable <Ret> tool-bar-mode and a new window pops up showing the customisation options for this variable (figure 3.5). You can use your mouse to move around the configuration screen. Using <Tab> and S-<Tab> moves the cursor between screen elements.

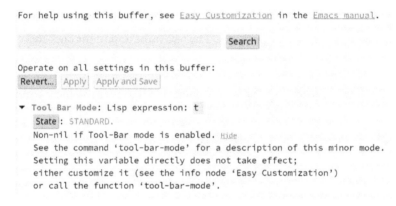

Figure 3.5: Customisation screen for tool-bar-mode.

In this case, the variable is a boolean, meaning it can be either true (t) or false (nil). Note that Lisp does not use false or f, but nil. In Lisp, an empty variable is the same as a false, and any content (or t) is interpreted as 'true'. Emacs documentation often employs a confusing double negative. Setting a variable to 'non-nil' is equivalent to setting it to true. Other variables can require different types of input, such as a drop-down list, tickboxes or free text.

The [Apply] button brings this change into immediate effect, but it will be reset when Emacs is restarted. Clicking [Apply and Save] applies the new setting and saves it to the `init.el` file so it is activated next time you restart Emacs. The 'q' key closes the customisation screen.

Use the ~ customise-group ~ function to see an overview of all parameters that a package provides, and select the one you like to explore. Move the cursor between the available variables with the Tab key and use the Return/Enter key to customise the variable of interest.

Throughout this book, suggestions will be provided for customising variables. Rather than writing Emacs Lisp, you can use the customisation system for a no-code method of configuring Emacs. Whenever this book suggests customising a variable, you need to evaluate the `customise-variable` command (`C-c w v`), type the name of the variable, complete the configuration screen and click "Apply and Save".

3.10   Exiting Emacs

Working with Emacs is so much fun you might never want to shut it down. However, all good things come to an end, so we may need to shut down (or kill) Emacs occasionally.

The `C-x C-c` shortcut (`save-buffers-kill-terminal`) kills the Emacs session, but not before checking for unsaved buffers. There are a few options to ensure you don't lose any unsaved buffers.

This function displays any unsaved files in the echo area and provides options for dealing with each or all of them. The safest option is to key ! and save all buffers that have changes without any further questions. Use the trusted `C-g` to exit this function without exiting Emacs or losing any text. Using `C-h` displays a help message describing all available options.

3.11   Next steps

If you would like to know more about the basic principles of Emacs, the built-in tutorial is a good start, which you can find with `C-h t`. If you like to see how other people use

Emacs, then you can find a lot of informative video content on the internet.

However, the best way to learn how to use Emacs is not to read about it or watch online videos but to play with it. A good place to find some interesting plain text files to practice with is the Gutenberg Project (`gutenberg.org`).

This book was written and published with the configuration it describes, so it is thoroughly tested in real-life conditions. The GitHub repository for EWS also contains the `documents` folder, which includes the Org source files for this book. You can download these files as an example of a book researched, written and published with Emacs.

```
https://github.com/pprevos/emacs-writing-studio
```

You now understand the basic principles of writing in Emacs. The next chapter explains how to install and use the EWS configuration, which installs a range of specialised packages for authors.

Chapter 4

Using Emacs Writing Studio

The previous chapter described how to use and configure vanilla Emacs to make it behave as you want. The *Emacs Writing Studio* (EWS) configuration converts vanilla Emacs to a bespoke tool for authors. This chapter explains how to utilise the additional functionality provided by the EWS configuration and introduces a workflow that spans from inspiration to publication.

EWS utilises a minimalist interface devoid of typical graphical software elements. This austere look minimises distractions from your screen so you can focus on what's important—writing words into a buffer. The second major change to vanilla Emacs is the completion system. EWS utilises the Vertico/Orderless and Marginalia packages to provide enhanced completion in the minibuffer, making it easier to find functions, files, and other necessary items.

The EWS configuration is an opinionated set of choices that might not suit everybody. Emacs users occasionally discuss what constitutes a sensible default configuration. No matter how interesting these debates might be, such a default does not exist. One person's sensible default is another person's computing nightmare; feel free to modify any aspect of EWS to suit your ideal workflow. The Appendix contains the complete annotated configuration and suggestions for making changes.

4.1   Installing Emacs Writing Studio

You don't have to learn to program in Elisp to use Emacs. You can start with the EWS configuration to get you going. But first, you need to install EWS and some additional software. To install the EWS configuration, download the `init.el` and `ews.el` files from the GitHub repository and save them in the configuration folder:

```
https://github.com/pprevos/emacs-writing-studio
```

The `init.el` file contains the EWS configuration, and the `ews.el` file includes a collection of bespoke functions.

The location of the configuration folder depends on your operating system. Type `C-h v user-emacs-directory` to identify its location in the popup help buffer. You can close this buffer by pressing q.

Copy the files from the EWS repository to this directory. EWS activates after you evaluate the `restart-emacs` command or the next time the program starts.

Emacs also integrates with other free software packages to extend its functionality. Some of the features provided by EWS require you to install this software. You don't need to know how to use these programs, as Emacs will control them for you. Each chapter in this book outlines the necessary software.

The `ews-missing-executables` function checks if external software is available on your system. This function runs when Emacs starts the EWS configuration and displays a message in the minibuffer indicating whether any of the recommended tools are missing. You can jump to the `*Messages*` buffer with `C-h e` to review the output. Emacs will function normally even if any of the listed software is missing, but some features may be unavailable.

If you are a Linux or Chromebook user, these packages will be available through your system's package manager. Windows users can use the Chocolatey package manager (`chocolatey.org`) or MSYS2 (`msys2.org`) to obtain this software. Apple users can install Linux tools using the Homebrew package manager (`brew.sh`).

4.2 Minimalist interface

Emacs is a place of rest and contemplation away from the cacophony of contemporary software filled with buttons and functionality you don't need. The EWS configuration removes the toolbar, menu bar and scroll bars. While drop-down menus are a valuable tool to discover functionality, there is no need to keep them on the screen. You can access the menu with F10 (menu-bar-open) and select menu options with the arrow keys and Ret to choose an item. You exit the menu with C-g (keyboard-quit). But after using Emacs for a while, you'll quickly build muscle memory and revert to keyboard shortcuts. If you prefer the graphical menu, icons and scroll bars to be visible at all times, then customise these variables:

- tool-bar-mode

- menu-bar-mode

- scroll-bar-mode

EWS uses C-c w as its default prefix key for its specific functionality, where the w is a mnemonic for writing and t for theme. In EWS, the customize-variable function is bound to C-c w v.

Themes

A theme is a set of instructions that describe the colours of defined text parts. Colours in a text processor play a different role than in a word processor. Colours in Emacs are semantic, which means that they indicate the function of the text, not how it looks when published. A heading might have a different colour than the text or metadata, which helps you find your way through the document.

Text processors use two types of themes: light and dark. Light backgrounds, familiar with most modern word processing software, can cause asthenopia (eye strain) after prolonged screen viewing. Dark colour schemes increase visual acuity and reduce visual fatigue, especially in low-light physical environments with complex backgrounds (Kim, Erickson, Lambert, Bruder, & Welch, 2019). Many text processor users prefer dark themes. Light themes are not bad intrinsically and are effective in a brightly lit room.

The EWS configuration installs and activates the most recent version of Prot's Modus themes. The Modus themes have two primary versions: the `modus-operandi` theme is the primary light theme, while the `modus-vivendi` theme is its dark counterpart. The primary Modus themes maximise contrast between the background and foreground, following the Web Content Accessibility Guidelines (WCAG).

The Modus themes comply with the triple-A standard of the WCAG, which specifies a minimum contrast ratio of 7:1 between the background and foreground. This high contrast ratio is legible for people with moderately low vision. Each of the primary themes has three modified versions: versions for red-green and blue-yellow colour blindness (deuteranopia and tritanopia) and a more colourful variety (tinted).

The tinted versions have a slightly lower contrast ratio and are suitable for people with normal vision. The Modus themes do not prescribe keyboard shortcuts, so EWS defines some. The `C-c w t t` shortcut toggles between the light and dark side (insert Star Wars pun here).

The Modus Themes package includes an extensive manual that explains in detail how to customise the look and feel of its collection of themes. This manual is available through Info Mode with `C-h R modus`. The Appendix provides additional information on customising the theme for your personal settings.

Emacs users have developed a ragtag collection of themes. To pick your favourite, you can browse the Emacs Themes Gallery (`emacsthemes.com`). If the theme is available in any of the package repositories, the `package-install` command can be used to install it for you. Type 'theme' to filter the list and pick your favourite. Once you have installed a new theme, you can use `C-c w t s` (`consult-theme`). This command provides a selection menu of all installed themes, allowing you to select a new one for the current session.

When you start EWS for the first time, it will use the default Emacs theme. To set your preferred default light or dark theme, run the `customize-themes` command and select your preferred version. Follow the prompts and click the 'Save Theme Settings' button to store your chosen default in the `custom.el` file

Setting fonts

The default font in Emacs is a fixed-pitch (mono-spaced) font designed for writing code. In a fixed-pitch font, all characters have the same width. An `i` or an `w` will use the same amount of space, just like mechanical typewriters. This type of letter, also called-mono-spacing, is ideal when writing code or tables because it helps to align the text. A variable-pitch font is easier on the eye when writing prose. Not all characters have the same width in a variable-pitch font, as is common in natural writing.

- `Fixed pitch font`

- Variable pitch font

Ideally, we want the best of both worlds and configure Emacs to use the most suitable font for each situation. Emacs can define a different font for certain parts of the text, for individual buffers, or for a major mode. The EWS configuration utilises variable pitch mode to achieve the ideal mix between font types.

The EWS configuration does not specify any particular fonts and uses the system's default fonts. You can configure your favourite fonts, provided they are available on your computer. You need to customise three font variables:

- `default`: The default settings (a fixed-pitch font).

- `fixed-pitch`: The font used for computer code.

- `variable-pitch`: The settings for prose.

In Emacs lingo, a 'face' is a collection of attributes to display text. It defines the font, foreground colour, background colour, optional underlining, etc. Various face attributes are available for configuration. The main ones to use are the name of the font and the font's height in units of 1/10 point. A point is exactly 1/72 of an inch, so one point is about or 0.35mm.

You can use the customisation menu by evoking `customize-face` and selecting `default`, `fixed-pitch`, or `variable-pitch`, then entering the font name in the *Font Family* box. Click `[Apply and Save]` for each font. This action saves the font settings to the `custom.el` file, which Emacs evaluates at the beginning of the startup sequence. Please note that any customisation you make overrides any theme settings, so ideally, only customise the font family and size.

To see which fonts are available, use `menu-set-font`. When you use the GUI to set the default font, the change is immediate but transient. Use `menu-bar-options-save` to save your default font and size to the `custom.el` file. This method only modifies the default font and should be a fixed-pitch font, which in most font names is indicated by the 'mono' prefix. You can also access the functions by pressing F10 and using the arrow keys to find the relevant functions in the options menu.

Note that fonts in Emacs are not the fonts used in the final published version. The typography of the final product is defined by the relevant templates (chapter 8).

The default margin settings can make the screen look a bit overfull. Hoping you don't suffer from *horror vacui* (fear of empty space), this configuration also installs Prot Stavrou's Spacious Padding package. This package increases the space inside windows and frames, preventing cramming a screen with symbols.

4.3 Exploring Emacs functionality

Emacs provides access to thousands of commands and hundreds of keyboard shortcuts. As you use the system for a while, these commands become second nature, and keystrokes are stored in muscle memory.

Section 3.3 discussed the completion system in the minibuffer, which helps find commands, files, and other information. EWS installs a series of packages that extend this functionality to make it even easier to find what you need.

Minibuffer completion

Even with the advent of speech-to-text software, the keyboard remains the most common method for converting thoughts into text. While computers might one day even read our minds, there is something to be said about using your fingers to do the talking. Who would want their 'ums' and 'ahs' or their uncensored stream of consciousness committed to text? Writing is as much about thinking and crafting a stream of words as it is about maximising keystrokes per minute.

Completion systems are like predictive text on a mobile phone. You start typing some characters, and the computer lets you complete your choice. Emacs has an extendable completion system that helps you complete long words, find files, remember function names and other menial tasks. Emacs has three types of completion systems:

1. *Minibuffer completion* assists with picking choices in the minibuffer, such as function names and files.

2. *Keychord completion*: Systems to help with keyboard shortcuts.

3. *Text completion* helps you complete words you type in the buffer.

The minibuffer is the place to find files, evaluate functions, and enter other information. The minibuffer completion system aims to make it easier to find what you need by providing a search mechanism that provides a list of possible options. The standard minibuffer Emacs completion system focuses on entering functions, filenames, buffer names and any other selection process in the minibuffer.

The minibuffer completion system is highly configurable, and several packages extend the vanilla functionality. The EWS configuration uses a set of connected packages developed by Daniel Mender to provide a seamless experience.

The Vertico package uses incremental search, meaning the list of candidates is shortened to match your entry as soon as you type one or more characters. For example, when opening a file with C-x C-f, you can start typing any part of the filename to locate the file you seek.

The Savehist package remembers your selections and saves your minibuffer history when exiting Emacs. This package ensures that your most popular choices remain on top for further convenience. To further refine Emacs' ability to find completion candidates, the Orderless package matches patterns, irrespective of the order in which they are typed. For example, typing emacs writing provides the same results as writing emacs.

Emacs is a self-documenting computing environment, meaning that every function and variable includes a text description of what it does. The Marginalia package displays the first line of these texts next to your completion candidates. This package also shows available keyboard shortcuts for relevant completion candidates (Figure 4.1). When you type M-x, you will see a list of functions and a brief description of what they do and whether there is a keyboard shortcut to access them.

```
17/8739 M-x []
emacs-uptime                    Return a string giving the uptime of this instance of Emacs.
bibtex-sort-buffer              Sort BibTeX buffer alphabetically by key.
normal-mode                     Choose the major mode for this buffer automatically.
org-metadown (M-<down>)         Move subtree down or move table row down.
eval-buffer                     Execute the accessible portion of current buffer as Lisp code.
scratch-buffer                  Switch to the *scratch* buffer.
common-lisp-mode                Major mode for editing programs in Common Lisp and other similar Lisps.
org-wc-count-subtrees           Count words in each subtree, putting result as the property :org-wc on that he...
org-wc-display                  Show subtree word counts in the entire buffer.
list-packages                   Display a list of packages.
```

Figure 4.1: Minibuffer completion with Vertico, Orderless and Marginalia.

Keyboard shortcuts

Completion shortens the amount of text you must type. It is ideal for discovering functionality you may not have realised existed. However, as explained in the previous chapter, we typically don't type function names but use keyboard shortcuts instead.

Remembering which keyboard shortcut you need takes some effort. The Which-Key package by Justin Burkett helps you remember which keyboard shortcut to use. This package displays the keybindings following the currently entered prefix keys in a popup (figure 4.2).

Many keyboard shortcuts have multiple parts, such as C-x C-f. Which-Key lists all the available options. When, for example, you press C-x, the menu will list all follow-up keys and the function they are bound to. Where it says prefix in the popup, this indicates a deeper level of detail. So, by pressing C-c w, the EWS prefix, you see a list of the available sub-menus and functions.

If the shortcuts are too numerous to fit in the minibuffer, then you can move to the next page with C-h n and the previous page with C-h p. Typing C-h inside the Which-Key menu displays additional options at the bottom of the screen.

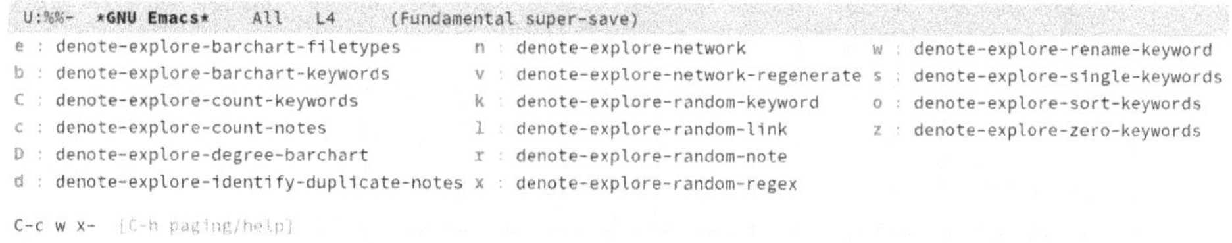

```
U:%%-  *GNU Emacs*    All  L4     (Fundamental super-save)
e : denote-explore-barchart-filetypes      n : denote-explore-network             w : denote-explore-rename-keyword
b : denote-explore-barchart-keywords       v : denote-explore-network-regenerate  s : denote-explore-single-keywords
C : denote-explore-count-keywords          k : denote-explore-random-keyword      o : denote-explore-sort-keywords
c : denote-explore-count-notes             l : denote-explore-random-link         z : denote-explore-zero-keywords
D : denote-explore-degree-barchart         r : denote-explore-random-note
d : denote-explore-identify-duplicate-notes x : denote-explore-random-regex

C-c w x-  [C-h paging/help]
```

Figure 4.2: Which-Key popup window for C-c w d.

Finding help

Emacs Writing Studio utilises the Helpful package by Wilfred Hughes. This package provides additional context to help screens, enhancing access to information. EWS overrides the regular keybindings for the help system:

- C-h x: Help about commands (helpful-command)

- C-h k: Help about a keyboard shortcut (helpful-key)

- C-h v: Help about variables (helpful-variable)

4.4 Recent files and bookmarks

Whenever you return to a new Emacs session, you can open a recently opened file. The recent files minor mode (`recentf-mode`) list the files you most recently opened. To access this list, use `C-c w r` and search for your target on the list.

This minor mode saves a list of the files with associated open buffers when you exit Emacs and go to your configuration folder. The `recentf-edit-list` function opens this list, so you can modify it manually should you need to. The Recent Files mode stores the last 50 files that have been opened. Recent files are transient and continuously updated as you open new files.

For a more permanent list of files you like to open, use bookmarks. You can store a file as a bookmark with `C-x r m` (`bookmark-set`). The bookmark will also store the cursor's location, so you can maintain multiple bookmarks for a single directory or file. The default name for the bookmark is the filename. You can also enter a bespoke name in the minibuffer before saving. To view a list of all available bookmarks in the minibuffer and select the one you like to open, use `C-x r b` (`bookmark-jump`). If you want to remove a bookmark that is no longer required, use the `bookmark-delete` function. This function has no default keybinding but is bound to `C-x r d` in EWS. Bookmarks are saved in the `bookmarks` file in your configuration folder when creating or removing a bookmark.

4.5 Introducing Org mode

The previous chapter explained how to write a plain text file. Now, we add a new layer of functionality by introducing Org mode. This powerful major mode comes with Emacs by default. This software was initially developed in 2003 by Carsten Dominik, a professor of astronomy at the University of Amsterdam. Since then, countless other developers have continued to advance Org. Many people use Emacs because Org is a perfect environment for writing.

You can use Org mode to publish websites, articles and books, keep a diary, write research notes, manage your actions, and more. Additionally, it is intuitive to use. This section shows you the basics of writing prose in Org. The remainder of the book explains the more specialised functionality of this extensive package.

Start by creating a file with a `.org` extension and start writing, for example, `C-x C-f test.org`. Emacs automatically enables Org for any file with the `.org` extension. Org is derived from text mode, so everything explained in section 3.8 also applies here.

Each Org document starts with a header that contains metadata and settings relevant to the buffer. Org mode metadata and settings begin with #+ followed by a keyword and a colon, and then the metadata. The document header can also contain other metadata, such as a subtitle, a date and other bits of information. Emacs packages can utilise this information when publishing the text and for various functionalities. If Shakespeare had used Org, the front matter for *Romeo and Juliet* would be:

```
#+title:   The Most Excellent Tragedy of Romeo and Juliet
#+author:  William Shakespeare
#+date:    [1597-05-08 Thu]
```

Document structure

One of the unofficial rules of writing is to define the structure before writing the content. Books have chapters, sections and paragraphs; articles have headings; poems have verses; and so on. Almost all forms of writing have a hierarchy. Org mode has a flexible set of commands to quickly define the structure of your writing project. Defining headings is as easy as starting a line with an asterisk followed by a space. To create deeper levels, add more stars:

```
* Heading 1
** Heading 2
*** Heading 3
```

When you press M-<Ret>, the following line becomes a new heading. With C-<Ret>, the new line is added after the text in the current section. You can also promote a standard paragraph to a heading using C-c * (org-toggle-heading). Org also makes it easy to move and promote or demote existing headings and associated subheadings and text (which in Org is a subtree). Just use the Alt and arrow keys to move a subtree around the document. You can also use these keys to move paragraphs.

A subtree cannot move past a superior level using the Alt and up/down arrow keys. A faster method to move a subtree to another section of the document is to use the refile command, which can be accessed by pressing C-c C-w (org-refile). This command prompts you to enter a headline to refile the selected heading and its associated text and then moves it accordingly.

When the cursor is on a heading, the Tab key collapses the text. Repeatedly pressing the Tab key shows the subheadings and then the full text again. To collapse the whole document, add the Shift key. Pressing S-<Tab> collapses the whole buffer, showing only the level one headings. Pressing S-<Tab> once again will show headings, and repeating it for a second time reveals all text. You can keep cycling through these modes with the S-<Tab> key (figure 4.3 and table 4.1). You can recognise folded headings by the ellipses (...) at the end of the line. The Org-Modern package (section 4.5) changes the asterisks to triangles. When the triangle points to the right, the heading is collapsed, and when it points down, the heading is open.

Figure 4.3: Global cycling in Org with S-Tab.

Org mode also provides a set of commands to facilitate easier navigation between headings. These commands allow you to move between headings of the same level and

Table 4.1: Org mode structure editing.

Shortcut	Description
`<Tab>` / `S-<Tab>`	(Un)fold headings
`M-<up>` / `M-<down>`	Move a heading or paragraph
`M-<left>` / `M-<right>`	Promote or demote a heading
`M-<Ret>`	Insert a new heading
`C-c *`	Convert paragraph to heading
`C-c -`	Convert paragraph to a list item

navigate up the hierarchy. Table 4.1 lists some of the available commands related to the structure of Org documents. Figure 4.4 visualises how to move between Org headings with the `C-c C-*` keys, where * stands for b, f, n, p or u. So `C-c C-n` moves the cursor to the next heading, irrespective of its level on the hierarchy and `C-c C-u` moves to the parent of the current heading.

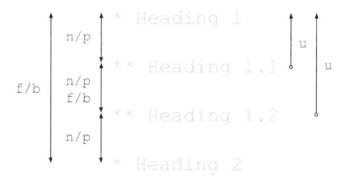

Figure 4.4: Moving between headings in Org mode with `C-c C-*` keys.

Text formatting

Writing all words in the same style can be boring, and some text needs emphasis. To change how Org displays text, you surround it with special characters:

`/italic/, *bold*, _underline_, +strikethrough+, =verbatim=`

In Vanilla Emacs, these markers remain visible but disappear when exporting the document to its published format. The EWS configuration hides these markers. The only problem with hiding emphasis markers that way is that rich text becomes hard to edit because it is unclear whether your cursor is on the marker or the first or last character. EWS, therefore, uses the Org-Appear package by Alice Hacker. This tool displays the rich text markers while the cursor is on a word but hides them otherwise, resulting in a less cluttered screen.

Lists

Writing lots of prose in long paragraphs can make content hard to understand, so non-fiction authors use lists to create clarity in writing. Writing lists in Org is as easy as it gets.

Start a line with a dash and complete the entry with M-<Ret> to create the next entry. Using the Alt and left or right arrow keys changes the depth of the item. The Alt key, combined with the up and down arrows, moves the line up or down in the hierarchy. You can change the list prefix with the Shift and left/right arrow keys. You can convert a paragraph to a list with C-c - (org-toggle-item). Repeatedly using this command changes the bullet type, just like Shift and the arrow keys.

```
- Item
  + next item
    1. Numbered list
    2. And another
```

Numbered lists start at one by default, but you can add a cookie to start the list at a different number. For example, to start the list at number 3, add [@3], as shown below.

```
3. [@3] First line
4. Second line
```

Links

A text, just like a person, cannot exist in solitude. People have family and friends, and so do texts. You might need links to connect related files or reference text from which your writing borrows ideas. Relationships between electronic texts are established with hyperlinks. Org mode recognises an extensive suite of link types, such as websites, Document Object Identifiers (DOI) and internal files.

Links in Org appear between double square brackets `[[ ]]` and start with an identifier, followed by the link itself. For example, websites begin with the usual `https:` and files start with `file:` and DOI numbers, you guessed it, start with `doi:`.

When the link location contains spaces, you need to surround it with quotation marks for it to become active: `[[file:"file name"]]`. Links can also contain a description using the following syntax: `[[type:link][description]]`. When a link has a description, Org hides the syntax and formats it like a hyperlink on a website. A link to a website in Org appears as an underlined hyperlink, displaying only the description. The `org-toggle-link-display` command switches this behaviour on and off. So this is what the syntax of a link to Wikipedia looks like under the hood:

```
[[https://wikipedia.org/][Wikipedia]]
```

You follow a link in Org with a mouse click or by pressing `C-c C-o` with your cursor on the link text (`org-open-at-point`). If you use this shortcut anywhere in the text that is not a link, Org presents a list of links in the current section.

You don't have to type the square brackets and create and edit links with `C-c C-l` (`org-insert-link`). This function first asks you to select the link type and then the full link address. The final step requests an optional description. To remove a link and retain only the description as plain text, use this command and delete the link address while keeping or modifying the description.

Org mode hides the link syntax by default. You can toggle this behaviour with the `org-toggle-link-display` command.

EWS includes Adam Porter's Org-Webtools package, which provides convenience functions for working with website links. To create a link to a website, copy any URL from the browser and use `org-web-tools-insert-link-for-url` (`C-c w w`). This command creates a fully-formatted link from the URL in the kill ring and fetches a description from the website. To find out what other functionality this package provides, use `C-h P org-web-tools`.

Images

Although Emacs is a plain text processor, it can also display images. Org does not embed images in the file but creates a link, so the text and the images remain separate files. Image links are links to other files without a description. To add an image, press `C-c C-l` (`org-insert-link`) and type `file:`. Press Enter and select the image filename in the minibuffer, but don't enter a description.

You can skip the `file:` part by adding the universal argument with the `C-u C-c C-l` shortcut, from where you can start selecting an image file. Your buffer will now contain a link that begins with `file:`, the directory and file name. Links to files can be absolute or relative to the directory the document you are linking from.

```
[[file:path/to/image]]
```

After adding the link, you can preview the image with `C-c C-x C-M-v`, which is bound to the `org-redisplay-inline-images` function. To toggle previewing pictures in the whole document, use `C-c C-x C-v` (`org-toggle-inline-images`). The EWS configuration enables default image previews in all Org buffers. When adding a new image, you need to enable the preview with the redisplay command (`C-c C-x C-M-v`).

Images in an Org mode buffer are always aligned to the left or right edge of the page, depending on the writing direction of your language. Images are 300 pixels wide in an Org buffer by default. You can configure the preview size to your preference by adding a line above the image, for example: `#+attr_org:  :width 600`. This line only changes the size of the image in the Org buffer but not in the final exported format. You can also add a caption and a reference name to an image. Chapter 8 explains how to set the image size, alignment, captions and cross-references for the final exported version. The example below shows what an image looks like in Org, including a caption, reference name, and attributes.

```
#+caption:  This is the image caption.
#+name:     fig-example
#+attr_org: :width 600
[[file:path/to-image]]
```

My writing projects contain a separate folder with image files to keep them separate from the text. Changing the name of an image file or removing it from the project results in a dead link. Emacs also has some facilities to manage image libraries through the Image-Dired package, discussed in Chapter 9.

Tables

A table is a common mechanism in technical publications to structure information instead of prose. Creating tables in Org uses an intuitive method to add, remove and move columns and rows. To create a table, start a line with a pipe (|) symbol, enter the content, and continue until you have defined all columns and end the line with a final pipe. You don't have to worry about aligning the text because the `Tab` key automatically adds spaces to adjust the column sizes. It also adds another row and places the cursor in the first cell.

When you start a row with |- and hit `Tab`, you create a horizontal line across the table. Start filling the cells with information. If the table becomes misaligned, then the `Tab` key or `C-c C-c` will realign the spacing. You can also add a horizontal line below the cursor and move to the next row with `C-c -`.

```
| Country   | Area |
|-----------+------|
| Singapore |  735 |
```

Org can also simplify creating an empty table or converting a region of text to a table with `org-table-create-or-convert-from-region`, which is bound to C-c |. When no region is selected, Org asks for the dimensions of the table. Entering 3x4 results in a table with three columns and four rows (including a header), or whatever size you seek. When you select a region when issuing this command, the region converts to a table, and any commas in the text become columns. This feature is useful when copying a table from another non-Org document, such as a website. If you have a table stored in a CSV (Comma-Separated Values) file, then you can import it with the `org-import-table` function.

Navigate forward through cells with the Tab or arrow up/down keys. Using S-<Tab> moves the cursor back one cell. To rearrange the structure of a table, combine the Alt and the arrow keys. So M-<up> moves a row up, and M-<left> moves a column to the left. Combining Alt and Shift with the arrow keys adds and removes columns and rows adjacent to the cursor. There is no need to sort your table manually. If you need to sort the table alphabetically or numerically, then use the `org-sort` function (which also sorts lists). This function provides a choice menu in the minibuffer to confirm your sort order. Lastly, if you find that your rows should become columns and vice versa, then the `org-table-transpose-table-at-point` does that job for you.

Moving within a cell is also possible with M-a and M-e (`backwards-sentence` and `forward-sentence`). Using these commands moves the cursor to the start or end of the cell's content. You can also use these commands to jump between sentences in a paragraph of prose outside a table.

The Column width defaults to the length of the widest cell plus two spaces. Columns that contain mostly numbers are automatically aligned to the right and other columns to the left. You can override this behaviour by adding a special row that indicates its alignment and width between angle brackets (<>).

The example below shows the top three counties by area in km². The width of the first column is constrained to the first 13 characters and centred. Use the C-c <Tab> shortcut to toggle between shortened and full-width columns. Possible alignment cookies are <l>, <c>, and <r>, which can be combined with a column width, as shown in the example below. Using C-c <Tab> without a width cookie will minimise the column to only one character.

```
#+caption: Top three countries by size.
|   Country   ...|     Area |
|----------------+----------|
|    <c13>    ...| <l>      |
|   Russia    ...| 17098242 |
|   Canada    ...| 9984670  |
|    China    ...| 9640011  |
```

Inserting special characters

A text is often more than a collection of letters, numbers and punctuation. Two methods are available to insert non-alphanumeric characters into your text.

The standard Emacs method is to insert special characters directly into your text. The insert-char function (C-x 8 <Ret>) provides a menu with hundreds of options. If you need any of the available arrow types, then search for the desired arrow with the arrow keys and select the one you need. The glyphs that you choose need, of course, to be available within the font that you use. This approach also lets you insert emojis, the twenty-first-century version of hieroglyphs, into the document. The C-x 8 e prefix key provides a menu with functions to select and insert emojis.

Org mode also provides a method to insert special characters inspired by LaTeX syntax. When, for example, you type \pi, Org displays this as π when pretty entities are enabled, which is the default in EWS. You can toggle this behaviour with the C-c C-x \

keys (`org-toggle-pretty-entities`). Greek letters (\alpha to \omega) and many other symbols are available.

To see a list of all these entities and how they translate to LaTeX or HTML, issue the `org-entities-help` command. Use the Org entity to insert the special character. Table 4.2 shows some of the special characters available in Org. Notice that most of the Org entities are identical to their LaTeX equivalents. Section 8.6 provides more details on using LaTeX in Org.

Table 4.2: Examples of Org mode entities.

Symbol	Org entity
Δ	\Delta
ℵ	\aleph
…	\dots
€	\EUR

To write super- and subscripts, use the caret and underscore notation, such as m^{2} or CO_{2}, which is displayed as m² and CO_2. By default, Org does not require curly braces for sub- and superscripts. But this can cause confusion if you like to write something using 'snake_case'. The EWS configuration limits applying sub- and superscripts to characters within curly braces.

Mathematical notation

Technical authors often rely on mathematical notation, which in Org is written in LaTeX syntax. A formula is surrounded by one or two dollar signs. A single dollar sign indicates an inline formula while using double dollar signs displays the formula as a separate paragraph with larger symbols. To give you a taste of what LaTeX formulas look like, this is Ramanujan's formula for π, both graphically and in LaTeX notation.

$$\frac{1}{\pi} = \frac{\sqrt{8}}{9801} \sum_{n=0}^{\infty} \frac{(4n)!}{(n!)^4} \times \frac{26390n + 1103}{396^{4n}}$$

A full explanation of LaTeX formula notation is outside the scope of this book. You can reverse-engineer this example to learn about the principles of LaTeX mathematical notation.

```
$$\frac{1}{\pi} = \frac{\sqrt{8}}{9801}
  \sum_{n=0}^{\infty} \frac{(4n)!}{(n!)^4} \times
  \frac{26390n + 1103}{396^{4n}}$$
```

When pretty entities are enabled, some LaTeX symbols are converted to mathematical notation, so you should disable this when writing math expressions with `C-c C-x \`.

Org mode can preview LaTeX fragments as images if the `dvipng` program is available (bundled with LaTeX). To preview the fragment under the cursor, press the `C-c C-x C-l` keys (`org-latex-preview`). This process converts LaTeX formulas to an SVG file stored in a subdirectory named `ltximg`.

The Org-Fragtog package by Benjamin Levy provides convenient functionality to toggle between plain text LaTeX fragments and image previews. When the cursor is inside a formula, Emacs displays the plain text; when outside a formula, it displays the graphical version, eliminating the need for manual switching between the two.

Ricing Org mode

Ricing is a slang term among software developers, referring to heavily customising the appearance of their editor. This prettification could involve themes, fonts, and other visual tweaks to create a unique style. Vanilla Emacs is an ugly duckling that can be configured into a beautiful swan. The EWS configuration file contains some modifications to the user interface.

The main difference between a plain text processor and a WYSIWYG word processor is that in Emacs, the design of the text (font, colour and so on) communicates meaning rather than design. Your Emacs theme sets the colours and fonts for your document. The purpose of this styling is to help you navigate the document. The way your document appears in the buffer is not what it will look like when exported to the final product.

The active theme, configurations, and packages define the look of an Org mode buffer. Emacs defines how a buffer looks through `font-lock-mode`. Font locking assigns faces to (or 'fontifies' in Emacs speak) parts of your text using logical rules. Evaluating `font-lock-mode` toggles between the fully configured version of your Org mode file and the plain text version. Run this function on an existing Org mode view to see the difference between plain text and fontified text. To take it a step further, you can open an Org mode file and run `text-mode` to disable all Org mode functionality and see the file in its raw beauty. To jump back to safety, run `org-mode` to restore the file.

EWS uses parts of Daniel Mendler's Org-Modern package. This package implements a modern style for your Org buffers using font locking and text properties. However, some of the styling is not implemented because, for beginning users, it is better to see the full syntax. The Appendix explains how to configure this package.

4.6   Checking spelling

Writing with a spellchecker has become the ultimate security blanket for authors. Without the squiggly red line, my writing would be littered with typos. The combined Ispell and Flyspell Emacs packages provide an interface to the Hunspell spell-checking software, so you must ensure that it is available on your computer, including at least one dictionary. The EWS configuration enables the Flyspell minor mode (spelling on the fly) for all text modes.

There are basically two ways to correct your writing. Either keep the juices flowing and check the complete text when you complete the session, or fix typos as detected.

The `ispell` function (`C-c w s s`) walks through all suspected spelling mistakes in the current buffer or selected region. This function displays the proposed corrections at the top of the window. You can choose the preferred correction by entering the relevant number. The minibuffer provides a menu to manage the error. Ignore the typo with the space bar; accept it for this session with a, insert it into your personal dictionary with i, and explore other options that C-h reveals.

Flyspell also has a handy command to jump between suspected spelling errors. The flyspell-goto-next-error function (C-,) places the cursor at the next word that needs a review. Adding the universal argument (C-u C-,) jumps to the previous error. To correct the suspect word, use ispell-word (M-$) and the options in the menu described earlier.

Checking single words requires you to move the cursor to that word and then return to the flow of your writing. Flyspell provides a more convenient way to correct words on the fly with flyspell-auto-correct-previous-word (C-;). This command replaces the first detected spelling error before the cursor is visible on the screen with the most likely alternative.

The most likely candidate is the dictionary word that has the shortest distance to the suspected type. The distance between two words is roughly defined by the number of steps it takes to convert one into the other. Repeatedly pressing C-; cycles through the available options until you return to the original version. The echo area shows the list of possible corrections. Typing any other key breaks the chain. So, to fix two spelling mistakes, you first correct one, type something other than C-; and correct the next problematic word.

The Hunspell software has access to a collection of dictionaries, including variations of English, which must be installed separately. The default dictionary for EWS is Australian English (en_AU). If you are not Australian, then you must customise the ews-hunspell-dictionaries variable to change the default language using the formal Hunspell dictionary name, for example, de_CH for Swiss German or nl_NL for Dutch.

If you write in more than one language, then add multiple dictionaries by adding them to the ews-hunspell-dictionaries variable in a comma-separated string. For example, to accept both Australian-English and Dutch words, customise this variable to "en_AU,nl_NL" and restart Emacs (restart-emacs). Any changes to dictionaries will only take effect when the chosen dictionary is available on your system. The `ispell-hunspell-dict-paths-alist` variable lists the installed dictionaries.

4.7 Learning more

These are the basics of the functionality that EWS adds to the vanilla Emacs system. The remainder of this book follows the EWS workflow by describing a linear writing process from inspiration to publication, as explained in section 2.6.

The EWS GitHub repository also contains the `org-demo.org` file, which includes examples of the functionality explained in this chapter. To play is the best way to learn, so boot up your computer and get ready for an adventure.

Chapter 5

Inspiration: Read, Listen and Watch

A common question for authors and other creative people is where they get their ideas from. The responses to this simple question are often mystical and vague, but a big part of the answer is straightforward. Authors need three resources for their inspiration: imagination, writing skills and the works of other writers. The thoughts and ideas of other thinkers are the foundation upon which authors build their works. In 1675, Sir Isaac Newton wrote a letter to Robert Hooke in which he penned the now-famous phrase, "If I have seen further, it is by standing on the shoulders of Giants". This quote may be a cliché, but it remains true, even in the era of generative AI.

Building on the works of other creators is essential, not only in academic writing, which has strict conventions regarding referencing. All authors need to read, listen, and watch to write effectively. Therefore, the first step in *Emacs Writing Studio* (EWS) workflow is consuming information created by others, either by reading, listening to, or watching content.

Even though Emacs is a text processor, it can invoke other software to display e-books and play media files. Besides being malleable software, Emacs is also an interface to other software. This means that we can use Emacs for tasks besides writing and editing text. You can also use Emacs to listen to music or podcasts and watch videos with the assistance of some additional software.

Keeping track of your collection of physical and electronic literature collection is another essential task of a scholar. Emacs can also assist with creating a searchable bibliography and media archive for easy access to your resources.

This chapter explains how to use Emacs to read electronic documents in the most common open formats, surf the web, and consume multimedia files. This chapter also demonstrates how to create a plain text database to manage your collections of electronic books and media files.

5.1 Reading e-books

In the pre-digital era, people shared information physically, from clay tablets to scrolls and paper books. Before the internet, the only way to find new information was to visit a library and spend hours and days wading through catalogues and books. Digital documents have become the norm over the last two decades, and the internet has all but eliminated the need to visit a library.

Most e-books are not distributed in plain text but in formats such as PDF, ePub, or DjVu. A notable exception is Project Gutenberg (`gutenberg.org`), an extensive electronic library of over 70,000 copyright-free e-books. This library started in 1971 and distributes books in plain text and other open formats. In addition to classic literature, it also distributes a variety of genres and subjects, making it a valuable resource of copyright-free literature.

Emacs can only render e-books in open formats. An open format, as opposed to a proprietary format, has a publicly available specification, allowing anyone to develop software to create and read these files. The most significant advantage of an open format is that any device can display the text. Emacs cannot read proprietary formats, such as Apple iBooks and Kindle books. Proprietary file formats pose a grave risk to cultural continuity. Some governments, therefore, require open document formats to enforce digital sovereignty and liberate themselves from the dominance of large corporations (Pohle & Thiel, 2020).

Emacs needs assistance from other software to display e-books and word processor documents. The diagram in figure 5.1 illustrates the programs necessary to render pages from the supported file formats. This software converts each page to a plain text buffer or a PNG image, which Emacs can display.

The following software is required to read the most common e-book formats:

- Ghostscript (`gs`) and/or MuPDF (`mutool`): These two packages can convert PDF files to images.

- Poppler (`pdftotext`): Another tool to render PDF files and convert them to plain text.

- LibreOffice (`soffice`): Office productivity software suite to view office documents.

- DjVuLibre (`ddjvu`): Reading DjVu e-books

- Unzip: Extract files from ZIP files to read ePub books.

The EWS configuration issues a warning when any of these packages are unavailable. Emacs will function normally, but some features may be unavailable. The warnings are displayed in the Messages buffer, which opens in another window with `C-h e` (`view-echo-area-messages`).

PDF files

Portable Document Format (PDF) is a versatile system developed by Adobe in the early 1990s. PDF presents documents consistently, regardless of the software, hardware, or

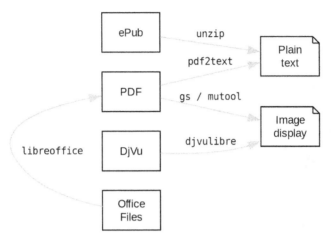

Figure 5.1: Reading electronic documents in Emacs.

operating system used to view them. PDF is codified in an international standard (ISO 32000) and has become the main open format for electronic literature.

Each PDF file includes a complete description of a fixed-layout document. The file contains the text, fonts, layout, typography, images, and other information needed to display the content.

A PDF file follows a traditional physical layout and typography, assuming that documents are printed. A PDF document is not an actual e-book because its layout is fixed, unlike other electronic formats that adjust to the screen size.

Emacs can display PDF files with the built-in DocView major mode with some assistance from GhostScript or MuPDF, which convert the files to images. Open a PDF file just as you would any other document. To navigate the file, use the arrow and Page Up / Page Down keys. Several other keyboard shortcuts are available to find your way through the document (table 5.1).

When the `mutool` program is available on your system, you can also use the `imenu` (M-g i) command to view a table of contents and jump to a chapter, assuming the PDF file has bookmarks.

To enable searching through a PDF file, you need the `pdftotext` tool, part of the Poppler software package. Fun fact: The name of this utility is based on an episode from the *Futurama* cartoon series.

You can search within a document with `doc-view-search` (bound to C-s), which creates a list of all matching pages and shows how many pages contain the search query. After the search, you can jump to the next page containing a match with an additional C-s.

DocView does not highlight the searched term, but pressing C-t shows the search results for this page in a tooltip (`doc-view-show-tooltip`). Poppler also allows you to view a PDF file as a plain text file with the C-c C-t shortcut (`doc-view-open-text`). This option makes searching and copying relevant text to your notes easier. To return to the graphical view of the text, press C-c C-c twice.

Table 5.1: Doc-View keyboard shortcuts.

Keystroke	Description
P	Zoom to the full page
W	Fit width to window
H	Fit height to window
+ / –	Zoom in and out
M-g g	Jump to page
M-< / M->	Jump to first or last page
k	Kill (close) the file
?	Help file

Office documents

The DocView package can also read Microsoft Office and LibreOffice documents. To enable this functionality, you must install the LibreOffice software package, a free and open-source office productivity software suite.

When opening an office document, Emacs invokes LibreOffice (`soffice`) to convert the file to a PDF and display it in DocView (figure 5.1), leveraging the functionality explained in the previous section. You can use this method to open not only word processor files but also presentations and spreadsheets, all of which are converted to PDF before viewing.

Office documents are compressed XML files, so when you open them with an archiving utility, you can view their content in plain text. Unfortunately, two standards for office documents exist. Free software, such as LibreOffice, uses an open standard, while commercial software vendors often adopt a different version. Differences between these standards can result in minor formatting issues when reading files created with commercial software.

DjVu books

DJVU (pronounced *déjà vu*) is a file format intended for scanned books. Since a DJVU file can contain high-quality colour images, photographs, text, and drawings, it's often used for archival documents. DjVu files use the `.djvu` or the `.djv` file extension. DocView can read DjVu files when DjVuLibre is available on your system.

DocView displays PDF, office documents, and DjVu documents, so the same functionality available when viewing PDF files also applies to these other formats. You can read more details about this package in the Emacs Manual, which you can quickly find with `C-h r g docu`.

Limitations of DocView

DocView has some limitations compared to other document viewers. The text is displayed as a PNG file, which limits search capabilities and makes copying text impossible.

The PDF Tools package by Vedang Manerikar is more versatile than DocView. Unfortunately, it is not included in EWS because it is complex to install on non-Linux systems. The Emacs Application Framework is another tool that provides an improved PDF reader, which relies on Python.

The final section of this chapter explains how to configure Emacs to open binary files such as PDF in other software.

ePub files

An ePub file (Electronic Publication) is a widely used open format for digital books, magazines, and other written content. Unlike PDF and DjVu formats, the content adapts to the screen's geometry, making it ideal for e-readers, tablets, and other devices. An ePub file is a website in a box. You can view the raw content of an ePub file when you open it with an archiving utility. The file consists of a collection of HTML files that define the content and design of the book, as well as any image files used for illustrations. This file format requires the Unzip package to view the content.

The nov package by Vasilij Schneidermann provides functionality for viewing ePub books inside Emacs. Open an ePub file and scroll with the space bar, the arrow keys or the page-up / page-down keys. Several keyboard shortcuts are available to move through the book (table 5.2).

Table 5.2: Keyboard shortcuts in the Nov package.

Keystroke	Function	Description
t	nov-goto-toc	Table of contents
n	nov-next-document	Next chapter
p	nov-previous-document	Previous chapter
q	quit-window	Quit
?	describe-mode	Help buffer

To increase or decrease the text size, use the C-x C-+ and C-c C-- keyboard shortcuts (text-scale-adjust). When enlarging the font, parts of the text may move outside the window. To reset the length of the lines, press g to re-render the document (nov-render-document).

You can copy and paste text from ePub files into your bibliographic notes (chapter 6) using the kill-ring-save command (M-w). You can also copy images from an ePub file. Open the file as an archive with the a key (nov-reopen-as-archive), which shows the document's internal structure. From here, you can navigate to the relevant image file, copy it with the C key (archive-copy-file), and select the new location and name. Unfortunately, there is no functionality to preview images inside an archive.

5.2 Managing your digital library

Maintaining a large collection of literature can quickly lead to chaos, so most scholars use an electronic bibliography to keep track of what they read. Emacs can help you build a plain text library catalogue to easily access your bibliography. This bibliography can also link to notes (chapter 6) and facilitate scholarly citations (chapters 7 and 8).

Creating and managing a bibliography requires three Emacs packages that seamlessly integrate with each other. The built-in BibTeX Mode assists with creating and maintaining a plain-text bibliography. The Biblio package by Clément Pit-Claudel searches online scholarly databases and inserts relevant items into your bibliography. Bruce D'Arcus' Citar package provides easy access to your bibliography using the minibuffer completion system. These three packages turn Emacs into a fully featured literature management system.

Getting started with BibTeX mode

BibTeX Mode is a major mode for creating and managing bibliographies. As the name suggests, this mode uses the BibTeX file format as your default literature database. BibTeX is a plain text format to organise literature and citations. It is typically used for typesetting scholarly publications with LaTeX (Lamport, 1994). A typical entry for a book will look like this:

```
@article{stallman_1981_emacs,
    title       = {EMACS the Extensible, Customizable
                   Self-Documenting Display Editor},
    author      = {Stallman, Richard M.},
    year        = 1981,
    journal     = {ACM SIGOA Newsletter},
    volume      = 2,
    number      = {1-2},
    pages       = {147--156},
    doi         = {10.1145/1159890.806466},
```

```
keywords   = {Emacs}
file       = {computing/stallman-1981-emacs.pdf}
}
```

Each entry starts with an @-sign and the publication type (book, article or other types), followed by a curly brace and a unique citation key. The following lines contain the relevant data about this entry. BibTeX can process various kinds of literature, including articles and conference papers, each with its own specific field types. BibTeX ignores unrecognised fields, which provides opportunities to use the format for other purposes, such as attaching files and keywords.

You can store one or more bibliography files in a folder to refer to them from anywhere in Emacs. In EWS, the `ews-bibtex-directory` variable defines this folder. You need to customise this variable to the desired location, which is set to `~/library` by default. The tilde at the start indicates the path to your home directory. After you customise this variable, run the `ews-bibtex-register` function to register the bibliography files in this directory. You need to run this function every time you add or remove a BibTeX file from this folder.

You don't need to install external software to get started. Just create an empty file in your bibliography directory with a `.bib` extension, and Emacs enables BibTeX mode when you open the file.

BibTeX is a venerable tool that remains relevant, albeit with some limitations. BibLaTeX is a modernised version that enables various output styles and integration with modern LaTeX document classes. Advanced LaTeX users can also use the BibLaTeX variant by setting the `bibtex-dialect` variable to `biblatex`.

Adding new entries

Emacs BibTeX mode uses templates to add new entries. To add a new reference, use the `bibtex-entry` function (C-c C-b) and select the relevant publication type. Emacs also provides shortcuts for each type of literature. You can read a list of these commands when inside a BibTeX file with C-c C-e ?.

Most fields are optional, but each literature type has at least one compulsory field. Optional fields start with 'OPT'. You must complete at least one field that begins with 'ALT', such as author or editor. For a book, as shown in the example below, the title, publisher and year fields are compulsory, and you have to complete either the author or the editor field or both. All other fields are optional. Each type of literature has its own template.

```
@Book{,
  ALTauthor    = {},
  ALTeditor    = {},
  title        = {},
  publisher    = {},
  year         = {},
  OPTkey       = {},
  OPTvolume    = {},
  OPTnumber    = {},
  OPTseries    = {},
  OPTaddress   = {},
  OPTedition   = {},
  OPTmonth     = {},
  OPTnote      = {},
  OPTkeywords  = {},
  OPTfile      = {}
}
```

Jump from field to field with C-j (bibtex-next-field) and complete all required fields and one of the ALT fields. When done, press C-c C-c (bibtex-clean-entry) to check the syntax and remove empty fields. This function also assigns a unique citation key to the entry using some configurable rules. You can override this citation key and set one manually, as long as it is unique. BibTeX mode issues a warning when it finds duplicate keys. To clean up the buffer and align the fields, use the bibtex-fill-entry function (C-c C-q). This command also removes redundant curly braces to create a clean look. Table 5.3 summarises the most salient keyboard shortcuts and functions in BibTeX mode.

To enter author or editor names, place the family name first, followed by a comma and the first name or initials. Separate additional authors by "and", e.g. "Hawking, S. and Penrose, R.". If you copy and paste an author name, the first and family name might be the wrong way around. A nice Emacs hack is to use the org-transpose-words function, bound to M-t, which swaps the order of two words left and right of the cursor. For example, transform "Stephen Hawking" to "Hawking Stephen" with M-t and add a comma after the last name to finish it off.

Table 5.3: Overview of keyboard shortcuts to add and edit entries.

Keystroke	Function	Description
C-c C-b	bibtex-entry	Add an entry for selected type
C-c d	bibtex-empty-field	Empty the current field
C-j	bibtex-next-field	Jump to next field
C-down	bibtex-next-entry	Jump to the next entry
C-up	bibtex-previous-entry	Jump to the previous entry
C-c C-c	bibtex-clean-entry	Clean the entry
C-c C-q	bibtex-fill-entry	Align the fields

This section provides a brief overview of the capabilities of this package. The documentation for this package is sparse. Jonathan Le Roux (jonathanleroux.org) hosts a comprehensive manual on his website that explains the functionality provided by this package in great detail. You can also explore other BibTeX mode functionality by using M-x ^bibtex and reviewing the options in the completion list.

Attachments

The EWS configuration provides additional fields to categorise literature with keywords and to attach one or more files. Your BibTeX attachments should also reside in the ews-bibtex-directory or a subdirectory. Any file paths for BibTeX entries start at this location.

For example, when the BibTeX entry states: `file={topology/article.pdf}`, the attachment is stored at: `~/library/topology/article.pdf`. You can have more than one attachment per entry, separated by a semi-colon. BibTeX attachments have no formal file naming convention, so you can use your favourite method. Section 9.2 provides guidance on constructing a consistent file naming convention.

EWS provides two convenience functions to assure the integrity of the links between the BibTeX files and the attachments. The ideal state is that all files mentioned in the BibTeX entries actually exist, and vice versa: all files in your bibliography directory are listed in BibTeX.

The `ews-bibtex-missing-attachments` function lists all missing attachments in the Messages buffer. To fix this discrepancy, you need to either remove or edit the `file` field in the relevant BibTeX entry or restore the name of the file in your collection. The `ews-bibtex-missing-files` function lists any attachments in your bibliography directory that are not registered in your BibTeX files. To fix any issues, either rename the relevant file or add it to the associated BibTeX entry in the `file` field. These two functions help you to ensure that you can always access your electronic literature through the Citar menu.

Add entries from online sources

BibTeX mode requires you to type all entries manually, which is inefficient and could easily lead to errors. Clément Pit-Claudel's Biblio package lets you browse and import bibliographic references from online sources to undertake a systematic literature review. Currently, the package enables you to search CrossRef, DBLP, arXiv, doi.org, and Dissemin.

Crossref interlinks millions of items from various content types, including journals, books, conference proceedings, research grants, working papers, technical reports, and datasets. Linked content encompasses materials from scientific, technical, and medical (STM) disciplines, as well as social sciences and humanities (SSH). DBLP is a computer science bibliography website featuring over seven million publications. The arXiv (pronounced "archive") is an open-access repository of pre-prints and post-prints approved for posting after moderation but not peer review. In mathematics and physics, almost all scientific papers are self-archived on the arXiv repository before publication in a peer-reviewed journal.

Most electronic publications have a Digital Object Identifier (DOI), a persistent identification code that links to metadata about the publication. The DOI system ensures that publications can be found, even when their addresses change. DOIs are widely used to identify academic, professional, and government information, including journal articles, research reports, datasets, and official publications.

To use the Biblio package, open the relevant BibTeX file, run `biblio-lookup`, select the appropriate database and enter a search query. Once the search results are available, a new buffer opens. Select your target with the arrow keys or search in the buffer with `C-s`. Once you have found the necessary literature, insert its BibTeX record into the buffer where you called the function with `i`. Alternatively, you can copy the BibTeX record with `c` and paste it into place later. You quit the search results with `q`. To see all possible commands in this buffer, use the `h` key.

The `biblio-doi-insert-bibtex` function inserts a BibTeX record based on a DOI number into the current buffer. You can enter just the identifier in one of the two formats mentioned above. You need to activate this command from within a BibTeX buffer with the cursor on the location you would like the new entry to appear.

Unfortunately, large corporate publishers still hold the world's academic knowledge behind closed doors. However, open access and pre-print publications are slowly becoming the norm. The Dissemin website searches for openly accessible copies of papers in an extensive collection of open repositories and websites. To use this service with Emacs, evaluate `dissemin-lookup` to show information about the open access status of a paper using a DOI number. You can also press `x` in the search menu for the `biblio-lookup` function to check for an open-access version.

The Biblio package is useful, but one minor inconvenience is that you must jump to the relevant bibliography file before inserting a new entry. It also provides two separate search functions, one for DOI and another for databases.

The bespoke `ews-bliblio-lookup` (`C-c w b b`) function lets you select the Bib-TeX file where you would like to store the search results before choosing one of the available sources. This function also combines searching for DOIs with the other sources, removing some steps from your workflow.

Access bibliographies

Maintaining one or more BibTeX files to store your library is a good start, but the content is not easy to search and access, especially when you have multiple bibliographies. We need an interface that makes it easy to locate and access literature on your computer, including resources such as links, attachments, and notes.

The Citar package uses minibuffer completion to access your bibliographies, providing access to hyperlinks and attachments. Citar also provides access to your literature notes (chapter 6) and integrates with Org's citation module (chapter 7).

The global Emacs bibliography is a set of BibTeX files available from anywhere within Emacs, located in the `ews-bibtex-directory`. Citar processes all bibliography files in the global folder and any files referenced in an active Org buffer. If you add a new file to the global bibliography, then you need to let Citar know about this addition with the `ews-bibtex-register` function (`C-c w b r`). This function registers all bibliography files in the nominated directory for Citar to use and displays them in the echo area. You only use this function to register new files; it is not required when adding new literature to an existing file.

You activate Citar with `citar-open`, which in EWS is bound to `C-c w b o`. A menu pops up in the minibuffer from where you can search your collection. The first three columns in the menu indicate which entries include a hyperlink (L), one or more attached files (F) and an associated note (N). The remainder shows the author, year, title, citation key and keywords (Figure 5.2).

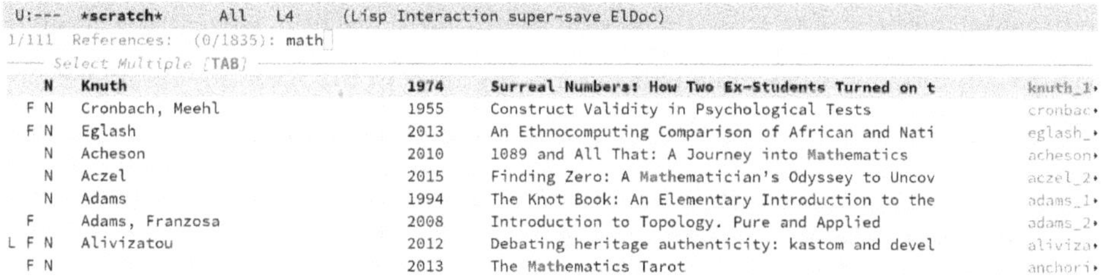

```
U:---  *scratch*   All  L4   (Lisp Interaction super-save ElDoc)
1/111  References:  (0/1835): math
──── Select Multiple [TAB] ────
     N   Knuth              1974   Surreal Numbers: How Two Ex-Students Turned on t    knuth_1▸
  F  N   Cronbach, Meehl    1955   Construct Validity in Psychological Tests          cronbac▸
  F  N   Eglash             2013   An Ethnocomputing Comparison of African and Nati   eglash_▸
     N   Acheson            2010   1089 and All That: A Journey into Mathematics      acheson▸
     N   Aczel              2015   Finding Zero: A Mathematician's Odyssey to Uncov   aczel_2▸
     N   Adams              1994   The Knot Book: An Elementary Introduction to the   adams_1▸
  F      Adams, Franzosa    2008   Introduction to Topology. Pure and Applied         adams_2▸
L F  N   Alivizatou         2012   Debating heritage authenticity: kastom and devel   aliviza▸
  F  N                      2013   The Mathematics Tarot                              anchori▸
```

Figure 5.2: Example of the Citar menu.

Finding literature with Citar is easy due to the power of the Vertico and Orderless packages, as described in chapter 4. After every keystroke, Citar narrows the list of options to relevant matches. Select your candidate with the arrow keys, or use the Tab key to select more than one entry. You can filter the Citar completion menu for entries with an attachment using ":f" and with links with ":l". After hitting the Enter key, Citar provides a popup menu in the minibuffer where you can open attachments or follow any hyperlinks listed in the BibTeX entry.

Using third-party software

If you already have a bibliography management tool, such as Zotero, you can continue using it to achieve the same result. Zotero users can export libraries as BibTeX or BibLaTeX files. The Zotero Better BibTeX package by Emiliano Heyns can synchronise the exported file with Zotero, allowing you to use it seamlessly within Emacs. Most reference management software packages have similar functionality.

5.3   Surf the web

Emacs also has a built-in web browser called the Emacs Web Wowser (EWW). This package prioritises readability over functionality by displaying websites as plain text. It can display images but does not render any CSS or run JavaScript. A wowser is somebody with strong moral views regarding temperance and abstinence. The plain text approach to browsing represents an ethical stance on the World Wide Web, particularly about its security and privacy issues. The name could also refer to the reaction you might have when you first see a website rendered in plain text. Reading websites in plain text is not visually appealing, but it is a more secure way of surfing the internet because EWW does not render any JavaScript.

You can open a URL or search the web with the command eww. If the input doesn't look like a URL, EWW will search the web with DuckDuckGo, a privacy-focused search engine that doesn't track your online behaviour. After the page loads, use the arrow and page-up / page-down keys to navigate the page. Several keyboard shortcuts are available to navigate the webpage.

- <, >: Beginning and end of the page

- R: Readable format (only display the main text)

- G: New search or website

- H: Browsing history

- M-I: Toggle images

- l / n: Previous and next page

- q: Quit the window

- w: Copy the URL under the cursor or the URL of the page

- &: Open the page in the external browser

- ?: Help file with list of other keyboard shortcuts

The enter button opens links (eww-follow-link). If you want the new page to open inside a new buffer, use M-<Ret> (eww-open-in-new-buffer).

The most useful option is R to ignore the navigation parts of the page and focus on the content. If the page does not render in EWW or you are warned about needing JavaScript, use ampersand (&) to escape to your system's default web browser.

When opening a link to a website from inside a non-EWW Emacs buffer, it is opened in the default browser for your operating system. Once you get used to browsing the internet in plain text, then you can set EWW as the default browser to follow links in Emacs. To make this change, customise the `browse-url-browser-function` variable, select 'Emacs Web Wowser' in the value menu and click `[Apply and Save]`.

If you find a website you like, bookmark it with `eww-add-bookmark`, bound to the b key inside EWW. The `eww-list-bookmarks` function lists all stored bookmarks, from which you can select one and visit the page. You can read the EWW manual with `C-h R eww` to find out more details.

Keeping a collection of bookmarks is helpful, but you have to regularly visit these sites to see if anything new has been published. Many blogs and podcasts use RSS feeds to notify their readers of new content, which is the topic of the next section.

Read RSS and Atom feeds

Finding engaging content on the internet can be like sifting through piles of garbage to discover something valuable. Social media can be fun and engaging, but the cacophony of irrelevant and abusive content driven by dark algorithms and bots is disheartening. RSS and Atom feeds enable subscriptions to the websites and blogs you enjoy. A feed is an XML file containing recent content from a website, either the complete text or just an excerpt.

RSS (Really Simple Syndication) is an elegant mechanism for consuming content, as it only displays the blogs or podcasts you have subscribed to. Atom feeds are a more recent format that clarifies some of the ambiguities in RSS. Both feeds are a form of XML, and you need an aggregator to display their content.

When you use RSS, no algorithm decides what you can and cannot see. Subscribing to RSS feeds is anonymous, so you won't be spammed with email funnels trying to sell you products or services. Some websites offer multiple feeds, allowing readers to subscribe to specific topics. For example, the RSS feed for Emacs articles on the accompanying website for this book is:

```
https://lucidmanager.org/tags/emacs/index.xml
```

Unfortunately, RSS feeds have lost importance due to the dominance of social media and website owners' preference for collecting email addresses. Finding RSS feeds used to be easy, but large internet companies prefer to rely on their black-box algorithms to feed content to users. Hence, RSS feeds are all but invisible. However, the technology remains alive and is still used on almost all websites, including those for podcasts and YouTube. Browsers no longer link to the feeds automatically, and websites rarely prominently link to them like they used to, but the feeds still exist.

Almost half of the world's websites use WordPress. You can find the feed for these sites by adding `feed` to the end of the URL. If all else fails, you can locate the feed by inspecting the page source (use the v key when viewing the page in EWW). Don't let the HTML code scare you. Search for `rss-xml` and copy the URL in the `href` specification.

To add YouTube channels, you need the channel ID. You can find this URL in the source code for the channel's home page by searching for `'channel_id='` and adding it to this template:

```
https://www.youtube.com/feeds/videos.xml?channel_id=<ID>
```

The Elfeed package by Christopher Wellons aggregates your favourite RSS feeds. You can list and categorise your favourite feeds. The Elfeed browser helps you navigate your unread articles, YouTube feeds, or podcasts. You must install the cURL program, which stands for 'Client for URLs'. This program assists with downloading files from the internet. If cURL is unavailable, then Elfeed uses the slower built-in Emacs method to extract data, which does not work on Windows computers.

The package creates a database to store the feeds. EWS sets the location of the downloaded content to your Emacs configuration folder. The EWS keyboard shortcut to start Elfeed is C-c w e. However, before reading feeds, you must first find some and add them to a configuration file, then download the data.

The Elfeed-Org package configures your list of favourite websites in an Org file. The package reads the nominated Org file(s) and collects internet addresses or links from the headers with the :elfeed: tag. You set a tag for an Org mode header with C-c C-q. The example below illustrates how to structure your Elfeed Org file. Note that a tag applies to all headings at a lower level, so the :elfeed: tag also applies to the Emacs and news headings. You can also add text comments, as Elfeed only reads headings.

```
#+title: Elfeed Configuration

* Feeds                                  :elfeed:
** Emacs                                 :emacs:
Emacs-related information.
*** https://lucidmanager.org/tags/emacs/index.xml
*** http://www.reddit.com/r/emacs/.rss

** News                                  :news:
*** https://www.abc.net.au/news/feed/2942460/rss.xml
```

You can either use a plain URL or an Org hyperlink. The Org-Webtools package inserts fully formatted hyperlinks into Org mode with C-c w w. When using the EWW browser you copy the current address to the kill ring with w.

The only configuration you need for elfeed-org is to customise the name and location of the Org file(s) you like to use to store your feed links. The location of the Elfeed configuration is stored in the rmh-elfeed-org-files variable, which by default is "~/elfeed.org". The GitHub repository for this book includes an example file to help you get started.

You need to customise this variable to match the file you like to use for your collection of feeds. To add or remove a feed, edit this file and update the database with elfeed-update. You are now ready to read your RSS feeds.

Press C-c w e to start the Elfeed browser, which shows a list with the date and title of each entry, the feed's name and any tags. When you press Enter, Elfeed displays the webpage or a summary with a hyperlink to the web version in a separate window. You can use the following keystrokes to manage your feed:

- G: Fetch feed updates from the servers

- b: Open the article in the system browser

- c: Clear the search filter

- g: Refresh view of the feed listing (remove read items)

- q: Quit Elfeed

- r Mark the entry as read

- s: Update the search filter

- u: Mark the entry as unread

All new entries are tagged as unread by default. The other tags derive from your list of RSS feeds. When you remove a feed from your list, all articles that you previously downloaded will remain in the database and will show on your list until you read or remove them. Elfeed also has a powerful search filter that can be used to filter by tag, feed name, and dates.

5.4 Emacs Multimedia System

Music is an excellent tool for boosting productivity. Playing J.S. Bach's transcendental fugues or Sepultura's polyrhythmic metal soothes the soul while writing your next great work of art. Psychologist Sara Bottiroli and her colleagues studied the psychological effect of background music and found that it can improve episodic memory, intelligence, and verbal and visual processing speeds (Bottiroli, Rosi, Russo, Vecchi, & Cavallini, 2014).

Emacs might be a humble text processor, but it can also facilitate playing background music while you write, listen to podcasts or your field interviews. You might already have a great music player on your computer, but not having to switch applications to play music helps to retain your focus. The Emacs Multimedia System (EMMS) is a comprehensive music and video player for Emacs. It features an intuitive browser that displays album covers and metadata, transforming your Emacs system into a personal jukebox.

Emacs requires access to an external music player to produce sound and to image software to convert album covers into thumbnails. To play sounds with Emacs, you must install one of the compatible sound players (ogg123, mpg321, MPlayer, MPV, or VLC). When you run the EWS configuration, the system checks whether one of these players is available. Any missing software is listed in the messages buffer when you start EWS, which you can access with `C-h e`.

The last step in playing music is caching the music files by scanning your collection of media files. Evaluate the `emms-add-directory-tree` command to scan your collection. EMMS creates a cache in your Emacs configuration directory. EMMS reads metadata in music files for Ogg Vorbis, Opus, FLAC, and MP3 files, as well as some video file types. This process also caches thumbnails and may take some time, depending on the size of your collection. You can start playing music when `EMMS: All track information loaded` shows in the minibuffer. You can view the scan progress in the Messages buffer, which you access with `C-h e`. To add new music to an existing collection, rerun this command and point to the new collection.

The basic principle for playing music files is to move tracks to the playlist buffer.

Figure 5.3: Screenshot of the EMMS browser.

The browser is the most convenient way to select the music of your liking. You start the browser with `emms-browser` (C-c w m b), shown in figure 5.3. Loading the browser for the first time in an Emacs session might take a moment if you have an extensive music collection.

When using the EMMS browser, press the b key followed by a number to browse by artist, album, genre, year, composer, or performer. The browser is collapsed by default, displaying only album covers, artist names, or the selected browsing category. The browser is hierarchical. For example, when browsing by genre, the hierarchy has four levels: *Genre > Artist > Album > Track*. Use the 1 to collapse and the 2-4 keys to expand the categories at levels 1 to 3.

As is the case in most Emacs applications, press ? for a list of available keystrokes, such as:

- r: Jump to a random entry

- s: Search by album, artist, title, performer, or composer

- `Ret`: Add selection to playlist

- `C-j`: Add selection to playlist and play

- `W`: Lookup entry on Wikipedia

Being an Emacs buffer, standard search commands will also work for visible entries. When the cursor is on a category, such as an album name or a composer, it will add all tracks belonging to that category to the playlist. So when the cursor is on an album, it will add all tracks.

When the cursor is on a single track, it will only add that track to the playlist. Jump to the playlist with `emms` (`C-c w m e`), from where you can manage what you play. Press ? for a list of keyboard shortcuts, some of which are:

- `n` / `p`: Next or previous track

- `r`: Play a random track.

- `D`: Remove selected track from playlist

- `C`: Clear playlist

The EWS configuration also configures the multimedia buttons on your keyboard (play, pause, next, previous). The MPRIS (Media Player Remote Interfacing Specification) extension ensures that these buttons also work outside of Emacs.

Once you have curated a funky playlist, you can keep it for future reference in m3u or pls format for use in Emacs or other multimedia players using the `save-buffer` command (`C-x C-s`). The `emms-play-playlist` function (`C-c w m p`) lets you load and play a saved playlist.

EMMS offers numerous advanced features that enable you to manage your sound collection. Some other useful EMMS functions are:

- `emms-play-directory`: Add a directory to the playlist.

- `emms-play-find`: Plays all files in the music directory that match a given search criterion.

The Emacs Multimedia System has a plethora of additional options to fine-tune your listening experience. Read the EMMS manual with the Info Browser (`C-h R emms`) for detailed information about the multitude of options.

5.5   Opening files with other software

Emacs is a Swiss Army chainsaw for plain text, but it cannot do everything. Sometimes, you need to open a file in other software, such as an image editor or video player.

The OpenWith package by Markus Triska allows you to open files with your favourite PDF viewer or multimedia player. This package associates file types with software external to Emacs. To create such an association, customise the `openwith-associations` variable. Click on the `[Ins]` button and Add the following three parameters:

- `Files`: The file extension (for example 'pdf' or 'mp4')

- `Program`: The name of the program to open your files (for example, 'evince' or 'mpv')

- `Parameters`: This should be '(file)' by default which instructs Emacs to send the filename to the program.

The advantage of this approach is that you can open files with their ideal application from the comfort of your Emacs interface, thereby preventing additional context switching by first having to open other software.

This package offers more advanced features for associating files with external software, including the use of regular expressions, which are beyond the scope of this book.

Now that you know how to inspire yourself with Emacs, it is time to solidify your thoughts by committing them to an electronic notebook. The next chapter explains how to use EWS as your personal knowledge management system.

Chapter *6*

Ideation: Record and Manage Ideas

As you read literature, websites, or consume any other source of information, you might like to take notes about what you have learned. Perhaps a random inspiration strikes, and a thought pops into your mind. Note-taking has become a popular topic in recent years. The market for ideas is flooded with methods for taking and maintaining notes, all promising to create a digital second brain, also known as a Zettelkasten.

This chapter explains how to use the Org and Denote packages to keep an electronic notebook and cultivate your digital ideas garden. The combination of these packages empowers you to collect notes, maintain a personal diary or journal, write a literature review, record laboratory results in a notebook, or any other imaginable use case. The approach described in this chapter is agnostic to any formal method. Emacs is flexible enough to allow you to implement almost any workflow you prefer.

This first part of this chapter explains how to use Org as a frictionless note-taking tool, using a single file to capture your thoughts. The remainder of the chapter describes the Denote package ecosystem, as developed by Protesilaos (Prot) Stavrou and others.

This package offers flexibility in managing a comprehensive collection of textual notes and other file types, enabling developing an interconnected second brain.

6.1 Thoughts on taking notes

Before the invention of writing, our ancestors shared knowledge by memorisation. People from these prehistoric cultures could recite thousands of lines from great works, such as the Iliad and the Mahabharata, and other epics from memory, aided by songs and rhymes (Kelly, 2016). Words that rhyme are much easier to remember than plain prose. We can memorise hours of song lyrics flawlessly but fail to memorise a shopping list. When writing became common, the Greek philosopher Socrates lamented in his dialogue with *Phaedrus* that it erodes our memory. More recent insights show that Socrates' argument was factually correct (Kahn, 1997).

However, writing has freed our minds from being a storehouse of factual knowledge to being a creative machine. Human development accelerated when writing allowed people to free their minds from facts and use this brainpower to create new ideas. Productivity guru David Allen expressed it succinctly when he wrote, "The mind is for having ideas, not for holding them" (Allen, 2005). Philosophers refer to Allen's intuition as the *extended mind thesis*, which suggests that the mind does not exclusively reside in the body but extends into the physical world (Clark & Chalmers, 1998), leading to the concept of the second brain.

Taking notes to extend the fragility of human memory is as old as the art of writing itself. Since the 1970s, humanity has transitioned from writing words on paper to storing them electronically. In recent years, the need to keep notes has given rise to a cottage industry of blogs, books, YouTube channels, and note-taking applications to help people organise their minds and lives. Whether Luhmann's *Zettelkasten*, Carroll's *Bullet Journal*, or Forte's *Second Brain*, they all claim to solve personal knowledge management challenges by following a specific method (Forte, 2022; Kadavy, 2021; Ryder, 2021).

These rigid workflows inevitably lead to failure because everybody has different needs.

When taking notes creatively, the formal workflow only matters little. As your collection of notes expands, your methodology emerges organically. So, rather than worrying about some method promoted online, start writing and creating a process as your needs evolve.

The best note-taking method is the one you invent, and that progressively grows in complexity. An electronic second brain does not automatically lead to success. Your organic brain should dictate the second one, not vice versa (Stavrou, 2024).

In my three decades working with paper and digital journals, I've learned that structure is only one critical aspect. What truly matters is the authenticity and originality of the recorded thoughts. Even Luhmann, the creator of the Zettelkasten method, saw his system as a "septic tank for ideas" (ZK II Zettel 9/8a2 niklas-luhmann-archiv.de).

Using Emacs to take notes or any other text processor has limitations. My personal ideation process starts with a physical notebook. This might be a strange thing to admit by somebody who professes admiration for the electronic virtues of Emacs. Physical notebooks have some advantages in the creative process. Firstly, you can use them anywhere without batteries, and they work in full sunlight. The only exception might be in the shower, which paradoxically is where we get our best ideas. Writing longhand in a notebook is also a slower process than using a keyboard, which might seem a disadvantage, but using a pen forces you to think more deeply. Writing on paper enhances creativity by triggering deeper neural pathways than writing electronically (Mueller & Oppenheimer, 2014; Umejima, Ibaraki, Yamazaki, & Sakai, 2021). Writing on paper also makes it easy to combine graphics with text. Doodling and sketching are artistic ways to conceptualise knowledge, which is one thing a text processor such as Emacs cannot provide.

Once my notebook's ideas germinate, some find a place inside my Emacs filing system. My workflow also includes scans of sketches from my notebook, photographs, videos, and electronic files from the web or emailed to me. All files are stored in an organised system, which makes it easy to find information and germinate new ideas. This workflow combines the flexibility of working on paper with the power of electronic information.

The practical reality of taking notes is that we can distinguish between two categories: fleeting and permanent notes (Ahrens, 2017). You take fleeting notes on a napkin or the back of your hand. Most fleeting notes have a short lifespan, but some are promoted to a permanent status. As the name suggests, a permanent note is information you like to keep in perpetuity. Your permanent notes form your personal wiki, second brain, Zettelkasten, digital garden or whatever neologism you prefer.

6.2   Fleeting notes

Fleeting notes capture the unexpected ideas that flit through the mind at unpredictable moments. A sudden insight, a movie quote, a to-do list reminder or anything else. These fleeting notes are temporary parking spots for thoughts. They might be ideas for a future project, tasks to complete, or something interesting to revisit later. A frictionless capture system, such as a trusty paper notebook, a phone app, or even the back of our hand, prevents these ideas from disappearing.

The need to take fleeting notes also arises while using Emacs. Imagine writing a book when you suddenly remind yourself that you need to buy some milk; Org capture mode lets you capture this fleeting thought with just a few keystrokes, saving it for future review without derailing your current focus.

Capturing a fleeting note with Org's capture feature is frictionless. Press C-c c (org-capture), and a selection screen pops up. Select 'Fleeting Note' with f, write your thoughts into the popup buffer, and press C-c C-c to save the note under the 'Notes' heading in your inbox as a list item. The capture system adds consecutive fleeting notes below the previous ones. If you decide it is not worth storing this thought, press C-c C-k to cancel the input.

Once you're done, Emacs returns to where you left off, and you can happily proceed with your work with minimal disruption. The capture menu also has an option to add an item to your to-do list, stored in the same file but under a different heading. Chapter 9 discusses managing projects and action lists.

The `org-default-notes-file` variable defines the name and location of the inbox. By default, this variable is `~/.notes`. The dot indicates that this file is hidden. You can customise this variable to set your preferred inbox filename. The file is automatically created when you first use the capture mechanism. You are, of course, free to directly add other information to this file outside the capture system.

As you create more fleeting notes, your inbox steadily fills with random musings. Undertaking a weekly review is a good habit to keep your inbox as empty as possible. This review involves converting promising thoughts to a permanent note or trashing them after they expire. Ideally, your inbox should trend towards zero content, as discussed in chapter 9.

You can use the universal argument with the `org-capture` command (`C-u C-c c`) to jump to the file for your chosen template. Using a double universal argument jumps to the most recently captured item (`C-u C-u C-c c`). Adding information through the capture system also creates a bookmark so you can find your latest notes with `C-x r b` (`bookmark-jump`) and select the `org-capture-last-stored` option.

The capture functionality is a versatile system that enables you to create templates for various notes. EWS only defines two types of fleeting notes, but you can customise this system to add bespoke capture templates. You could, for example, create a separate entry for a shopping list and synchronise that file to your phone. Org opens the customisation screen for the `org-capture-templates` variable with `C-c c C`, which includes an extensive help file that describes the myriad of capture options. The Org manual (`C-h R org <Ret> g capture`) discusses developing capture templates in detail.

6.3 Permanent notes

Permanent notes form an external electronic storehouse of information you can structure and search to create new insights. Don't worry too much about which method to use when you start your collection of electronic notes. You can start with a single file and write. The key to writing good notes is not worrying about the second brain, as your first brain is much more critical in the creative process (Stavrou, 2024). The second brain will organically emerge from the primordial soup of ideas that is your note-taking system.

Two methods are available to write permanent notes. You can either cram all your notes into one Org mode file and utilise its internal capabilities to manage your information or maintain a collection of hyperlinked notes in line with the popular Zettelkasten approach.

The following section explains how to use a single file to take notes. The next section introduces the Denote package, a powerful tool for managing an extensive collection of notes, including binary files such as photographs and PDF files.

Single Org file

To get started, create an Org file, give it a suitable title, and start writing. Use a descriptive heading for each note. You can also group your notes using level one headings as categories and lower levels for the note titles.

To add a timestamp to record when you took the note, use the `org-time-stamp` function. Calling this function with `C-c .` (control and full-stop) adds a date, and with a universal argument, the time is also included (`C-u C-c .`). A note under the philosophy category could look something like this:

```
#+title: Notes

* Philosophy
** Socrates against writing
   <2024-04-20 Sat>
   In the Phaedrus, ...
```

Org helps to manage an extensive collection of notes in a single file. To view the table of contents of a file when you open it, add `#+startup: content` to your front matter. With this keyword, Org only shows headings when the file is first opened. Org's ability to fold and unfold headings with `S-<Tab>` lets you focus on what is essential.

Some other startup options are `overview` to only show the first level and `showall` to unfold the whole document. The default option is `showeverything`, which does not hide any part of the document.

Another method to create focus within large files is to narrow the buffer to show only the section you are working in. The `C-x n` prefix brings you to the narrowing functionality. The `org-narrow-to-subtree` function (`C-x n s`) narrows the current buffer to only show the content of the subtree that the cursor is in. The other text is not erased; it is just hidden from view. To revert to the complete buffer, use the `widen` command, bound to `C-x n w`. The narrowing functionality has a few other options, which you can explore through the popup menu when you invoke the prefix key.

Yet another method to focus on relevant parts of your document is to construct a sparse tree with the `org-occur` function, evoked with `C-c / /`. Sparse trees offer filtered views based on search criteria, highlighting relevant text while hiding unrelated content. After entering the search criterion, Org highlights the requested words and only shows the sections where the search term occurs. Two shortcuts let you jump between the matches: `M-g n` jumps to the next match and `M-g p` to the previous one. Using any editing command or pressing `C-c C-c` exits the search. The main difference between a sparse tree and the regular search functionality (section 3.8) is that a sparse tree collapses your document to only show the parts where the search occurs.

Adding notes to categories by structuring headings is helpful but limited because a note can only be a member of one subdirectory. Org can also add tags to each heading to relate ideas to one another. A tag is a label for a headline to categorise related headings. Tags appear after the heading text, nested between colons. Tags are inherited properties, meaning any tag at a level one heading also belongs to the relevant subheadings. In the example below, all subheadings under the "Philosophy" heading inherit the `:philosophy:` tag. Any subheadings under the note about Socrates will also inherit both the `:philosophy:` and `:writing:` tags. A headline can have multiple tags, which allows you to create a detailed classification of your ideas.

```
#+title: Notes
* Philosophy                        :philosophy:
** Socrates against writing         :writing:socrates:
   <2024-04-20 Sat>
   In the Phaedrus, ...
```

You add a tag to a note with `C-c C-q` (`org-set-tags-command`). Type the name of the new tag in the minibuffer. Any tags already used in the document are displayed in the minibuffer completion list. You can also set a library for each file by adding something like this to the front matter of the Org file: `#+tags:  philosophy(p) writing(w)`. The letters between parentheses become a shortcut in the minibuffer menu for fast selection. To create a new tag, type free text into the minibuffer. Once you have a file with tagged entries, you can use them to search notes by category using the functionality of the sparse tree. To select one or more tags for a sparse tree, use `org-match-sparse-tree` (`C-c \`). This function collapses the whole document and highlights the segments where the selected tags occur.

Moving around large Org files can be cumbersome. The `org-goto` command makes this easier. When you press `C-c C-j`, Org displays all headings in the minibuffer completion menu from where you can select your destination. The Consult package by Daniel Mendler includes a convenient function for moving around large Org files. The `consult-org-heading` function (`C-c w h`) lists all headings in the current Org file in the minibuffer, from where you can navigate to the desired location. The Consult package offers a comprehensive range of search and navigation commands to enhance your use of Emacs.

You can structure headings with the Alt and arrow keys, as section 4.5 explains. A convenient tool to manage large files is the `org-refile` function, bound to `C-c C-w`. This command allows you to effortlessly move sections within your document. When evoking this function, a list of chapter names appears in the minibuffer. The subtree that the cursor is currently in will move to the selected chapter. To jump to the relevant entry after refiling, use the C-u C-u C-c C-w shortcut (two universal arguments before the command).

Lastly, you might want to create links between notes in a file. We have already seen file links in section 4.5, but we can also link to a heading within an Org file. The easiest way is to create an internal link with C-c l, enter the name of the heading without asterisks and add a description. The link now looks something like this:

```
[[Heading name][Description]]
```

The problem with this approach is that the name of the heading might change, or perhaps you misspelled it. When following a link to a non-existing target, Org mode does not throw an error; instead, it asks whether you want to create a new heading. A better approach to linking is giving the heading a unique ID.

To insert a link between notes in a single note document, move the cursor to the heading you want to link to and press C-c l (org-store-link). This function creates a drawer underneath the heading. A drawer consists of collapsible text that can store metadata about a heading. Drawers are helpful for many tasks and are further discussed in chapter 7. The drawer might look something like this:

```
:PROPERTIES:
:ID:       d454979b-2d40-4f95-9f85-f5d9314c28d7
:END:
```

The random string of letters and numbers is a Universally Unique Identifier (UUI), which creates a random ID. The likelihood of a duplicate ID is so astronomically small that we can consider it unique. A link to this ID is now stored in memory, and you can insert it elsewhere with org-store-link. A link to an ID looks like this under the hood:

```
[[id:d454979b-2d40-4f95-9f85-f5d9314c28d7][Example]]
```

Using one large file for your notes is a great way to start commuting your thoughts to Emacs. However, the file can become unwieldy over time. If you become highly productive, a large file can slow down the system. The following section shows how to use the Denote package to create a collection of interconnected notes.

6.4 Writing notes with Denote

Using a single file is a nice way to start your journey, but once these files grow to gargantuan sizes, they become unwieldy. Most note-taking systems, therefore, use separate files to create a network of ideas. Emacs users have developed a slew of packages to write and manage collections of notes. EWS uses the Denote package. This package does not enforce any specific methodology or workflow. It can process both written notes in three plain text formats and binary files, such as photographs, PDF files, or any other file type you would like to store in your digital archive.

The Denote package categorises your files using keywords. There is also an option to add a signature, which can designate a semantic order. Notes can also link to each other to form a network of thoughts. With these three mechanisms, you can use Denote to create an organic digital garden or implement a formal system, such as the Zettelkasten, Johnny.Decimal, or PARA method, or work according to your personal preferences.

The driving force of the Denote package is its file naming convention. This approach embeds metadata in the filename, eliminating the need for a database or any other external dependency to navigate your jungle of notes. The Denote naming convention consists of five parts (all in lowercase by default), of which only the ID and file extension are required. The file naming convention in Denote limits your freedom in naming files. However, these restrictions provide incredible power by introducing predictability and uniformity, which makes it easy to find notes. An example of a fully formatted Denote file is.

```
20210509T082300==9=a=12--duck-rabbit-illusion__perception.org
```

1. Unique identifier (ID) in ISO 8601 time format.

2. Signature (lowercase letters and numbers), starting with a double equals sign.

3. Title separated by dashes (`kebab-case`), starting with a double dash.

4. Keywords separated by an underscore (`snake_case`), starting with a double underscore.

5. Filename extension.

The timestamp orders our notes chronologically and creates a unique and immutable identifier that Denote uses to link files. The signature lets you order your notes just like the Dewey Decimal System orders books on the shelves of a physical library. The keywords or file tags group notes that share a common theme. The signature, title and tags are flexible and can change over time. The timestamp should always stay the same to maintain the integrity of links.

To maintain the system's integrity, the Denote signature can only contain letters, numbers, and equal signs. The title only has letters, numbers and dashes (kebab-case). Keywords start with an underscore and can only contain letters and numbers (snake$_{case}$). Denote cleans (sluggifies) file names to enforce compliance with the convention.

Denote stores new notes in the folder signified by the `denote-directory` variable, which defaults to `~/Documents/notes`. You can customise this variable to suit your needs.

Denote can store notes in subdirectories within `denote-directory`, but there is no need to do so. When using subdirectories to categorise files, a part of the metadata for that file changes when you move the file to another location. Modern operating systems can effortlessly manage tens of thousands of files in one directory, so there is no need to use subdirectories. Instead of subdirectories, you can use file tags, which makes it easy to view files that logically belong to the same group. File tags are more flexible than subdirectories because each file can have multiple tags, but it can only reside in one directory.

Create new notes

Denote functionality is available under the C-c w d EWS prefix. The denote command, which you activate with C-c w d n, creates a new note as an Org file. It first asks for a title and then for the relevant keywords. You either select a keyword from the completion list of existing notes in the minibuffer with the Tab key or enter new ones as free text, separated by commas. The timestamp is automatically generated using the date and time you create the note. You can also activate this command with the Org capture system and select 'Permanent Note' (C-c c p).

When creating a new note, it first opens as an unsaved buffer. You will need to save it to disk with C-x C-s to make it permanent. Creating a permanent note with the Org capture mechanism saves the note when exiting the capture popup screen with C-c C-c. Some functionality might not work unless you have saved the note to disk, so if you get a warning that says "Buffer not visiting a Denote file", you might have to save the buffer first so Denote recognises it.

The default EWS configuration does not require a signature or a subdirectory for new notes. You can customise the denote-prompts variable to define the default way Denote generates and renames files by ticking the items you like to include when creating a new note.

The date and identifier are also part of the file's header. Keywords become file tags, which are similar to the tags we saw in the previous section but apply to the entire file. Now, fill the buffer with relevant content and save it to disk. The front matter of the note in the example above would appear as follows:

```
#+title:     Simultaneous Contrast
#+date:      [2021-05-09 Sun 08:23]
#+filetags:  :colour:illusions:
#+identifier: 20210509T082300
```

This workflow applies to generic notes. However, not all permanent notes are created equal. The relevant workflow within Denote depends on the purpose of your note. Broadly speaking, we can distinguish between four types:

1. *Journal entries*: Experiences related to a specific time.

2. *Literature notes*: Notes about a publication.

3. *Attachments*: Read-only notes, such as photographs or PDF files.

4. *Meta notes*: Notes that link to all notes meeting a search criteria.

Keeping a journal or diary

You can use Denote for personal reflection, to create a journal or laboratory logbook, to add meeting notes, or to record any other notes related to an event.

Writing a journal with Denote is easy because the identifier for each note indicates the date and time you created it. Adding a standard tag, such as _journal, makes your journal entries easy to distinguish from other notes or whatever makes sense in your native language.

If you create a note for an entry in the past, use the denote-date function (C-c w d d). You enter the date in Year-Month-Day (ISO 8601) notation like 2023-09-06. Optionally, you can add a specific time in 24-hour notation, for example, 2023-09-6 20:30. Denote uses the present date or time if no date and/or time is provided.

The Denote-Journal package provides further specialised functionality for keeping a journal or diary. You can set a standard keyword so you don't have to select it every time you create a new entry. This package also lets you access your notes through a calendar view. You can read the manual with C-h R denote-journal.

Literature notes

A literature or bibliographic note contains a summary or an interpretation of a book, journal article or any other published format. A literature note is a special category of permanent notes that link to one or more publications.

The Citar-Denote package integrates your Emacs bibliography and Citar with the Denote note-taking system. This package provides extended functionality for creating and managing literature notes. Refer to chapter 5 to find out how to create a bibliography and use Citar.

Citar-Denote enables a many-to-many relationship between notes and entries in your BibTeX files, providing a complete solution for documenting literature notes. This means you can add multiple notes per bibliographic entry or one note for more than one piece of literature. You could write a note about each book chapter or create a single literature note for a collection of journal articles, whatever method suits your workflow.

Literature notes are regular Denote files but with some additional metadata to link the file to one or more entries in your bibliography. Citar-Denote relates a note to an entry in your bibliography by using the citation key as a reference in the front matter. Each bibliographic note is also marked with the `_bib` file tag to reduce the number of files the system needs to track. The front matter for a bibliographic note could look something like this: (note the `_bib` tag and the reference line):

```
#+title:      Marcuse: An Essay on Liberation
#+date:       [2022-11-12 Sat 19:23]
#+filetags:   :bib:culture:marketing:philosophy:
#+identifier: 20221112T192310
#+reference:  marcuse_1969_essay
```

Open the Citar interface with `C-c w b c` (`citar-create-note`) to create a new note. Select the entry you want to write a note for, hit Enter, and follow the prompts. If a note already exists for this entry, you can create additional notes or open the existing one.

Once you have collected some bibliographic notes, you will want to access and modify them. You can access the attachments, links and other notes associated with the references from within via the Citar menu with C-c w b o (citar-open). Entries with a note are indicated with an N in the third column. From this menu, you can also create additional notes.

To only show those entries with a note, start the search with :n. Alternatively use citar-denote-open-note (C-c w b n) to open the Citar menu with only entries with one or more associated notes. Furthermore, the citar-open-note function lists the file names of all literature notes in the minibuffer.

The citar-denote-add-citekey function (C-c w b k) adds citation keys or converts an existing Denote file to a bibliographic note. When converting a regular Denote file, the function adds the bib keyword to the front matter and renames the file accordingly. This function opens the Citar selection menu and adds the selected citation keys to the front matter. You can remove citation references from a note with the C-c w b K shortcut (citar-denote-remove-citekey). When referencing more than one publication, select the unwanted item in the minibuffer first. When the note only has one reference, the bibliography keyword is removed, and the file is renamed, converting it to a generic permanent note.

Several functions are available to manage the current buffer when inside a bibliographic note. The citar-denote-dwim function (C-c w b d) provides access to the Citar menu for the referenced literature in this note, from where you can open attachments, other notes, and links. When a note has more than one reference item, you need to select the relevant item first.

What is the point of building a bibliography without citing or using each item at least once in a bibliographic note? The citar-denote-nocite (C-c w b x) function opens the Citar menu and shows all items in your bibliography that are neither cited nor referenced. From there, you can create a new bibliographic note, follow a link or read the file. This function can act as a checklist of the literature you have not yet read or reviewed.

To learn more about functionality in the Citar-Denote package, read the manual with `C-h R citar-denote`.

Attachments

Your digital notes garden can be much more than just text. You can manage your photographs with Denote and store an archive of PDF files, such as bank statements, course certificates, or scans of your paper archive. Extending Denote with attachments converts your list of notes into a comprehensive personal knowledge management system featuring intuitive heuristics for finding and linking documents to notes.

There are numerous use cases for extending Denote to binary files. I save my photographs and videos in the Denote file format. I also store PDF files, such as scanned paper documents or files received via email, including invoices.

Denote's reliance on a filename to store metadata allows you to manage files other than the three plain text types Denote can generate (plain text, Markdown or Org). An attachment is a file with a compatible filename, except those files that Denote creates. Denote recognises any file stored in the Denote directory that follows its file naming convention.

The first step in registering an attachment in Denote is to ensure it has a compliant name. You can rename a file manually after opening it with `denote-rename-file` (`C-c w d r`). This function uses the filename as a default title, which you can modify and add relevant keywords as needed. The last modified timestamp of the file will serve as its identifier. However, the creation date on the file system is not always the actual creation date. When working with attachments, there are three options for a valid timestamp, being the date and time when the:

- A digitised document was created

- Electronic file was born (first creation date)

- Electronic file was created on the file system (Denote default)

The first scenario mainly relates to historical documents. Over the years, I have gradually digitised my paper archives. The earliest identifier timestamp in my Denote library is 13700623T120000, a scan of a medieval mortgage contract of my birth house in the Netherlands. The original creation date of the document (when it was scanned) is in 2021, and the date on my file system is in 2023. The Denote renaming function would use the file system date, which is not ideal. This document requires manually entering a timestamp that places the document in the distant past.

The second scenario mainly occurs with photographs. The timestamp on the file system may differ from when the picture was taken, so we need to know the exact time the photo was taken. For recent images, you can extract the creation date from the file's metadata. Several tools, such as ExifTool, are available to extract metadata from photographs and PDF files.

Meta notes

Once you have written many notes, you might want to add some structure to them. One method of doing this is to create a meta note. These notes are gateways to other notes on a similar topic. A meta note might contain links to related notes or the content of other notes on a topic.

We can achieve this with Org mode and the additional package Denote-Org, which leverages dynamic blocks in Org. Dynamic blocks are a versatile Org feature that can aggregate your thoughts and link to relevant notes. A dynamic block is a section of text that can be dynamically updated as your Denote collection evolves. A meta note could contain a dynamic block that shows a list of all notes within a category or an ordered list of notes that matches a signature or even includes the text of other notes.

Let's say that you are working on a project to write a paper about the *Daimonion* (inner voice) that spoke to the ancient Greek philosopher Socrates. You read the literature and create a bunch of permanent notes that use the _daimonion keyword. When gathering your thoughts into an integrated view, you can make a meta note.

Use the `org-dynamic-block-insert-dblock` function (`C-c C-x x`) to see a selection list of available dynamic blocks and select `denote-links`. Next, provide a regular expression that matches the notes you want to list (in this case `_daimonion`). A regular expression is an advanced search term, much like using a wildcard in a filename. Denote inserts a block in your Org file that lists links to all notes matching this search criterion, for example:

```
#+BEGIN: denote-links :regexp "_daimonion"
- Plato Apology
- Socrates and Plato
- Plato: Crito
#+END:
```

Using this approach, you can collate your journal notes for a particular month with the magic of regular expressions. Using `^202309.*_journal` lists all journal entries for September 2023. This regular expression lists filenames that start with 202309 and include the `_journal` keyword. The tilde (`^`) denotes that you are searching at the start of the filename. The `.*` in the middle of the regular expression indicates that any character (`.`) can appear multiple times (`*`). Regular expressions are a powerful tool for searching, but a detailed discussion is outside the remit of this book.

As your notes collection changes, the dynamic block needs to be updated with `C-c C-x C-u`. This command (`org-dblock-update`) recreates the list of links based on the latest information. Adding the universal argument updates all dynamic blocks in the current buffer (`C-u C-c C-x C-u`).

Other dynamic block types are available in Denote, allowing you to list backlinks to a note or include the text of other notes. The `denote-missing-links` dynamic block inserts a list of links to files that match a regular expression but are not listed in the remainder of the buffer. Another dynamic block with links is `denote-backlinks`, which lists all notes that link to the current buffer.

Dynamic blocks with links can include parameters that define how to display the information. The first parameter is mandatory, and the others are optional:

- `regexp`: The regular expression of the files you seek to link.

- `excluded-dirs`: Directory to exclude from the list.

- `sort-by-component`: Sort the list by either title, keywords or signature. The default sorts by identifier. Other options are title, keyword or signature.

- `reverse-sort`: When set to t reverses the order of the list.

- `id-only`: When set to t, it only shows the identifiers, not the descriptions.

- `include-date`: include dates in the list.

The last type of Denote dynamic block enables transclusion, which includes the content of other notes into the meta note. This can be useful when you have many notes with small quotes or thoughts and want to see them all on one screen. The `denote-files` dynamic block works like the other versions but has some additional parameters.

- `no-front-matter`: When set to t excludes the front matter from the files.

- `file-separator`: When set to t adds a separator between subsequent files.

- `add-links`: When set to t, add a link to each file at the start.

The Denote-Org manual contains detailed information (`C-h R denote-org`).

Linking notes

The Denote signature and keyword offer a unique way to order and categorise ideas. Additionally, Org can become a personal wiki by linking notes. While the term 'personal wiki' may seem contradictory, given that wikis are collaborative writing tools, linking notes enables the creation of an interconnected web of ideas.

Org features a versatile link system. Previous chapters explored adding hyperlinks to external and internal sources (sections 4.5 and 5.3). Linking to other documents adds additional structure to your notes. Still, this method has a problem because the link breaks when the target file changes name or location.

Denote enhances Org's functionality by creating stable links between notes. A Denote link only stores the identifier of the target file, so the signature, name and keywords can change freely without the risk of creating dead links.

You can link notes and attachments to links with the `denote-link-or-create` function (`C-c w d i`). This command lists all available notes using the minibuffer completion system, from which you can select a target and hit enter. To modify the link's label, press `C-c C-l` (`org-insert-link`) while the cursor is on the link and follow the prompts. The source of a Denote link looks something like this:

```
[[denote:20210208T150244] [Description]]
```

Because Denote links only use the identifier, you can freely change the title, signature and file tags without severing the link.

If you enter a name for a note that does not yet exist, Denote will let you create a new note and then link to it. Denote links are indicated with italics in EWS to distinguish them from links to other resources, such as websites.

You can also link to attachments inside a Denote note. However, it is not possible to link back from an attachment using Denote, as these files are not notes. Denote can only create links in Org, Markdown or plain text files.

You don't need to search through a document to find relevant links. Jump to any linked note without moving the cursor with `denote-link-find-file` (`C-c w d l`). This function shows all notes linked from the open note in the minibuffer, where you can select the one you like to jump to. To find out which notes link to the one you are currently reading, use the `denote-find-backlink` function (`C-c w d b`).

Finding notes and attachments

When collecting thousands of notes and attachments, you need tools to find the information you need or make new connections between ideas. The most straightforward method to find files is opening one with the standard `find-file` function. The minibuffer completion system helps you to find what you need by searching through the file names.

If, for example, you like to filter notes tagged as 'economics', type `C-x C-f`, move to your notes folder, and type `_economics`. Minibuffer completion narrows the available options. If you need a note with economics in the title but not as a tag, use `-economics`. If you type `economics` without a prefix, the minibuffer shows all posts with this search term in the signature, title, or tag. Regular expressions (section 6.4) increase your search power. As the minibuffer completion uses the Orderless package, a space acts as an AND operator. So typing `^2022 ==9a _art` searches for all notes with a file name that starts with "2022" (the hat `^` symbol matches the start), and include a signature that starts with 9a (`==9a`) and have the `_art` file tag.

The Consult-Notes package by Colin McLear merges the capabilities of Denote and Daniel Mendler's Consult package to help you find notes using regular expressions. This package also provides facilities to search through the content of your notes. To find a note by any part of its filename, use the `consult-notes` function bound to `C-c w d f`. The Consult package provides live previews of the files that match the search. To search within a subdirectory of the Denote directory, start the query with a slash, for example, `/attachments`. This package accepts regular expressions, as explained in the previous paragraph. For more advanced users, this package also allows you to define separate silos of Denote files, which can be helpful when, for example, you want to separate work files from private information.

One note of caution when using Consult previews. The OpenWith package (section 5.5) can interfere with the preview functions in the Consult package. The system will preview file types configured in OpenWith with external software, disturbing the workflow. Using this package requires customising `consult-preview-excluded-files` to exclude any file types mentioned in the `openwith-associations` variable. You only have to register the file extension and add a $ symbol, which is the regular expression symbol for the end of the string. So adding "mp4$" instructs Consult not to preview video files. Click in INS button in the customisation menu to add multiple file types.

Searching for titles, tags, and other metadata is a powerful way to access your information due to the Denote naming convention. While this is a good start, sometimes you need to search through the content of your notes rather than just titles and metadata. The Consult package provides a valuable interface to achieve this objective.

The `consult-notes-search-in-all-notes` function (`C-c w d g`) activates a deep search inside your notes. The package uses Grep, a utility for searching plain text files for lines that match a regular expression. Grep must be installed on your computer for this to work, which is typically the case for Linux and Apple computers.

The search is incremental, just like minibuffer completion. As you type your search criterion, a list of results appears that can be narrowed. The results show the filename and the matching lines within each file. The search term starts with a hashtag; when you type another such symbol, for example, `#topology# homotopy`, the next phrase will be searched within the results that match the first regular expression. This example finds all notes that contain the word "topology" and narrows to those files that also contain the word "homotopy".

Denote also has a built-in search function that leverages the Grep software, which is explained in the manual. This function provides all the matching files in a separate buffer, which you can use for further exploration.

6.5 Implementing note-taking methods with Denote

The Denote package is flexible and malleable, so you can implement any published note-taking methodology. EWS does not promote any note-taking systems and this section only provides some hints on implementing three popular methods with Emacs and Denote.

Try not to get distracted by 'shiny-object syndrome' and focus on writing rather than chasing the latest ideas. The ideal method is one that you grow organically, tailored to your specific needs. The power of the Denote file naming convention and regular expressions basically provide everything you need at your fingertips.

PARA

Tiago Forte has developed the PARA method to organise your digital life (Forte, 2022). In his system, all digital assets form part of one of four folders:

1. *Projects*

2. *Areas*

3. *Resources*

4. *Archives*

Forte uses a cooking example to illustrate the PARA method. The *Projects* are the pots and utensils you need to prepare a dish. Files in this category are the material you need to work on for your current deliverables. The *Areas* are like the ingredients you store in the fridge. These are notes that you need to access regularly. The third category is *Resources*, which relates to items stored in the freezer. These are topics that interest you or research material. Lastly, the *Archive*, which we can refer to as the pantry, contains completed projects or those on hold.

The key to this method is that each file belongs to only one of these four categories. A file could start as a resource, become a project, and end its life in the archives. In his original idea, Forte suggests using four directories to store material from each category. You can implement this method in Denote by associating each note with one of four tags. Ideally, each note can only belong to one of these four categories. To list all notes in your *Projects* category, open `consult-notes` and search for `#projects`, and so on.

EWS includes a bespoke function to implement Forte's PARA method with Denote. The `ews-denote-assign-para` function moves a note to one of the four PARA categories by assigning a keyword to the note. If a PARA keyword already exists, it is replaced with the new version.

The `ews-para-keywords` variable contains the keywords used in this method. You can customise this variable to translate into your native language or use a different set of exclusive categories. You can, for example, also configure this variable to implement Nick Milo's ACCESS system by changing the options to Atlas, Calendar, Cards, Extras, Sources, Spaces and Encounters. This function can replace any file management system that depends on folders with Denote keywords.

If you insist on using folders instead of keywords, Denote also allows you to do so. Customise the `denote-prompts` variable to ask for a subdirectory when creating a new note.

Johnny.Decimal

The Johnny.Decimal System uses a numbering scheme to organise files, created by Johnny Noble. The basic idea is to divide your digital life into fewer than ten broad areas. You can begin with, for example, just *work* and *personal*. These main categories are the virtual filing shelves in your digital library. Each shelf can accommodate up to ten boxes. For instance, in our example, we could have boxes for *finance*, *writing* and *travel* on the *personal* shelf.

The next step involves assigning numbers to each category. Johnny.Decimal identifiers start with 10–19 because lower numbers are reserved for system maintenance. The 00 folder typically contains an index to help you navigate the numbering system.

In our example, *personal* is shelf 10–19, and the boxes are numbered from 11 to 19, for example, *finance* (11), *writing* (12), and *travel* (13). There is room for seven more boxes, but wait to use that capacity until the need arises. In the original system, the numbers form the start directory names.

The Johnny.Decimal system is similar to the Dewey Decimal system in a library but with fewer categories. The Johnny.Decimal system describes your life, while the Dewey

Decimal system describes humanity's knowledge. Of course, you could also categorise your notes using the Dewey Decimal approach; the choice is yours.

You can implement Johnny.Decimal, Dewey Decimal, or any other system using ordered numbering with Denote signatures. Denote does not use signatures by default, so you will need to customise the `denote-prompts` variable and tick 'signature'.

For example, a note about EWS could have 12=03 as a signature, indicating it belongs to the *writing* box on the *personal* shelf. You could use a third level in your box to number individual files, so a file in the *writing* box could be numbered as 12=03=01. 12=03=02 and so on. You can use meta notes (section 6.4) to list all the files within this box by changing the `sort-by-component` to `signature` to order the links in the list. Without this sorting instruction, notes are ordered by ID.

```
+BEGIN: denote-links :regexp "==12=03" :sort-by-component signature
- 12=03=01 ews purpose
- 12=03=02 zettelkasten
 - ... etc.
+END:
```

Zettelkasten

Many people are inspired by Niklas Luhmann's Zettelkasten concept. Zettelkasten is a German word for a box (Kasten) that contains notes (Zettels). Luhmann was an influential sociologist renowned for his prodigious productivity and expansive note collection, comprising over ninety thousand interconnected index cards (Kadavy, 2021). His Zettelkasten facilitated his extensive research output.

Trying to emulate Luhmann to the letter is not a great idea. The main reason for his productivity was that he was a workaholic, so using his system does not magically make you more productive. His method is not unique. I was taught how to use index cards for research in my arts degree almost 30 years ago. I remember spending evenings rearranging index cards to structure essays at the dining table. What sets Luhmann apart is his unwavering discipline in note-taking, a trait that continues to inspire.

Luhmann's method for his Zettelkasten included a signature that links cards sequentially in a branching hierarchy. Johnny.Decimal and Zettelkasten differ in that in the former, numbers signify categories. In contrast, in a Zettelkasten, the numbers create a logical relationship between notes. Luhmann's original Zettelkasten has at least six levels of nested categories. This is a minuscule extract from his original work, sourced from `niklas-luhmann-archiv.de`:

- 76: Causality

  - 76,2: Causality — motivation
  - 76,5: Causailty as regular order

    * 76,5a: Causality: Equivalence of cause and effect

Notes in the Zettelkasten method are ordered to form a coherent idea, which is why Luhmann was such a prolific writer. His articles and books grew as he added notes to the system. In the Zettelkasten method, each note has a unique ID, which can be signified with the signature in Denote. Please note that the Denote package does not enforce unique signatures.

The individual files are the 'Zettels', and your Denote directory is the 'Kasten'. You cannot precisely copy Luhmann's syntax because he uses characters that are disallowed in Denote signatures that you cannot use in filenames, such as the slash symbol (/). In the example listed above, the last category would have 76=05=a as a signature, and individual notes would be something like 76=05=a01. You should use leading zeroes with numbers to ensure that notes are ordered appropriately when using dynamic blocks to list or transclude notes.

You can implement this method using the Denote-Sequence package, which is enabled in EWS. This package uses kinship relations, as each node can be a parent, child, or sibling. In the example above, the note with sequence (signature) 76 is the parent. This note has two children (76,2 and 76,5), and these notes are each other's siblings. The note with 76,5a as signature is a child of 76,5.

Within the Denote-Sequence package, the individual elements of a sequence are separated by an equals symbol. Figure shows the family tree for the above example using the Denote syntax.

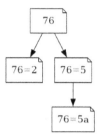

Figure 6.1: Sequence of Denote files.

The `denote-sequence` command creates a new note that is either a new parent, sibling or child of an existing note. The package automatically assigns numbers to a note based on the input choices. This package can use two types of schemes: either only numbers, such as 1=13=3, or alternating letters and numbers, which would be 1=m=3. Customise the `denote-sequence-scheme` variable to select the desired behaviour..

Read the Denote-Sequence manual for a more detailed description of the additional functionality that this package offers with `C-h R denote-seq`.

6.6   Managing your digital garden

Your collection of notes requires regular maintenance as ideas and thought structures evolve over time. The names, keywords and signatures of notes can change over time as your digital garden grows and blossoms.

Org files in Denote include metadata in the file name and the file's front matter. Ideally, the file's name and the front matter are in sync. You can also change the title and the keywords by editing the text. For more convenience, use the `denote-keyword-add` (`C-c w d k`) and `denote-keyword-remove` (`C-c w d K`) functions to change tags with minibuffer completion. These last two functions will also rename the file.

Using `denote-rename-file-using-front-matter` (`C-c w d R`) changes the filename using the data in the front matter. This function leaves the identifier unchanged, even when edited in the front matter.

The Denote-Explore package provides convenient functions for managing your collection of Denote files. You can find the shortcuts for the Denote-Explore package with the `C-c w x` prefix. You can find keyboard shortcuts for individual commands in the Which-Key popup menu. This package provides four types of commands:

1. *Summary statistics*: Count notes, attachments and keywords.

2. *Random walks*: Generate new ideas using serendipity.

3. *Janitor*: Manage your denote collection.

4. *Visualisations*: Visualise your Denote files as a network.

Summary statistics

After a day of working hard in your digital knowledge garden, you may want to review the notes and attachments in your collection. Numbers are great, but a graph is worth a thousand numbers. The built-in `chart.el` package by Eric M. Ludlam is a quaint tool for creating bar charts in a plain text buffer. Two Denote-Explore commands visualise basic statistics leveraging functionality from `chart.el`:

1. `denote-explore-keywords-barchart`: Visualise the top *n* keywords (figure 6.2).

2. `denote-explore-extensions-barchart`: Visualise used file extensions. With a universal argument, it only visualises attachments.

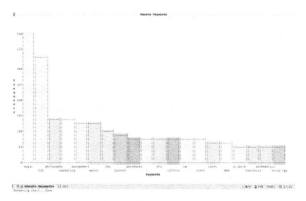

Figure 6.2: Example of a bar chart of top-twenty keywords.

Random walks

Creativity springs from a medley of experiences, emotions, subconscious musings, and the connection of random ideas. Introducing random elements into the creative process generates avenues of thought you might not have travelled otherwise. This method can be beneficial when you're stuck in a rut or prefer to browse through your files randomly. A random walk is an arbitrary sequence of events without a defined relationship between the steps. You randomly wander inside your second brain by jumping to a random note, connected or unconnected to the current buffer. The Denote-Explore package provides four commands to inject some randomness into your explorations:

1. `denote-explore-random-note` (`C-c w x r`): Jump to a random note or attachment.

2. `denote-explore-random-link` (`C-c w x l`): Jump to a random linked note (either forward or backward) or attachments (forward only).

3. `denote-explore-random-keyword` (`C-c w x k`): Jump to a random note or attachment with the same selected keyword(s).

4. `denote-explore-random-regex` (`C-c w x x`): Jump to a random note matching a regular expression.

The default state is that these functions jump to any Denote text file (plain text, Markdown or Org). The universal argument (`C-u`) includes attachments as candidates for a random jump.

When jumping to a random file with the same keyword(s), you can choose between one or more keywords from the current buffer. When the current buffer is not a Denote file, choose any available keyword(s) in your Denote collection. The asterisk symbol * selects all keywords in the completion list.

The janitor

Just like any building needs a janitor to keep it clean and perform minor maintenance, your digital home also requires assistance. After using Denote for a while, you might need a janitor to keep your collection organised.

The Denote package prevents duplicate identifiers when creating a new note. However, sometimes you may need to manually create a date and time for an old document if the creation date differs from the date on the file system, as explained in section 6.4. Adding the Denote identifier manually introduces a risk of duplication. Duplicates can also arise when exporting Denote Org files, as the exported files have the same file name but a different extension.

The `denote-explore-identify-duplicate-notes` command lists all duplicate identifiers in a popup buffer. Be careful when changing the identifier of a Denote file, as it can destroy the integrity of your links. Please ensure that the file you rename does not have any links pointing to it. Use `denote-find-backlink` (`C-c w d b`) to check whether a file has any links pointing to it.

Denote-Explore provides several functions to manage keywords and keep your collection organised. A keyword signifies a category, so ideally, all keywords are used at least twice. The `denote-explore-single-keywords` command provides a comprehensive list of file tags that are only used once, making it easy to identify and address any issues. The list of single keywords is presented in the minibuffer, from where you can open the relevant note or attachment, streamlining your note management process.

Depending on your Denote structure, notes should have at least one keyword. The `denote-explore-zero-keywords` command presents all notes and attachments without keywords in the minibuffer, allowing you to open them and consider adding a keyword or leaving them as is.

You can rename or remove keywords with `denote-explore-rename-keyword`. Select one or more existing keywords from the completion list and enter the new name of the keyword(s). This function renames all chosen keywords to their latest version. It removes the original keyword from all existing notes when you enter an empty string as the new keyword. This function cycles through all notes and attachments containing the selected keywords and asks for confirmation before making any changes. The new keyword list is stored alphabetically, and the front matter is synchronised with the file name.

Denote stores metadata using its ingenious file naming convention. Some of this metadata is copied to the front matter of a note, which can result in discrepancies between the two metadata sources. The `denote-explore-sync-metadata` function checks all notes and asks the user to rename any file where these two data sets are mismatched. The front matter data is the source of truth. This function also ensures the alphabetical ordering of keywords, which facilitates the retrieval of notes.

6.7 Visualising notes as networks

Committing your ideas to text requires a linear way of thinking, as you can only process one word at a time. We reading text from top to bottom from beginning to the end, which means thoughts need to be pre-ordered. In my paper notebook, I regularly use diagrams, such as mind maps, rather than a narrative to convey thoughts. Visual thinking is another way to approach ideas as it can reveal previously unseen connections. One of the most common methods for visualising interlinked documents is a network diagram.

Linking ideas in a network is not a modern tool. Medieval monks sketched diagrams in the margins of books they read, connecting their short notes with lines. These diagrams are the source of the curly braces }, which initially indicated branching an idea (Even-Ezra, 2021).

Viewing your thoughts as a network helps you discover hitherto unseen connections between them. Visualising your Denote digital garden as a network can also help your creative process. A network diagram has nodes (vertices) and edges. Each node represents a file in your Denote system, and each edge is a link between notes (figure 6.3).

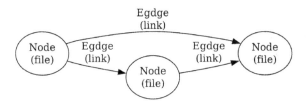

Figure 6.3: Principles of a Denote file network.

The Denote-Explore package uses the functionality provided by external software to visualise the structure of parts of your Denote network. You need to install the Graphviz software to visualise networks. This tool converts plain text descriptions of a network into an image file. The network diagrams in this book are all created with GraphViz.

Denote-Explore does not provide a live environment for viewing the structure of your Denote collection. This functionality is intended to analyse the structure of your notes, not to act as an alternative user interface. Live previews of note networks are dopamine traps. While seeing the network of your thoughts develop before your eyes is satisfying, it can also become a distraction.

The `denote-explore-network` command provides entry to three network diagram types to explore the relationships between your files:

1. Community of notes

2. Neighbourhood of a note

3. Keyword structure

A community consists of notes that match a regular expression. For example, all notes with Emacs as their keyword (_emacs) are shown in figure 6.4. The graph displays all notes matching the regular expression and their connections. Any links to non-matching notes are pruned and not displayed (dotted line to the _vim note in the example). The graph will also show any orphaned notes, such as those without connections. Using an empty regular expression generates a network of all available files.

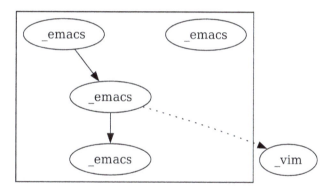

Figure 6.4: Community of Denote files with _Emacs keyword.

The neighbourhood of a note consists of all files linked to it at one or more steps deep. The algorithm selects members of the graph from linked and backlinked notes (such as A to B and C to A in figure 6.5). This network type visualises the possible paths to follow with the `denote-explore-random-link` function discussed in section 6.6.

Generate a neighbourhood graph with `denote-explore-network`, select 'Neighbourhood' and enter the graph's depth. When building this graph from a buffer, not a Denote note, the system also asks to choose a source note. A depth of more than three is

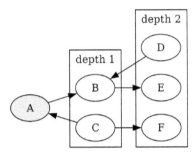

Figure 6.5: Denote neighbourhood of files (depth = 2).

usually not informative because the network becomes large and difficult to read, or you hit the edges of the island of interconnected notes of the selected origin.

There will be files without connections, the lonely isolated notes. Depending on your note-taking strategy, you may want all your notes to be linked to another note. The `denote-explore-isolated-notes` function lists all notes without links or backlinks for you to peruse. You can select any unlinked note and add some links. Calling this function with the universal argument `C-u` excludes attachments in the list of lonely files.

The last available method to visualise your Denote collection is to develop a network of keywords. Two keywords are connected when used in the same note. All keywords in a note create a complete network. A complete network is one in which all nodes are interconnected. The union of all complete networks from all files in your Denote collection defines the keywords network. The relationship between two keywords can exist in multiple notes, so the links between keywords are weighted. The line thickness between two keywords indicates the frequency (weight) of their relationship (Figure 6.6).

While the first two graph types are directed (arrows indicate the direction of links), the keyword network is undirected as these are bidirectional associations between keywords. The diagram below illustrates a scenario with two nodes and three possible keywords, showing how they combine to form a keyword network.

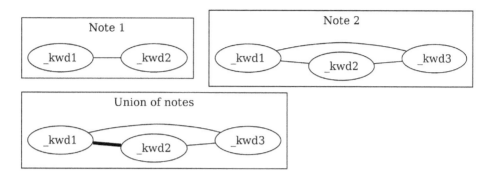

Figure 6.6: Denote network of keywords.

The size of each node is proportional to the number of notes linked from or linked to it. When the degree is more than two, the name of the node is displayed. When viewing the SVG file in a web browser, hovering the mouse over a node shows the note's metadata (figure 6.7).

Clicking on a link will open the relevant file. You will need to configure your browser to open Org files with Emacs. Ideally, you should configure Emacs as a server so it does not open a new version for every link you click.

You can regenerate the same network after you make changes to notes without having to enter new parameters. The `denote-explore-network-regenerate` command recreates the current graph with the same parameters as the previous one, which is useful when you want to see the result of any changes without entering the search criteria again.

Adding more connections between your notes may improve your second brain, but this is not necessarily the case. The extreme case is a complete network where every file links to every other file or one without any links. These situations lack any interesting structure, which wouldn't offer any insights. So, be mindful of your approach to linking notes and attachments so that your network diagrams help you to connect ideas instead of just being eye candy.

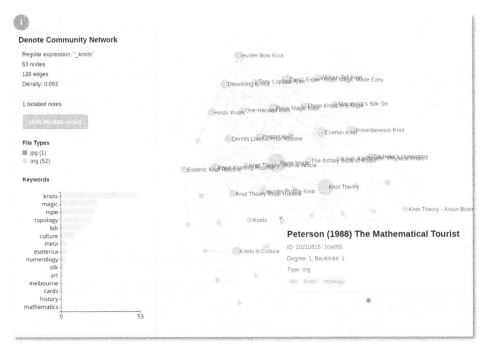

Figure 6.7: Screenshot of a Denote community network in D3.js.

6.8 Learn more about Denote

This chapter provides a brief introduction to the Denote package and some of its auxiliary packages. These packages offer extensive functionality to customise Emacs according to your preferences.

The extensive Denote manual describes its full functionality in great detail, with numerous options to configure how it works (`C-h R denote`). Prot, the maintainer of the Denote package, has also published some extensions, some of which have been mentioned above. Each of these auxiliary packages ships with a detailed manual.

The *Denote-Silo* extension makes working with silos (separated collections of Denote files) a bit more convenient. Silos can be useful when, for example, you like to keep your private and work notes separate. The *Denote-Markdown* package extends functionality for working with Markdown files. You can access these manuals with `C-h R denote` and selecting the relevant package.

Denote, combined with other Emacs functionality, provides a bewildering multitude of options and configurations. Don't be tempted to dive straight into the weeds to define your ideal system. The best advice is to spend most of your time on writing notes rather than finetuning your system in great detail. As computer science pioneer Donald Knuth once wrote:

> Premature optimisation is the root of all evil.

Now that you have collected and organised a lot of notes, it is time to start a writing project. The next chapter shows how to work on an extensive writing project using Org.

Chapter 7

Production: Prepare a
Manuscript

Chapter 3 laid the groundwork for writing plain text documents, establishing essential concepts that serve as a crucial foundation for effective writing. Chapter 4 then introduced the basics of Org syntax, allowing you to organize and structure your text in a meaningful way. Building upon these fundamental principles, this chapter provides a comprehensive guide to preparing a manuscript specifically for publication in *Emacs Writing Studio* (EWS). It explores the unique capabilities of Org mode and integrates additional tools designed to streamline and enhance your writing process.

Throughout this chapter, you will learn how to add editorial notes, seamlessly incorporate citations, and create cross-references that enhance the clarity and cohesiveness of your document. To further improve the richness and variety of your prose, you may want to utilize Emacs' integrated dictionary and thesaurus tools. Additionally, this chapter delves into crucial techniques for managing large writing projects, including version control strategies and collaborative writing approaches that facilitate teamwork with fellow authors.

In the final section, this chapter introduces a range of other text modes that might captivate authors. Among these are Markdown, which is particularly well-suited for creating technical documentation, and the specialized Fountain mode designed for writing film and theatre scripts. With these insights, you'll be well-equipped to explore diverse writing styles and formats, expanding your capabilities as a writer.

7.1   Adding notes, citations and references

A typical writing project is more than just the words of the manuscript. Org's comprehensive set of features, including smart plain text constructs for comments, citations, and cross-references, ensures that your manuscript is enriched. We've already covered some of the metadata in the front matter of an Org file, such as `#+title:`. Org also provides a syntax to include images, tables, and drawers, as explained in the previous chapters.

This section adds more Org functionality to your toolkit to prepare a manuscript for publication. Org has provisions to add notes to a document, which are ignored in the final product. This section also explains how to add citations from your bibliography and create cross-references to headings, tables and other parts of your document.

Adding document notes

The previous chapter detailed the versatility of note-taking in Emacs, whether within a single Org file or a network of interconnected files. You can also write notes inside your writing projects, outside your formal note-taking system. These notes serve as reminders of pending tasks or anything else you'd like to keep hidden from the final product. For instance, you can include a checklist, links to websites or notes in your Denote digital garden, or any other crucial information about the writing process. If you need to jot down any notes unrelated to the current document, then use the Org capture system to store a fleeting note in your inbox (chapter 6).

Org mode offers three flexible mechanisms for adding editorial notes. The first approach is straightforward. Any line that starts with a hashtag/pound symbol (#) is a comment, which Emacs disregards when exporting the text to the final output.

```
# This is an editorial comment.
```

You can also add notes within a structural block, an Org mode construct used to add various types of content. For a note, use `C-c C-,`, which pops up a menu to insert templates (`org-insert-structure-template`). Press C to add a comment section, which adds two lines to your manuscript. Anything you write between these two lines is a comment. To keep your writing surface tidy, you can collapse comment blocks with the Tab key when the cursor is on the `#+BEGIN` or `#+END` line. Some of the other options in the structure template menu are discussed in the next chapter.

You can also use this construct to store text that is no longer part of the main document, but you don't like to remove. When you issue this command after selecting a text region, the selected text is converted into a comment. You can include dynamic blocks inside comment blocks. This is useful for adding links to a collection of notes relevant to your manuscript.

```
#+BEGIN_COMMENT
- This is a comment
- Another comment
#+END_COMMENT
```

The third method involves using a drawer under the current heading, which acts like a comment structure block. The main difference is that drawers have a name, for example, `:NOTES:`. You can open or close a drawer with the Tab key when the cursor is on it. The example below shows what a drawer in your text can look like.

```
:NOTES:
- This is inside the drawer.
- You can fill this with notes.
:END:
```

Drawers are commonly placed directly under a headline, but you can insert them anywhere. Calling `org-insert-drawer`, bound to `C-c C-x d` interactively inserts a drawer at the current location. You enter the drawer's name in the minibuffer (by convention in uppercase, for example, NOTES) and fill in the drawer's content. If you select a text block and create a drawer, that text will appear inside it. You can also use this method to hide parts of the text in the final product that are worth keeping.

A bespoke (EWS) function (`ews-org-insert-notes-drawer`) generates a note drawer bound to the `C-c w n` keyboard shortcut. This function moves the cursor below the heading of the section you are writing and generates the drawer names as NOTES. If a notes drawer exists for this section, the function creates a new line at the end of the existing ones. After writing your notes, `C-u C-<spc>` takes you back to the original position in the text.

These note drawers are helpful to add a checklist of actions to be taken to complete a chapter of your manuscript. Section 9.1 explains how to create a checklist to track the progress of your to-do list.

Adding citations

Citations are the essence of scholarly writing and the currency of an academic career, signifying the influence and impact of your work. Org mode can be your ally in this journey, offering a citation management tool to read BibTeX, BibLaTeX, or CSL files. To start, you'll need to create a bibliography. This can be done manually, or you can link a file from a bibliography management tool, such as Zotero, as discussed in Chapter 5.

The `org-cite-insert` (`C-c C-x @`) command is your go-to when inserting citations. In *Emacs Writing Studio*, this command opens the Citar menu, allowing you to select one or more publications. To select multiple references, use the `Tab` key after each selection. Org inserts a citation, which looks like this:

```
[cite:@einstein_1905; @newton_1728]
```

The Citar menu indicates whether an entry is cited in your current file with a C in the list of publications. Use the `:c` keys in Citar to view only cited entries.

The Citar package also provides some convenient functions for managing citations. To change the order of citations in a block, use the shift and left/right arrow keys when the cursor is on the citation (`citar-org-shift-reference-left` / `-right`).

A citation can have a prefix and a suffix, for example:

```
[cite:see@darwin1859 p. 123]
```

This citation can be rendered as "(Darwin, 1859 p. 123)", depending on the citation style, discussed in the next chapter. You can edit the prefix and suffix when the cursor is on a citation with M-p (`citar-org-update-prefix-suffix`). Section 8.2 of the next chapter discusses how Org's citation management system exports them and how to format them.

To access the resources related to a citation, use the `org-open-at-point` (C-c C-o) command. This opens the Citar menu for the citation under the cursor. When no existing note or attachment is available and you follow a citation link, the system asks you to create a new note. Citations not found in the bibliography are marked in red.

A bibliography can be global or local. The global bibliography is accessible from any place in Emacs. It is defined by the BibTeX files inside the `ews-bibtex-directory` variable. In contrast, the local bibliography file is only available within the current Org buffer. The global bibliography is set in your configuration. As discussed in section 5.2, it can consist of one or more files. The local bibliography is linked to the current buffer with a keyword in the front matter, for example:

```
#+bibliography: bibfile.bib
```

Captions and references

When reading a comprehensive document like this book, leveraging internal links enhances the readability of the text. This feature in Org empowers you to guide your reader to specific sections, figures, or other parts of the manuscript, making your writing easier to navigate.

Referencing figures and tables is a breeze. Assign a name to the item using the #+name: keyword below the caption, for instance: #+name: fig-example. When referring to this item, enclose its name in double square brackets ([[fig-example]]). Org automatically creates a link to the location of the image or table, as explained in section 4.5. These references can point to other documents, as long as they are part of the same project.

References to sections or chapters consist of links to the name of the targeted heading. So, a link to this particular section would be [[Captions and references]]. This approach risks producing broken links when you change the heading name but forget to modify the links that refer to it.

You can also add a property to a heading with a custom ID. Use org-set-property (C-c C-x p), select CUSTOM_ID, and enter the desired ID. Links to a custom ID require an octothorpe, also known as a hashtag or pound symbol. So, a link to this section of the book could have a custom ID of sec-references with links defined as [[#sec-references]]. Without the hashtag, Org mode will link it to a section with that same name. Confusingly, cross-references to named tables and images don't require a hashtag.

The name of internal links can be anything you like, as long as the names are unique in your manuscript. It is good practice to categorise your links with prefixes such as fig-, tab-, chap-, and so on to create clarity and lower the risk of duplication. Please avoid using a colon in the name, as it may cause issues when exporting to HTML. Org can add a unique identifier to a heading using a string of random letters and numbers to ensure unique link names, but using these makes the manuscript hard to follow (section 6.3). Org exports cross-reference links as hyperlinks within the final document discussed in chapter 8.

7.2 Productivity tools

Emacs can help you maximise productivity and maintain quality by streamlining your writing processes with various tools, such as text completion. Writing demands undivided attention, so Emacs also provides a serene environment that is free from the distractions of graphical software. Lastly, Emacs offers facilities to integrate with grammar tools, a dictionary, and a thesaurus to enhance the quality of your writing.

Searching the content of your project

The `consult-grep` command searches through the content of all files in the current folder (C-c w g). This command requires the Grep external software, as explained in section 6.4. When using this command with a universal argument, you can first select the directory to search.

The search function provides flexibility. You can search using regular expressions. The search term between hashtags offers a list of files that contain the word. Any subsequent search terms narrow the list.

- `#alpha omega`: Search for alpha and omega in any order.

- `#alpha.*beta`: Search for alpha before omega.

- `#alpha#omega`: Search for alpha, quick filter for omega.

Expanding abbreviations

Governments and businesses litter their writing with abbreviations and acronyms. Abbreviations are not a modern problem and have been popular since the start of writing. Roman stone inscriptions are mostly abbreviated, making reading hard even if you understand Latin. Roman writers abbreviated words because it saved a lot of effort chiselling the text into marble. However, in the age of electronic writing, we no longer need abbreviations, as the effort to write complete words or phrases is negligible. Electronic writing systems can automatically expand abbreviations into their full context, making a text easier to read.

An Emacs 'abbrev' is a predefined snippet of character that expands into something else. Technical writing is often formulaic, so an academic might want to automatically replace "stbl" with "shown in table" or similar typical academic phrases (Fox & Tigchelaar, 2015).

Emacs Abbrev mode is a built-in library that defines a library of personal snippets that expand into a larger chunk of text. EWS enables Abbrev mode by default for all text modes. The basic functionality is that the user defines an abbreviation, for example, "ouat". The next time you type this abbrev, Emacs expands it into "once upon a time".

Abbreviations (abbrevs) can apply to all modes (global) or only to a specific mode. This section only discusses global abbreviations, but the same principles apply to mode-specific ones.

The `define-global-abbrev` function defines a global abbreviation. You enter the abbrev and its expansion in the minibuffer, and you are set. Next time you type the abbreviation, it will expand into the chosen word when followed by a space or punctuation mark. The expansion will also be capitalised when you start an abbreviation with a capital letter, so in our example above, "Ouat" expands into "Once upon a time".

To define a global abbreviation from within the text you are currently working on, type `C-x a g` (`add-global-abbrev`). The characters before the cursor, up to the start of the previous word, become the expansion, as indicated in the minibuffer. Next, you enter the abbreviation and hit `Ret` to store it. The `inverse-add-global-abbrev` function defines the abbreviation and then the expansion, which you activate with `C-x a i g`.

Abbreviations can expand into multiple words or even standardised text sections of multiple paragraphs. Select the relevant text, use `C-x a g` to define the abbreviation, and press `C-g` to cancel the selection.

Emacs abbrevs are a bit like passwords. They should be memorable but not identical to a dictionary word. However, unlike passwords, they cannot contain punctuation marks. Using a dictionary word can lead to frustration as it expands into something you don't want. You can use this problem to your advantage by defining a commonly misspelled word as an abbreviation, for example, expanding "teh" into "the". There is a workaround if you need to display an abbreviation in the text. Type C-Q after the abbreviation and keep typing.

A negative prefix argument (C-u -) before any abbreviation command removes them from the table. To remove a global abbreviation, use C-u - C-x a g, enter the chosen abbreviation, and press Return.

To review your collection of abbreviations, use list-abbrevs. This command opens a new read-only buffer containing a list of all abbreviations for each relevant major mode; search for "global-abbrev-table". The abbrev table might look something like this:

```
(global-abbrev-table)
```

```
"stbl"           3     "shown in table"
"ouat"           7     "once upon a time"
"teh"           10     "the"
```

This list displays the abbreviations, numbers, and their corresponding expansions. The number in the centre indicates how often an abbreviation has been used, which is helpful if you need to prune an extensive collection.

The abbreviations table is editable, allowing you to define or modify your arsenal of shortcuts. Type the new abbreviation between quotation marks, followed by a zero and the quoted expansion, and you can start using it in your manuscript after you save it to disk.

When you save the file you are working on, and the current abbreviations table is not the same as the saved version, Emacs will also ask you to store the defined abbreviations in your init directory. This mechanism ensures that your collection of time savers is also available in future Emacs sessions.

The Emacs manual provides extensive documentation on using and configuring abbreviations, including advanced functionality (see C-h r g abbrev).

Placeholder text

Lorem Ipsum is a pseudo-Latin placeholder text used in web design, typography, and printing to demonstrate how a page will look in the final product. The text originates from the Roman statesman and philosopher Cicero's treatise *De Finibus Bonorum et Malorum* (The Extremes of Good and Evil), written in 45 BCE. The first two words (*lorem ipsum*) are a truncation of *dolorem ipsum* ("pain itself").

The primary purpose of this text is to focus the viewer's attention on the layout, typography, and visual elements rather than the content itself. This package allows you to design a layout without being distracted by the meaning of the text. The next chapter provides a more detailed discussion of document typography and layout. This package was used to design the layout of the paperback version of this book and is useful when testing functions.

EWS includes a package to generate *Lorem Ipsum* paragraphs, which you can access with `C-c w s i` keys. To insert multiple elements, use a numeric prefix. For example, `M-6 C-c w s` inserts six random paragraphs.

Converting text casing

Emacs has built-in functions to convert words and regions to lowercase and uppercase (section 3.8). When writing prose, we sometimes require book titles, chapters, and other headings to be capitalised following defined rules.

The Titlecase package by Case Duckworth provides title-casing for English prose. The `titlecase-dwim` function (`C-c w s t`) converts the selected region or the current line/paragraph. There is no single method to capitalise a phrase or sentence. You can set the casing convention by customising the `titlecase-style` variable to your preferred method. The customisation menu provides a drop-down box with options to set the style of the title-casing according to the conventions of the APA style guide.

EWS includes a convenience function (`ews-org-headings-titlecase`) that cycles through all headings in the current Org buffer and capitalises them. Use `C-c w s c` to access his function. With the universal argument (`C-u`), the headings become sentence case, which only capitalises the first word. By default, this function converts all headings to the desired case. When you configure the `ews-org-heading-level-capitalise` variable, you can either add a number to convert only headings up to a certain level or retain the default of converting all headings. So, when, for example, you set this variable to one, only the top-level headings are capitalised, while lower-level headings don't change.

Unfortunately, due to the whimsies of written English, it is impossible to capitalise titles perfectly using an algorithm. For example, the computer does not distinguish between a word and an acronym. So, never trust a computer and proofread your titles before publishing.

A clean writing interface

Writing creative prose takes total concentration, and distractions are the author's natural enemy. While your computer is a vital writing tool, it can also be a distraction. Most writing software is littered with icons and options to change the document's design. These are rarely useful and mostly distractions. Distraction-free writing tools eliminate these distractions from the screen, making the computer more akin to a mechanical typewriter that allows the author to focus on content over form.

Olivetti is an Emacs minor mode that facilitates distraction-free writing. The name Olivetti derives from the famous Italian typewriter brand. This minor mode reduces the width of the text to seventy characters and centres the text in the middle of the window. The width of the text is changeable with the `olivetti-set-with` command (`C-c \`).

EWS enhances the use of Olivetti mode with its user-friendly function (`C-c w o`). This command activates Olivetti mode (`ews-olivetti`) and stores your current window configuration and cursor position. It enhances your writing environment by increasing the text size and creating a focused screen. Reactivating the function restores your previous window and cursor settings, allowing you to effortlessly switch between distraction-free and regular writing modes.

Quality assurance

While automated spellchecking is a fantastic tool to ensure your writing is syntactically correct, sometimes you must look up words in a dictionary to get more context. Emacs has a built-in dictionary search function that connects to an online source. The default for EWS is the *Collaborative International Dictionary of English* (CIDE), derived from the 1913 Webster's Dictionary (`dict.org`). Volunteers from around the world manage the content of this dictionary, which you can access at your fingertips from within Emacs.

To find the definition of the word the cursor is currently on in the dictionary, use `dictionary-lookup-definition` (`C-c w s d`). A dictionary screen appears, providing the relevant definitions. You can scroll through the window as with any other buffer. The dictionary buffer contains links to other defined words, which you follow with the Enter key. Using the `n` / `p` keys, jump between hyperlinks. To look up a new word, type `s` or click on the `[Search Definition]` button on top of the window. The `h` key lists the available options in dictionary mode.

Being lost for words is a common ailment for authors, and the cure is, in most cases, a thesaurus to help you add some variety to your prose. The dictionary lookup command also includes acces to the Moby Thesaurus. While in dictionary mode, type `D` to change the search strategy and select the thesaurus.

The core skill in writing is choosing the correct words. Equally important is knowing which words not to use. WriteGood mode, by Benjamin Beckwith, reviews your text for three fundamental problems: weasel words, passive voice, and duplicates. Writegood mode highlights issues in your text with coloured squiggly lines. Hovering the mouse over a marked word provides context on the identified transgression.

Weasel words are often used by politicians and marketers to obscure their intentions. They are weasel words because they suck the meaning out of language, just like a weasel sucks eggs (Watson, 2004). You can find the defined list of weasel words with `C-h v` `writegood-weasel-words`. Customise this variable to remove or add your words or create a list relevant to your native language.

Another area for improvement in writing that authors should avoid is the use of passive voice. Passive voice is like telling a story backwards. Instead of saying, "The dog chased the cat," which shows who is doing what, you say, "The cat was chased by the dog." Passive sentences tend to obscure the subject performing the action, making sentences often more verbose. This form can lead to ambiguity, particularly in technical and formal writing, where clarity and precision are paramount. Moreover, active voice generally makes the prose more dynamic and engaging, improving readability by emphasising the actor and their actions, which aligns well with the principles of clear communication. Passive voice has its place in writing but should be avoided when possible (pun intended).

Writegood mode detects passive voice and marks it as such. It achieves this by detecting "to be" forms followed by a word ending in "ed". The software also contains a list of irregular verbs, which you can view and modify to your personal settings or own language by customising the `writegood-passive-voice-irregulars` variable.

Duplicate words are a common artefact of copying and pasting text. Our minds are not particularly good at detecting duplicate words, as the brain often skips words and fills in missing parts (Rayner, Slattery, Drieghe, & Liversedge, 2011). Writegood mode underlines duplicated words words (pun intended).

The WriteGood package can also calculate the Flesch reading ease score to assess how easy or difficult an English text is to understand. The score ranges from 0 to approximately 120. You can perform this test with the `writegood-reading-ease` function (C-c w s r). For the mathematically inclined, this formula calculates the readability index as follows:

$$206.835 - 1.015 \left(\frac{\text{words}}{\text{sentences}} \right) - 84.6 \left(\frac{\text{syllables}}{\text{words}} \right)$$

This test confirms what we intuitively know. Texts with long sentences (words per sentence) and long words (syllables per word) are more challenging to read. The lower the readability score, the easier a text is to understand. For reference, the readability index of *Reader's Digest* is about 65, *Time Magazine* scores about 52. The *Harvard Law Review* has a general readability score in the low 30s (Lipovetsky, 2023).

Note that counting words and sentences depends on assumptions on what constitutes a word or a sentence, as explained in section 7.3.

7.3   Manage the writing project

A writing project is about more than just smashing as many words as possible into a document. Some functionality is available in Org to manage your project by splitting it across several files, tracking word counts, and monitoring the overall progress of your manuscript.

Writing large projects

Working with large files can be cumbersome and, in some cases, slow down Emacs; therefore, splitting larger projects across multiple files is often a good approach. Org can split a writing project over multiple files with references.

When writing this book, I created a main file and a file for each chapter. The main file contains the references to each chapter. For example, adding the line below includes a file named `chapter-02.org` inside the document at the location where this line appears during export.

```
#+include: "chapter-02.org"
```

You can visit the child document with `C-c ’` (`org-edit-special`) when the cursor is on the inclusion line. Org has additional options to determine which part of the child document to include. You can, for example, exclude the title line of the included file by adding `:lines "2-"` to the keyword. This parameter instructs Org mode to only include the text from line two onwards:

```
* Chapter Two
#+include: "chapter-02.org" :lines "2-"
```

When you include a document this way, the heading level will be one below the subtree it is embedded in. So, for example, when you include a document under a level one heading in the source, the level one heading in the linked document will become level two headings, level two becomes level three, and so on. The example above results in something like this:

```
* Chapter Two
** Level one heading in "chapter-2.org"
*** Level two heading in "chapter-2.org"
```

This method allows you to work on a book or dissertation and store each chapter in a separate file, as is the case with this book. When you export the main file to the final publication, all included files are exported as one.

When working with multiple files in a project, it is essential to be mindful of two key issues. You can add links to cross-references in other files, but these links will not be functional until you export the project to a single file or website. Secondly, when you rely on a local bibliography, you need to ensure that it is referenced in all individual files that use it, as referenced files do not inherit properties from the bibliography.

Counting words

Counting words is a standard activity for any author. I aim to write between 5,000 and 10,000 words for each chapter in this book. To count the number of words in a highlighted part of the active buffer, use M-= (count-words-region). This function displays the number of lines, sentences, words, and characters in the echo area.

Adding the universal argument counts the words in the whole buffer (C-u M-=). The count-words function, which has no default keyboard shortcut, tallies all words in the buffer or the marked region. A line in this context is a logical line, which is the same as a paragraph when using Visual Line mode.

Counting words is not an exact science because the outcome depends on the definition of a character, a word or a sentence. When counting characters, Emacs also counts spaces and semantic constructions, such as the metadata of an Org file. Being primarily a computer code editor, Emacs counts hyphenated words or any words separated by punctuation as two words.

By default, Emacs defines a sentence as a sequence of characters that end with a full stop and double spaces. This default setting generates wrong results when counting sentences, as most authors use single spaces, so EWS disables this behaviour. Adding double spaces at the end of a sentence made sense in the days of typewriters. Modern typesetting software no longer requires this archaic practice. Most style manuals, such as the *The Chicago Manual of Style*, recommend using single spacing . When exporting text to the final product, the typesetting software inserts appropriate spacing between sentences. Double spaces after a full stop do make sense when the output is in a monospaced font, as is common in writing software code. The only disadvantage of this method is that abbreviations such as "E. W. S." count as multiple words and sentences.

To count the number of words in each chapter or section of your text, you would have to run `count-words-region` for each part of your document. EWS provides a convenience function to automate this task and display a word count for each heading. The `ews-org-count-words` (C-c w c) function cycles through all headings and adds the word count in a property drawer, which is another type of drawer that works much like the notes drawer described above. The word count for higher-level headings includes the content for their lower headings. This method also allows you to add targets for each section, enabling you to monitor progress. Use C-c C-x p (`org-set-property`), type TARGET, and enter your desired word count. You can also manually edit the drawer, of course.

```
* Heading
  :PROPERTIES:
  :WORDCOUNT: 305
  :TARGET: 300
  :END:
```

Property drawers are a powerful feature that can convert an Org buffer into a database.

You can view these properties in table format. First, you need to define the desired properties to display by adding the following line to the front matter of the Org buffer:

```
#+columns: %40ITEM(Section) %10WORDCOUNT(Words) %10TARGET(Target)
```

The numbers after the percentage sign indicate the size of this column, and the text after the number matches the property name; here ITEM stands for the header text. The text between parenthesis is the display name for the column. You can now view the word count and target for each heading in a table with C-c C-x C-c (org-columns). Ensure you evaluate this function when the cursor is positioned at the highest level in the hierarchy (at the beginning of the document). This view creates an overlay, with the top line of the buffer as a table heading.

All headings have a grey background and contain the values of the defined properties. A table appears at the overview and contents level of the document by cycling through the document with S-<Tab>.

The headlines become read-only and contain the properties defined as columns. You have a few options when the cursor is on one of the headlines. The c button collapses the headings so you see only the table and not the underlying text. You can still edit the text, but visual line mode is disabled.

Navigate through the table with the arrow keys. You can edit a property with the e key. Change the content in the minibuffer and hit Enter. The g key resets the columns. Place the cursor on a column overlay to remove the overlay and press q.

Tracking the status of your writing

The typical writing workflow progresses through various stages, from early drafts to edited versions and ultimately to completed texts. As you work on various parts of your writing project, it might be good to know the status of each chapter. Org mode includes an extensive system to manage projects, which you can deploy to keep track of progress in your document. This section is only a brief introduction to this functionality. Section 9.1 provides a more detailed explanation of project management.

Each heading in Org mode can have a status token, such as TODO, DRAFT, or EDITED, or any other workflow you prefer. You add a status token with the shift and left/right arrow keys when the cursor is on a heading. You can also use the C-c C-t shortcut (org-todo). By default, the system only recognises the TODO and DONE status. However, Org mode allows you to add additional workflow states, providing the flexibility to tailor the system to your specific needs. The example below instructs Org mode to cycle through these four status tokens, but only in this file. The tokens before the vertical line (pipe symbol) are in progress and usually marked in red. Items after the vertical line are completed and marked in green.

```
#+todo: TODO DRAFT EDIT | FINAL
```

If you would like to add the status of your heading to the summary table discussed in the previous section, then add %20TODO(Status) or something similar to the column definition in the front matter.

7.4   Control versions and collaborate

It's not uncommon to revise the flow or structure of your text during the writing process. To ensure you retain valuable information, it's essential to understand how Emacs manages different versions of a buffer or a file. Writing may seem like a solitary activity, but more often than not, you collaborate with other authors and editors. In such scenarios, version control plays a pivotal role in maintaining the collaborative spirit.

While Emacs may not boast the flashy cloud collaboration systems found in office software, it offers various methods to control versions. At the lowest level, we have the version in the current buffer and the one saved to disk. The undo system meticulously tracks all changes within the current buffer at a more granular level. Another method involves using the built-in backup system, which saves older versions of files, preserving your manuscript's evolution. For more advanced needs, Emacs also interfaces with version control software, allowing you to formally check files in and out, which is useful when collaborating with other authors or an editor.

Reverting the current buffer

There are always at least two versions of a text you are working on. The last saved version and the current buffer. You can discard all changes since the buffer was last saved with the `revert-buffer` command, which reloads the file from the disk, erasing all edits made since the last save of the file. Use this as a nuclear option with care. Reverting a buffer only applies when you made colossal mistakes or updated the file outside your current Emacs session.

The undo system

Section 3.8 discussed correcting mistakes using Emacs' powerful undo system. However, after repeatedly issuing undo and redo commands, it is easy to get lost in the previous states of a document. The Vundo package by Yuan Fu helps you keep track of edits by visualising them as a tree, creating a writing time machine.

The `vundo` (C-M-/) command visualises the various edits in your file as a horizontal tree in the minibuffer. This function allows you to navigate through previous versions using the arrow keys. The current buffer changes as you wander through history. Hit Enter to select the chosen edit and continue writing. The C-g keys jump out of the tree without making changes.

Most of the time the tree is simply a straight line. In some cases, the document has parallel versions visualised as branches when combining undo and redo commands. The Vundo tree for the simple example in figure 3.4, where we started with Socrates, changed to Plato and back again and added some text, would look like this:

```
o--o--o--o
   '--o
```

The Vundo package provides an intuitive interface to manage the various document since you opened the file. The manual for the Vundo package provides some further information, which can be read by typing C-h P and selecting vundo.

Automated backups

Rewriting a file destroys its previous contents, which can sometimes mean losing hours of writing in a split second. To prevent such disasters, Emacs can keep a backup of every file.

Emacs backs up a file the first time you add content to a buffer. The first backup of any new file is, therefore, an empty file. No matter how often you save the file in the current session, its backup remains unchanged until you kill the buffer and revisit the file. So, backup files contain the versions just before starting a new writing session. This backup will remain the same as the current file until you save the buffer again. The current version will become a backup file if you save the buffer with a prefix argument (C-u C-x C-s).

By default, Emacs stores backup files in the same directory as the original file, resulting in clutter. EWS stores backups in the Emacs configuration directory under backups. Emacs appends the original file name with a tilde to indicate that it is a backup, so the backup for chapter-02.org would be chapter-02.org~. EWS is also configured to keep the last three versions of the file. Emacs appends version numbers to the end of the filename: ~1, ~2, and so on.

The directory editor (dired) allows you to view the available backup files. Use the C-x d shortcut and enter the location of the backup folder (in your Emacs configuration directory). Using the arrow and enter keys, select and open a file. Chapter 9 provides a detailed explanation of how to use the directory editor.

The way Emacs manages backups can be confusing, so let's visualise it (figure 7.1). When you create a new file and start editing, the system creates a backup, which is an empty file at this stage, or the content of the file as it was first opened in Emacs. While editing and saving intermediate versions, new backups are only created if you save the file with the universal argument. When you close the buffer and then reopen it, a new backup is created. The Undo-Tree package manages versions within an open buffer. These intermediate versions are discarded when you close (or kill) the buffer.

These mechanisms provide fine-tuned version control that minimises the risk of losing information to close to zero. Read the relevant Emacs manual entry with C-h r g backup to find out more about the Emacs backup system.

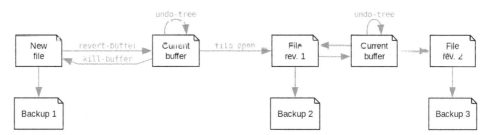

Figure 7.1: Emacs backup system logic.

Comparing file versions

As your writing project progresses, you might end up with different versions of the same file, either through your own doing, by an editor or by another collaborator. This situation may raise a problem, as you are unsure which file is the most recent version, or you may need to create a new version that contains all the latest changes.

The ediff command helps you solve this problem. It provides a rich interface for comparing two or three files and managing changes. Ediff visualises differences between files and lets you select the parts of each file you like to merge into the main version.

Using Ediff is straightforward. Start the ediff command and select two files in the minibuffer, which are then displayed in the Emacs frame in two windows side-by-side. Ediff refers to the left window as file A and the right one as file B. The Ediff control panel is below the two file windows. The control panel enables you to issue commands to either of the two open buffers, making the process of file comparison and merging effortless.

When you type n, Ediff takes you to the next difference. The paragraph where the difference occurs is highlighted, with the actual differences in a more intense background. Repeatedly typing n takes you through successive differences and p to the previous one. The mode line of the control panel displays the number of differences and your progress through them. The highlighted sections are effectively the tracked changes used in word processing software.

Ediff offers a flexible approach to handling differences. You can synchronise parts of file A with B or vice versa by either typing a or b in the control panel. Using a synchronises the two files to the content in file A for the highlighted section, while using b makes both files the same as the highlight of file B. Ediff's adaptability allows you to choose the version of the file that best suits your needs, giving you complete control over the merging process.

You can also move the cursor into either file buffers to edit them manually as you would normally. However, this can cause confusion, as it will be difficult to distinguish between what you typed and the original content. Any text added during the Ediff session is not recognised as a new difference. To end the session, type q in the control panel and follow the prompts to either save or kill the two buffers.

Ediff is useful when you work with an editor (a person who edits a text, not a computer program). You can send them a plain text file that the editor improves, and you process it with Ediff. When receiving the modified file, you can then use Ediff to manage any proposed changes to the text. If your editor is uncomfortable using plain text files, the next chapter explains how to export Org files to common word processor formats.

Ediff has a lot of functionality outside the scope of this book. Type the question mark when the cursor is in the control panel for a list of options. You can read the Ediff manual for a comprehensive description with `ediff-documentation` or `C-h R ediff`.

Version control

The traditional method of version control, often used by authors, involves changing the filename to distinguish between different versions of their writing. For instance, you might have a file named `article-draft.org` and almost identical copies of this file named `article-draft-02.org` and so on. While this approach can be practical when all collaborators follow the same process, it can become cumbersome and confusing. With the power of Ediff, you can easily track changes between files; however, this approach can be cumbersome.

Using file name versions litters the project directory with multiple copies of your files. The Emacs backup system prevents the need to keep multiple versions of the same file. However, the backup system provides limited active control over the stored versions.

Software developers often collaborate with other coders. They solve issues between versions of the same code with a Version Control System (VCS). These tools are not only suitable for hackers but also benefit authors who write texts for humans.

A VCS is like a supercharged filing cabinet. It is your personal assistant that tracks every change to a document, lets you go back to a previous version, and even allows you to work on multiple drafts without getting confused. This tool can also inform you who made which changes and when, making collaboration effortless.

Version control systems can also define different branches of your work. Think of branching as creating parallel universes. You can work on different storylines without mixing them up. When ready, you can merge the changes into the main document. Let's say you're writing a novel. You can create a main branch for the current draft. When you write an alternate ending, you can create a new branch called "alternate-ending" and work on it without disturbing the primary draft. If you collaborate with an editor, they can make changes and suggest edits in their branch. You can review and merge these changes into your primary draft when ready.

If you're co-authoring a book or receive feedback from an editor, a version control system (VCS) can prevent conflicts between versions. You can see who made which changes and resolve any potential conflicts when two people edit the same part of the document.

Since a VCS saves versions of your document, it also serves as a reliable backup. You can recover your work if your computer crashes or if you accidentally delete something. Lastly, VCS tools can store comments on specific changes. This is useful for reminding yourself why you made a change or communicating with collaborators. A VCS brings order to the turbulent writing process and ensures you never lose a great idea or a critical revision.

The Emacs built-in VC package can interface with the most common version control systems, of which Git is the most popular. So, for this functionality to work, you will need to install Git, a decentralised version control system developed by Linus Torvalds to support Linux development.

Let's say you are working on a project with a bunch of Org files and some illustrations in a directory and subdirectories. When a directory of files is under version control, it is known as a repository or repo in hacker-speak. Start by initialising the current directory as a repository with the `vc-next-action` command (`C-x v v`).

This command detects the next logical action, which in this case is creating a new repo. You will need to select a backend (Git) and the folder in which to implement version control. VC stores the version control data in a hidden folder inside your project directory. For Git, this is `.git`. Manual changes to this directory can break your version control, so leave it as is. Please note that the Emacs backup system ignores files in directories managed under version control to prevent duplication.

The next logical action in this process is to commit a file to the repository. Committing a file to a Git repository means saving a snapshot of the file's current state to the repository's history (figure 7.2). When you change a file in your repository and commit those changes, Git records them as a new commit in the repo's history. Each commit has a unique identifier and includes information about the changes, including the name of the person who made the change, as well as the date and time it was made. You commit a file with the same command (`C-x v v`).

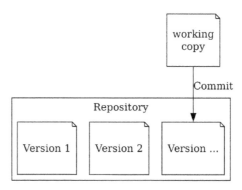

Figure 7.21 Version Control System.

VC commits the current version of your file and asks you to describe the changes in a short statement of no more than fifty characters. Below the summary (under the horizontal line), you can write a more detailed account of the changes, but this is not compulsory. This summary of changes provides a running commentary on the evolution of your manuscript. At the bottom of the screen, VC lists the file(s) in this commit. You finalise the commit with C-c C-c. If you decide you are not yet ready to commit the changes, use C-c C-k.

The mode bar of your file will now display an indicator that it is under version control, along with the branch it belongs to, typically Git: master. This means you are using Git to manage versions for this file and working in the master branch. The vc-diff command (C-x v =) shows a popup buffer that visualises the differences between the current version and the most recent commit.

You can produce a list of current file changes with C-x v l or vc-print-log. This list shows the unique commit ID, the author, the change date, and a summary of the changes, with the most recent version at the top. Navigate between the various versions with n (next) and p (previous). You can view the changes between versions with the d key. Selecting more than one commit with the m and arrow keys and then d shows the differences between the oldest and latest versions. To quit this view, use the trusty q key.

To view changes in the whole repository, use C-x v L (vc-print-root-log).

There is also a command to show the development history of a selected text region. Select the part of the text you are interested in and use C-x v h (vc-region-history). This buffer operates in the same manner as the previous two examples. The vc-annotate command (C-x v g) shows the relevant commit for each line in the text, coloured by the age of the contribution.

The vc-dir command (C-x v d) lists the status of all files in the current directory and its subdirectories. The first line shows the backend for this version-controlled directory, which, in our case, is Git. The following four lines show the directory under version control and other metadata. This buffer lets you act on individual files. Press the question mark key to see a list of available options.

Version control has much more functionality, and a full explanation is outside the scope of this book, such as creating separate branches of your work and synchronising the repository with an online version to share it with collaborators. You can find the Emacs manual chapter about version control with C-h r g version. The manual is written with software development in mind, so please use your imagination to see how it applies to writing prose.

Collaborating with other authors and editors

Unfortunately, writing in plain text with advanced version control systems is not the most common approach to collaborating on writing projects. This raises the question of how you collaborate with coauthors or editors. There are three options, collaborator(s) either:

1. Neither use a VCS or plain text files

2. Don't use a VCS, but write in plain text

3. Uses both VCS

The fourth possible scenario, where somebody uses a VCS but not plain text files, makes little sense. Let's briefly discuss each of these three scenarios.

Even if your collaborator does not use a VCS or understands the benefits of plain text, you can still collaborate effectively. The next chapter will guide you on how to export your work to the most common word processor file formats (section 8.3). This allows you to send your manuscript to an editor or other collaborator. When you receive the result, you can easily accept all tracked changes, save it as a text file, and use Ediff to manage differences with your last version. This process ensures that you can still participate in the collaborative writing process, regardless of the tools your collaborators use.

Your collaborators don't necessarily need to use Emacs because any text editor can read and write Org files. However, the fancy Org functionality is unavailable when not using Emacs. When a collaborator sends you a new version of a file, Ediff is the ideal tool to resolve differences between versions.

When all collaborators use a VCS and can write in Org mode, either in Emacs or with another text editing program, you should push your repository to an online platform, such as GitLab. Uploading a repository to online storage is called pushing a repo. Users can then 'clone' the online repository and work on the manuscript. Collaborators can push their changes to the central repository. The repository owner can then merge the changes into the main branch and resolve potential issues.

Another collaboration method is to share the project folder with a sharing system, such as NextCloud. This method has the risk that you both open the same file simultaneously. Emacs can lock a file for opening by another user, but the EWS configuration disables the use of lock files. To use a shared folder, you must customise the `create-lockfiles` variable. If this is set to `t`, then a file can only be opened by one user simultaneously. It achieves this by storing a file that prevents other users from making changes.

7.5 Other text modes

This book is a comprehensive guide to using Org mode for your writing projects. Org is just one of the many text modes available in Emacs. Understanding these other formats, which are based on text mode, is crucial for making informed choices and enhancing your writing process.

The most basic version is a plain text file, typically denoted by a `.txt` file extension. These files are plain in that they don't contain any formatting and generally consist only of alphanumeric characters, spacing and punctuation. If we want to publish a work as a website, a book or any other type of media, a plain text file will not suffice because there is no way to define what the final result should look like, such as the page layout, font types, hyperlinks and other such vital parts of a published work.

Other text modes consist of styled or rich text. These files contain plain text and additional information about the document's design, such as font style and links. Org and HTML are examples of styled plain text. The styling instructions are the markup of the document. Traditional publishing markup is a system of annotations in red or blue pencil that instruct the printer on how to style a manuscript. Marking up a document was laborious, and editors and typesetters used symbols (the markup) to indicate how the text should appear on the page. In digital publishing, we use sequences of characters and punctuation as markup to instruct the computer to display a document.

Graphical word processors hide the markup and show the text in its printed form. This method might seem convenient, but it can also become a nightmare as you try to wrangle the system to obtain the desired result using these invisible instructions. Plain text is easier to use because the markup is directly visible in the document, so you have direct control over the design of your manuscript.

Many plain text modes exist for all sorts of purposes. You have already seen how Org uses plain text snippets to add instructions. There are two types of markup. Presentational markup provides instructions on how to present the text, including boldface, italics, lists, and headings. Procedural markup consists of symbols to instruct the computer about aspects such as page size, text position, citations, metadata, and other more complex elements of a publication (Travis & Waldt, 1995).

Styled text modes are available in two types, regular markup and lightweight versions. A regular markup language, such as HTML or LaTeX, includes instructions that resemble a computer language to define the document's design output. For example, to write a heading in HTML and LaTeX, you need:

- HTML: `<h2>This is a heading</h2>`

- LaTeX: `/section{This is a heading}`

Regular markup languages offer powerful capabilities to define all the details of the final output of your project. The disadvantage is that your text is littered with angled brackets, curly braces, and instructions. In lightweight versions, the number of characters required to define a document is reduced, simplifying the writing process. Org is an example of a lightweight markup language. It is not lightweight due to its limited capabilities but rather because of the simplified instruction set. To create the same heading in Org, add an asterisk at the beginning of the line, which removes some clutter from the screen.

The next two sections explain the principle of two standard text modes used by authors. The next chapter describes how to export Org manuscripts to create an e-book, PDF file, or printed book or to export them to LaTeX or HTML.

Introducing Markdown

Markdown, a markup language introduced by internet pioneers John Gruber and Aaron Swartz in 2004, is designed to be easy to read and understand, with minimal use of semantic characters. Unlike the more complex HTML, Markdown's simplicity is its key feature, hence the name 'mark-down'. It's a versatile tool, widely used for instant messaging, online forums, and software documentation. The fundamental principles of Markdown are similar to those of Org, as demonstrated below.

```
# Heading
## Sub-Heading
Text attributes: _italic_, **bold**, `monospace`.

Bullet lists nested within numbered lists:
1. Fruits
    * Apple (sub-lists indented with four spaces)
    * Banana
2. Vegetables
    - Carrot
    - Broccoli

A [link](http://example.com).

![Image](Icon-pictures.png "icon")
```

Various markdown flavours exist, most of which provide additional functionality to the standard syntax. The Markdown Mode package by Jason R. Blevins implements the original version. The developer has also published a detailed book on how to use Markdown in Emacs (Blevins, 2017). The EWS configuration activates Markdown by default, but a complete description of this format is outside the scope of this book.

Markdown is often used in technical documentation and is more commonplace than Org mode to share information.

The Denote package can create notes in Markdown in two varieties. Unlike Org, Markdown has no native provisions for storing metadata about the document. Denote provides two methods to achieve this: TOML (Tom's Obvious Minimal Language) or YAML (YAML Ain't Markup Language). You can set the denote-file-type variable to either markdown-toml or markdown-yaml to start creating Markdown notes.

Read the Denote manual for more details and try the different varieties yourself. You can also consider using the Denote-Markdown package, which provides additional functionality for writing Markdown Denote files.

Screenwriting with Fountain

Who wouldn't want to write a screenplay for the next Hollywood or Bollywood block-buster? Writing movie or theatre scripts follows some strict principles and formatting rules. The standard font for screenplays has a fixed pitch, giving the document an old-school typewriter feel.

However, you can unleash your creativity with Fountain, a plain text format for writing screenplays in any text processor. The Fountain file format is quite special as it contains almost no markup. Given the strict conventions in screenplays, Fountain can logically determine how to format the document.

Fountain Mode implements this text format in Emacs and is enabled in *Emacs Writing Studio*. To become the next Shakespeare or Stanley Kubrick, read the extensive manual with `C-h R fountain`.

Chapter *8*

Publication: Share with the World

Emacs Org mode is not just an ideal tool for writing without distractions; it's a power-house for publishing. Working with plain text allows you to focus on content instead of design. With Org's export capabilities your work can exist in various formats. Org can export your manuscript to PDF for a printed book, a journal article, a website, or a word processor document. Additional packages can export your manuscript to other formats, such as an e-book in ePub format.

This chapter guides you in preparing Org files for export by defining the layout and typography. The first section explains the principles of the export process and how Org interfaces with other software to create the desired output. The second section provides the generic settings that apply to all output formats, equipping you with the practical knowledge to prepare your document for publication. The remainder of this chapter explores the intricacies of the most common export formats, PDF, HTML and word processor docuuments. It guides you in configuring Emacs and your manuscript to achieve the desired output.

8.1 Export Org files

Preparing a document for export used to be the responsibility of a typesetter. The type-setting process determines the sizes of fonts and graphical elements, as well as their place-ment on the page. In traditional printing, typesetting involves arranging physical mov-able type to form a page. With electronic publishing, we no longer have to move physical pieces of lead but issue instructions. Typesetting in Org starts with adding appropriate metadata to the manuscript, depending on the chosen export format.

The basic principle of exporting Org files to the desired format is that Emacs converts the text and associates it with a document class, CSS style sheet, or other type of template. The template defines the typography and layout of the document. You don't need to know CSS, HTML, or LaTeX, but it will help fine-tune the output. Your text file can also link to a local or global bibliography to manage citations.

When exporting to PDF or a word processor format, the exported file is passed to either LaTeX or LibreOffice and then compressed with Zip to generate the final result. The Zip program is necessary because ePub and office documents are websites packaged into a single file. Figure 8.1 shows the Org export workflow and the tools used to render the output from the Org file to the desired output. You can export the same file to any of the available formats. For example, the source files for this book produce a print-ready PDF file for the paperback version, an e-book in ePub format and a website.

For example, if you create a website or e-book, any Org text surrounded by for-ward slashes (`/example/`) translates to `<i>example</i>/`, while for LaTeX it becomes `\emph{example}`. The default setting for this example is italic text, but it could be something different depending on how you configure your export.

The Org and Emacs configuration includes instructions on the layout and typogra-phy of the document (the "what you mean" in WYSIWYM). Each export format has its own method for linking syntax to typography. When exporting to HTML, a Cascading Style Sheet (CSS) specifies the design, while in LaTeX, the document class and preamble determine how this syntax looks in the final output. An OpenDocument Text Template

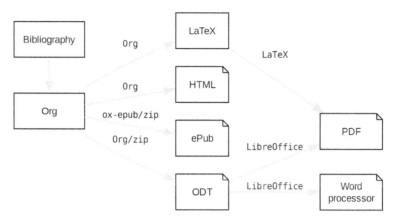

Figure 8.1: Org mode export principles.

(OTT) defines the final design when exporting to word processor format.

Exporting an Org file starts with the `org-export-dispatch` function with the default C-c C-e keyboard shortcut. A new buffer pops up with a large number of options. The first letter you type determines the export format, and subsequent letters the specific options. Using q exists the export dispatcher.

8.2 Document settings

Your manuscript can store metadata and configurations to guide the export process. Numerous settings control how Org exports your document. The use of this data depends on the export format. Some generic metadata applies to all formats. The following keywords apply to all formats:

- `#+title:` Document title.

- `#+author:` Author name.

- `#+date:` Date of publication.

You can define the order of the year, month and day to suit your preference with the `org-export-date-timestamp-format` variable. This variable utilises an encoding commonly used in programming languages to display a date. For example, `%e %B %Y` means that it starts with the day number (without leading zero), indicated by `%e`, then the full name of the month (`%B`), followed by the four-digit year (`%Y`) and separated by spaces (3 June 2024). To use the American date format, customise this variable to `"%B %e, %Y"` (June 3, 2024). The help page for the `format-time-string` variable lists the available formats.

The author name appears by default in every exported document, even when not defined in the Org file. When this keyword is not used, the exports defaults to the content of the `user-full-name` variable. Adding `#+options:  author:nil` negates this behaviour. This option can also remove a title, author and/or date.

```
#+options: author:nil date:nil title:nil
```

Org has a fine-tuned mechanism to control the export using the options keyword. These settings only apply to the buffer under consideration. All available options also have a matching variable that you can customise so it applies to all exports. You can read about all available options in the manual with `C-h R org` and search for the relevant chapter with `g export settings`.

The title, author and date are the basic metadata. Each export format also uses specific variables in the front matter. You can obtain a template for exporting to your target format with `org-export-insert-default-template`, which inserts the keywords relevant to the chosen export format in the current Org buffer. Access this function through the export dispatcher with `C-c C-e #`. Using more than one export format for one manuscript is perfectly fine. However, using this function more than once leads to some duplicate keywords.

Org saves the result of the export process in the same directory as the source document. The exported file has the same name as the source file but with a different extension. Exporting Denote Org files can create a filename conflict because it results in two files with the same identifier. You can change the exported file's name by adding `#+export_file_name:   <filename>` to the header. The filename can be any string without the file extension. You can export files to another folder, but this can cause errors.

Typography

A published manuscript includes more than just letters and numbers. It also includes special typographic characters, such as ellipses, foreign characters and varying types of dashes. The Org export module parses LaTeX characters, such as `\alpha`, to their respective font values. See section 4.5 for more information on special symbols.

For a typographer, a simple dash is not so simple at all. While most electronic writing uses only the plain dash as a hyphen or to separate words and numbers, best practice typography is more subtle. There are four types of dashes, each with its own unique characteristics and use cases. The dash is the shortest, the En-dash is slightly longer, and the M-dash is the longest. The width of an En- and Em-dash is roughly the same as the capital letters N or M. You write these dashes in plain text as a single, double or triple dash. This method is only needed when writing text. In mathematical expressions, the display engine automatically uses the correct version.

- `-`: The dash links elements in compound words (short-term) or hyphenations at the end of a justified line of text.

- `--`: The En-dash separates numbers or words, replacing the word "to" (1–3, or Marathon–Sparta).

- `---`: The Em-dash sets thoughts apart and functions like a comma, a colon, or parenthesis: (—).

- `$-$`: Type a hyphen in mathematics mode for a minus sign ($a - b$).

Adding a table of contents

Org inserts the table of contents directly above the first headline of the file. You can toggle this behaviour by customising the `org-export-with-toc` variable. The table of contents can also be modified for each manuscript by adding the `#+options:` keyword to the front matter, for example:

- `#+options:` `toc:t`: Add the complete contents.

- `#+options:` `toc:n`: Only include n levels in the table of contents.

- `#+options:` `toc:nil`: Don't export a table of contents.

Numbered section settings

Numbered sections are standard in business and academic writing. When you add `num` to the startup keyword, Org mode numbers every heading (`#+startup:` `num`). The numbering appears in the Org buffer as virtual text, so the file content remains unchanged. Whether this numbering also appears in the published output depends on the export template for the relevant format.

Some parts of a manuscript, like the front and back matter of a book or a list of references, are usually not numbered. To exclude a heading from numbering in the export, type `C-c C-x p` (`org-set-property`) and set the UNNUMBERED property as `t` (true). When setting this property to `notoc`, the heading is also excluded from the table of contents. These properties only apply to the exported document for this heading and its children but not the Org buffer itself.

```
:PROPERTIES:
:UNNUMBERED: t
:END:
```

Enhancing tables

Org makes it easy to insert tables, as discussed in section 4.5. Within the source document, tables feature vertical lines for every column, and users can add horizontal lines as needed. However, this is not necessarily how a table looks in the final output.

Horizontal lines defined in the source appear in the final result, but vertical lines are omitted (University of Chicago Press, 2017, sec. 3.53). Most publications allow only horizontal lines because data in a table is aligned into columns, so the eyes don't need a vertical line to separate groups.

Occasionally, vertical lines can be helpful to structure a table into groups of columns. A row with a forward slash (/) in the first field specifies which columns form a group flanked by vertical lines. The other fields either contain a lesser-than symbol (<) to indicate that this column starts a group or a greater-than (>) symbol to indicate the end of a column. Using <> inside a column creates a separate group surrounded by vertical lines. Effectively, the symbols point towards the location of a vertical line. It is also possible to insert the column group starters (<) after every desired vertical line. However, this method does not add a line to the left and right edges of the table. The example below illustrates these principles, with the exported version in the table 8.1 below.

```
#+caption: Example of a table with vertical lines and alignment.
#+name: tab-lines
| n | n^2 | n^3 | n^4 |  Animal  |  a | b  |
|---+-----+-----+-----+----------+----+----|
| / |  <  |     |  >  |          | <> |    |
|   |     | <r> | <c> |    <r> |    |    |
| 1 |  1  |  1  |  1  | Aardvark |  3 |  4 |
| 2 |  4  |  8  | 16  |     Bird |  5 | 12 |
| 3 |  9  | 27  | 81  |      Cow |  8 | 15 |
|---+-----+-----+-----+----------+----+----|
```

Org mode can only handle simple tables without spanning information over multiple columns or rows. To create more complex tables, Org integrates with the builtin

Table 8.1: *Example of a table with vertical lines and alignment.*

n	n^2	n^3	n^4	Animal	a	b
1	1	1	1	Aardvark	3	4
2	4	8	16	Bird	5	12
3	9	27	81	Cow	8	15

Table package by Takaaki Ota. These tables have a slightly different syntax to Org, as illustrated in the overview of German articles below.

To convert a standard Org mode table to the more complex format, use `C-c ~`. To edit an advanced table in Org, use `org-edit-special (C-c ')`, which opens a new buffer with only the table. The same keyboard shortcut takes you back to the document. To learn more about the syntax for this package, read the manual with `C-h P table`.

```
+------------+-----------+----------+----------+-------------+
|            |           Singular              | Plural      |
|            +-----------+----------+----------+-------------+
|            | Masculine | Neuter   | Feminine | All genders |
+------------+-----------+----------+----------+-------------+
| Nominative | der       | das      | die      | die         |
| Accusative | den       | das      | die      | die         |
| Dative     | dem       | dem      | der      | denen       |
| Genitive   | dessen    | dessen   | deren    | deren       |
+------------+-----------+----------+----------+-------------+
```

Table 8.2: *Table exported with the Table package.*

	Singular			Plural
	Masculine	Neuter	Feminine	All genders
Nominative	der	das	die	die
Accusative	den	das	die	die
Dative	dem	dem	der	denen
Genitive	dessen	dessen	deren	deren

Quotations and other structures

The best advice to any writer is to use original words when expressing their thoughts. However, there are times when the words of other authors are so powerful that they not only need to be quoted but also inspire and motivate us. The most direct way is obviously using "quotation marks". Most export formats define a separate typography for quotations, such as indenting the paragraph or using an italic font. Instruct Org to use the quotation structure template with C-c C-, q.

```
#+begin_quote
  Good writing is essentially rewriting (Roald Dahl)
#+end_quote
```

Org structure templates are predefined bits of text to quickly insert commonly used structures. They streamline your workflow by reducing repetitive typing. You have already seen a structure template for notes in the previous chapter. The structure templates most relevant to this book's topic are notes, quotations, verses, and centred text. These structure templates instruct the export workflow to treat these parts of the text accordingly.

Macros

Org also has the functionality to use macros in a manuscript. A macro consists of a string of characters between triple curly braces. Org expands the macro to the full text during the export process. For example, for this book the macro {{{ews}}} is replaced by: *Emacs Writing Studio*. You define a basic macro in the document's front matter:

```
#+macro: ews /Emacs Writing Studio/
```

Org also includes a series of built-in macros. One example provides dynamic timestamps in the date field. Timestamps in Org are static, but you can use an export macro to insert a date dynamically. Using `{{{time(format)}}}` inserts the current date in the output with `format` as described above.

Org macros are a versatile toolkit that can help expand commonly repeated passages. Macros can also include variables and Emacs Lisp functions to create dynamic expansions. The Org manual provides some more advanced examples of macro expansion (`C-h r org <ret> g macro`). The sections about HTML and LaTeX export include further information about macros.

Excluding content from export

Not everything you write should be shared with the world. Org excludes any comments from the final format as discussed in section 7.1. The EWS configuration also doesn't export drawers, so your notes remain private.

Furthermore, you can exclude a section and associated subsections (the subtree) of your writing from export by adding the `:noexport:` tag to a heading with `C-c C-q` (`org-set-tags-command`). You enter the tag name in the minibuffer and can use completion to find tags already used in the current buffer. The tag appears on the right side of the heading name between two colons.

Org mode will export the heading name with any associated tags. You can nullify this behaviour by adding `tags:nil` to the options keyword.

Exporting citations

Org has a built-in citation manager that can use BibTeX / BibLaTeX or CSL bibliography files to reference bibliographic items such as articles and books. The basics are straightforward and work without configuration or external software.

You already know how to create a global and local bibliography and insert citations into Org buffers (sections 5.2 and 7.1). This section explains how Org converts constructs such as `[@cite:wittgenstein_1922]` to a formatted citation, for example, "(Wittgenstein, 1922)."

All you need to export citations is a global or local bibliography, one or more citations and a list of referenced literature (the bibliography), as in this example:

```
#+bibliography: references.bib
"The world is everything that is the case" [cite:@wittgenstein_1922].
* References
#+print_bibliography:
```

You need a citation processor to convert citations in an Org file to the exported version. Org uses the basic export processor by default, which is suitable for simple projects and applies to all export formats. Other processors provide more flexible citation management, as discussed in the sections 8.3 and 8.6.

The basic citation processor can be configured with a keyword in the metadata of your document. This keyword specifies the processor (basic), followed by a bibliography style and a citation style:

```
#+cite_export: basic [bibliography style] [citation style]
```

Org converts the citations to formatted text during the export process and adds a list of references. To include a list of references, add #+print_bibliography: at the location where it needs to appear. The list of references does not include a heading when using the basic engine. The second part of the #+cite_export: keyword defines the bibliography style, which can be one of three options:

- author-year: Default mode.

- numeric: Vancouver system with numbered entries.

- plain: Same as the default, but only author family names.

The basic export processor supports various citation styles. When no citation style is provided, the default is to use the author(s) and year(s) in parentheses, such as "(Toulmin, Stephen, 2003)". There are two ways to define the style of citations. The third part of the

`#+cite_export:` keyword provides the default, which you can override in individual citations. The following citation styles are available:

- `author` (/a): Only author(s) "Toulmin, Stephen"

- `noauthor` (/na): No authors "(2003)"

- `text` (/t): Inline text citation "Toulmin, Stephen (2003)"

- `nocite` (/n): No citation, but add an entry to the list of references.

- `note` (/ft): Citation as footnote.

- `numeric` (/nb): Numbered references between parenthesis (Vancouver system).

You can override the default by adding a style marker before the citations (listed in parentheses above). For example, `[cite/t:@rorty_1979]` is exported as "Rorty (1979)" in author-year citation systems.

Another configuration option is to add a citation variant. This indicator determines whether to remove parenthesis (/b) or capitalise the first letter (/c). You add the variant after the style. For example, `[cite/ft/b:@rorty_1979]` results in a footnote without parenthesis: "Rorty, 1979."

Some combinations of bibliography and citation styles don't make sense. For example, the numeric bibliography and footnote citation styles are incompatible. Org ignores impossible combinations of style and variant.

Org can also include prefixes and suffixes to citations. For example `[cite: See @rorty_1979 p.12]` results in "(See Rorty 1979 p.12)". There is also a global prefix and suffix when using multiple citation keys. So, a citation with all the trimmings could look like this:

`[@cite/s/v: global-prefix; prefix @key1 suffix; prefix @key2 suffix; global-suffix]`

8.3   Create office documents

There are many use cases when we need to share our work with people who prefer to use word processors. In my personal workflow, I often write memoranda and technical reports in Emacs and export them to word processor format to share with my colleagues and facilitate collaboration.

The export function in Org can create documents in formats readable by word processors such as LibreOffice Writer, Apple Pages, or MS Word. Exporting to a word processor format is useful when writing for corporate clients or collaborating with coauthors or an editor. The Org export process results in an OpenDocument Text format (ODT).

An ODT file is a compressed collection of XML files and embedded images, which requires the Zip program to be available. Extensible Markup Language (XML) defines and stores data, inducing text documents, in a shareable manner. When you open an ODT file with an archive program, such as Unzip, you find the following files:

- `meta.xml` contains the metadata for this file.

- `styles.xml` is a stylesheet defining the layout and typography.

- `content.xml` contains the actual document.

When Org exports a buffer to ODT format, it generates two files: `meta.xml` and `content.xml` plus a stylesheet. The stylesheet is either copied from the default configuration or from a user-supplied file. The ODT export tool has some additional front-matter keywords to customise the output. The subtitle is added to the content, while the description and keywords are available in the file's metadata.

- `#+subtitle:` The document subtitle.

- `#+description:` File description.

- `#+keywords:` The exported file(s) keywords.

If you have LibreOffice installed, you can also create a DOCx file to make it easier for MS Word users to share the joy of reading your writing. When you enable this option, the export process will result in both an ODT and a DOCX file. You can change the output format by customising the `org-odt-preferred-output-format` variable. You can also customise this variable to instruct LibreOffice to generate a PDF file.

Images and tables

To control how to export tables and images in an ODT file, use the `#+attr_odt:` line just above the item. Various properties to size and place images are available:

- `:width` and `:height` control the size of an image in centimetres. You can use either only width or height or both. This parameter only accepts numeric values; it does not accept percentages.

- `:scale` defines the relative width of the source image.

- `:anchor` anchors the image `as-char`, to a `paragraph` or to a `page`.

For example, an image with the following properties becomes ten centimetres wide and is anchored as a character:

```
#+attr_odt: :width 10 :anchor as-char
```

When anchoring an image as a character (`as-char`), it is placed in the document like any other character. The image moves with the text as you add or delete text before the image. An image anchored to a paragraph moves with the paragraph. When anchoring an image to a page, it keeps the same position relative to the page margins and does not move. This method is particularly practical for publishing layout-intensive documents, such as newsletters.

Based on the properties mentioned above, the ODT export engine determines the image size in centimetres. The source image is embedded into the ODT document at a resolution of 96 dots per inch (DPI). Customise the `org-odt-pixels-per-inch` variable to use a different resolution. One has to wonder why the image sizing is in centimetres and the resolution uses imperial measurements. Alas, that is the way it works.

Org can export tables to ODT format. By default, tables have top and bottom frames and horizontal and vertical lines, as defined in the source. The `:rel-width` property controls the width of a table in percent of the text width. Any column sizes specified in the table will be relative to the total width (see section 4.5). The following property line above a table would export it at a relative width of 75% of the text width:

```
#+attr_odt: :rel-width 75
```

Mathematics

The Org export to ODT ignores LaTeX formulas; however, a workaround is available. The easiest method is to convert the mathematics into an image file by adding this keyword to the front matter: `#+options: tex:dvipng` for PNG exports. This method requires the dvipng program. Alternatively, use Image Magic with `tex:imagemagick`.

ODT documents have a native formula format (MathML), which Org can export. MathML expresses mathematical formulas in an XML-based notation. However, this option requires some advanced configuration and a MathML converter. The Org manual provides more detailed guidance on using MathML.

Style templates

Controlling the typography and layout for office documents requires an OpenDocument Text Template (OTT) file. These files hold settings to generate new documents, including typography layout and other artefacts. You specify the relevant template in the frontmatter of the current buffer with the `#+odt_styles_file:` keyword, followed by the path to a style file (either OTT or ODT format). To use the same template for all ODT exports, customise the `org-odt-styles-file` variable.

Creating a style file template is a straightforward process. Create an empty Org document, add #+options: H:4 num:t author:nil and export to ODT with C-c C-e o o. The options keyword creates four numbered heading levels. You can obviously modify these settings to suit your preference. Open the exported document with LibreOffice and edit the styles (F11).

Org mode uses some particular styles that start with "Org", so ensure you configure these. When the document is styled to your liking, save it as an OTT file and attach it to your manuscript. The next time you export the Org document, the output will be in the style defined in the template. Org extracts the styles.xml file embedded in your template file and copies it to the exported file.

When your styles contain images, such as a background image for a page, you also need to specify this in the styles file keyword, as shown in the example.

```
#+odt_styles_file: ("template.ott" ("styles.xml" "background.png"))
```

The styles.xml has to be specified, and the background.png file is the one designated as the background image in the template document. Note that LibreOffice renames files, so you need to open the template with Emacs and press C-c C-c to view the file structure and copy the image file name. This setup is ideal for writing corporate documents.

The ODT export process relies on specific templates and style names. Third-party templates can lead to mismatches when they use different style names. Please note that you can only create templates with LibreOffice. Unfortunately, commercial word processors are incompatible with the ODT format used in Open-Source software.

You can fine-tune how Org exports to OpenOffice at a detailed level. For a thorough discussion on Open Document export, read the *OpenDocument Text Export* section of the Org manual: C-h R org <ret> g open.

Citation Style Language

The basic citation processor works perfectly fine when exporting to ODT format, but it is limited in its ability to fine-tune your citations or meet the expectations of your university or publisher. Using the Citation Style Language (CSL) provides extensive options to style your citations. CSL was created by Bruce D'Arcus, who also developed the Citar package described in section 5.2. You can use the CSL citation processor for all export formats. This book uses the CSL citation processor for the published formats.

The CSL engine relies on a file that defines the output. You can find these through the `citationstyles.org` website. Many thousands of varieties are available in CSL for specific journals or universities. Download the style files relevant to your writing projects and store them for future reference.

By default, the CSL processor renders citations in Chicago author-date format. You can use another style file by specifying it within the document by adding the file name to `#+cite_export:` keyword, for example:

```
#+cite_export: csl /path/to/style-file.csl
```

If you maintain a collection of CSL files in the same folder, you need to customise the `org-cite-csl-styles-dir` variable to ensure that Org finds them. When this variable is defined, then you only have to specify the file name in the front matter.

The CSL processor supports the following citation styles, some of which are identical to those supported by the basic processor discussed above.

- `author` (/a): Author only.

- `noauthor` (/na): No author(s).

- `text` (/t): In-line citation.

- `nocite` (/n): Note cited but listed in the references.

- `year` (/y): Only the year

- `title` (/ti): Title of the entry.

- `bibentry` (/b): The full citation as listed in the bibliography.

CSL provides functionality to add a filtered list of references by keyword or publication type. You can combine this with the `nocite` option to create a themed bibliography. Using * as a key in a `nocite` citation includes all available items. The example below exports all books in the global and local bibliography with "Emacs" as a keyword. Note that the keyword is case-sensitive.

```
#+title: Emacs books
#+bibliography: ../library/emacs-writing-studio.bib
#+cite_export: csl

Show a list of books tagged with the "Emacs" keyword.

* Bibliography
[cite/n:@*]
#+print_bibliography: :type book :keyword Emacs
```

8.4 Generate web pages

Emacs includes a built-in major mode for editing HTML files. However, Org has perfect export capabilities for this format, so you can use its lightweight markup without worrying about technical syntax. You export Org to HTML to publish websites and to create ebooks in ePub format, outlined in section 8.5.

The HyperText Markup Language (HTML) is the engine that drives the World Wide Web. Org exports directly to HTML; let's export this small Org document.

```
#+title: HTML Example

Hello world!
```

The example converts to a simple file with HTML markup surrounded by angled braces (less- and greater than symbols). Indentation is optional but helps understand the document's structure.

```
<!DOCTYPE html>
<html>
  <head>
    <title>HTML Example</title>
  </head>
  <body>
    <div>
        <p>Hello world!</p>
    </div>
  </body>
</html>
```

The HTML export engine in Org allows you to set a wide range of document properties in addition to the ones already discussed. These configurations fine-tune the output of the HTML code, which requires in-depth knowledge of web coding and is therefore intended for advanced users and is outside the scope of this book. The Org mode manual describes the details (`C-c R org <ret> g html`). You can preview all available HTML settings with `C-c C-e #` and selecting `html`.

The default export adds a postamble to the page with some metadata. You can negate this behaviour by adding `html-postamble:nil` to the options keyword in the front matter.

Images and tables

Org provides a series of attributes to define how images and tables are exported. These configurations are directly translated into HTML attributes. The `#+attr_html:` keyword defines the attributes for both images and tables.

- `:alt` provides alternative information for an image if a user cannot view it (for example, due to a slow connection, a technical error, or if the user uses a screen reader).

- `:title` adds the image title. The information appears as a tooltip text when the mouse moves over the image.

- `:align` left, centre or right.

- `:width` and `:height` to set the image size (in pixels or percentage)

Images in Org can also be links when the description of the link is itself an image, either a local file or weblink. For example, to insert a thumbnail that hyperlinks to its high-resolution version, use something like this:

```
[[file:high-resolution.jpg][file:thumbnail.jpg]]
```

Tables are also modified by the `#+attr_html:` keyword, which provides three attributes:

- `:border` indicates the width of the border around the table.

- `:rules` set to `all` to draw all table lines.

- `:frame` specifies the visibility of outside borders. The default behaviour is no outside borderlines. Use `border` to show all border lines.

- `:cellspacing` and `:cellpadding` adjust the padding inside the cells and the space between them.

Mathematics

Exporting an Org file to HTML includes a reference to MathJax. This JavaScript library displays mathematical notation in web browsers. You can override this behaviour by directly adding images into the HTML output with `#+options:   tex:dvisvgm`, which converts formulas to SVG files so you don't rely on JavaScript.

Style sheets

While the HTML file contains the content and structure, Cascading Style Sheets (CSS) determine the layout and typography. The default export engine includes a basic style sheet in the front matter that you can replace with your own. The `#+html_head:` keyword lets you add lines to the document preamble.

```
#+html_head: <link rel="stylesheet" type="text/css" href="style1.css" />
#+html_head_extra: <link rel="stylesheet" type="text/css" href="style2.css" />
```

Citations

The HTML export module can process citations using both the basic and CSL processors, as described in sections 8.2 and 8.3.

Inserting bespoke HTML

If you know how to write HTML, insert it directly into an Org file. This technique allows you to add online forms and embed multimedia or non-standard typography. Insert an HTML structure template with `C-c C-,  h` and add your bespoke code. Your webpage includes all lines between the beginning and end markers as-is.

```
#+begin_export html
<some html code/>
#+end_export
```

These HTML blocks are only exported when the output format matches. If you prepare a document in multiple formats, you must include an alternative LaTeX or ODT variant.

Some HTML snippets may appear multiple times in your documents. Most web page development tools provide shortcodes, which are text snippets used to insert HTML. Org macros are ideal as HTML shortcodes. You can use them to embed complex HTML, such as forms and multimedia, or simple applications, such as changing the background colour for selected words.

The example below creates a macro that expands to an embedded YouTube clip using its identification code. The $1 part of the macro represents the first parameter in the macro. Any subsequent parameter will be $2 and so on.

```
#+macro: youtube <iframe src="https://youtube.com/embed/$1"></iframe>
```

This example embeds *Me at the Zoo*, the first YouTube video ever uploaded:

```
{{{youtube(jNQXAC9IVRw)}}}
```

This shortcode exports to:

```
<iframe src="https://youtube.com/embed/jNQXAC9IVRw"></iframe>
```

Publishing Websites

The standard export process only converts a single file and any included files. This could become tedious when working on a website that consist of a large number of individual files.

Org also includes a publishing system to generate websites that requires exporting a collection of Org files. You can customise it to nominate a source folder, as well as a range of other settings that determine the design of the website.

Using this functionality requires technical knowledge of developing websites and familiarity with Emacs Lisp; therefore, it is not explained in detail in this book. You can find the section in the Org manual about publishing documents with `C-h R org <ret> g publish`.

8.5 Create e-books

Most ebook publishers use the ePub format for distribution. The ePub format is a compressed file with the contents stored as a website optimised for an e-reader. Mark Meyer's ox-ePub package adds this functionality to the Org export dispatcher. This package utilises the built-in Org to HTML export feature to create the e-book, allowing you to utilise any of the features described above to fine-tune the output. This package produces a file following the EPub version 2.0.1 standard.

There are some specific export options for this format beyond the ones already discussed, which you can add with `C-c e # epub`:

- `#+uid`: Unique ID of the document, otherwise known as URI, could be a website address or an ISBN. This property is mandatory.

- `#+publisher`: Name of the book publisher.

- `#+license`: Copyright or copyleft license.

- `#+epubstyle`: The CSS file used for export.

- `#+epubcover`: The image of the book cover.

The default configuration for HTML export adds a postamble to the bottom of the last page, including a timestamp, author, and a link to an HTML validation service. Adding `#+options: html-postamble:nil` to the Org file header removes these from your e-book.

The ox-ePub package does not convert Org timestamps, such as `[2024-07-08 Mon]`, to a date format that complies with the ePub standard. You can correct this by removing the square brackets and the name of the day and time from the timestamp. Alternatively, use the time macro to set the date format to ISO 8601 format:

```
{{{time(%Y-%m-%e)}}}
```

It is recommended to use only open formats, such as PNG, when including images in your content. Some e-book readers are unable to display JPG files and other proprietary formats. The e-book will display correctly on your computer, but it may not pass any publisher's quality checks. The ePub export process breaks when any image files are missing. While you can export to HTML and PDF without any errors, your ePub will not render if any linked images are missing.

We should not judge a book by its cover, but it is essential to your publication. The `#+epubcover:` keyword contains the path of the cover file. The ideal dimensions for e-book covers are 2,560 x 1,600 pixels or any other size with an aspect ratio of 1:1.6.

The output from this package is perfectly readable by ePub readers. However, two issues cause the manuscript to fail ePub validation. When your manuscript references other files for inclusion as described in section 7.3, the table of contents is not generated correctly. Secondly, Org exports footnotes in a way that does not comply with the W3C standards for e-Pub files. Both issues can be either avoided or corrected manually with an advanced ePub editor such as Calibre.

8.6   Export to LaTeX and PDF

When computer science pioneer Donald Knuth received the proofs of the second edition of his *The Art of Computer Programming* he was unhappy with the result. In the 1970s, publishers transitioned from traditional fixed-type printing to electronic versions. He turned his disappointment into a positive and decided to develop an electronic typesetting system called TeX (*tekh*) that recreates the aesthetic of traditional books (Knuth, 1984). The original language is complex, so Leslie Lamport developed a TeX macros library called LaTeX (Lamport, 1994).

LaTeX results in beautiful print-ready documents. This tool is widely used in academia and technical fields. LaTeX optimises documents for printed works, so it is also great for writing non-technical paper books. The paperback version of this book was created with Org and exported to PDF with LaTeX.

You don't necessarily need knowledge of LaTeX, but it will help you fine-tune the design of your publication. The basic syntax of LaTeX is easy to explain. All LaTeX instructions begin with a backslash and parameters enclosed in curly braces (`\command{}`). The example below provides a minimal working example of a LaTeX file.

```
\documentclass[11pt, b5paper]{book}
\usepackage{ebgaramond}
\begin{document}
\title{Lorem Ipsum}
\author{Peter Prevos}
\date{July 2024}
\maketitle
\section{Nunc eleifend}
Nunc aliquet, augue nec adipiscing interdum.
\end{document}
```

The area between `\documentclass{...}` and `\begin{document}` is the *preamble*, which contains commands that affect the entire document. The content is enclosed between the `\begin{document}` and `\end{document}` commands after the preamble. The first line defines the type document class. The default class used by Org is an article. The document class defines the layout and typography of the final output. LaTeX developers and publishing companies have created document classes for various types of publications. The most common document classes are:

- `article`: Journal articles

- `report`: Small book or thesis

- `book`: Writing long-form books

Each document class has configurable options between square brackets, such as the standard font and paper sizes. The above example defines the book class with 11-point fonts and B5 paper size (176 × 250 mm).

The next part of a LaTeX document initiates the packages. LaTeX is extendible with packages just like Emacs. These packages enhance the design of your document. In the above example, the `\usepackage{ebgaramond}` command instructs LaTeX to use the Garamond font used for the paperback version of this book.

The following lines are the top matter that defines the title, author, and date. The top matter closes with the `\maketitle` command, instructing LaTeX to typeset the title block.

The actual manuscript starts after the `\maketitle` command. The example defines a section header with the `\section{}` command. Standard paragraphs don't need LaTeX syntax.

Writing documents directly in LaTeX can be confusing because the text is cluttered with backslashes, curly braces, and other syntactical distractions. The AUCTeX Emacs package assists with writing LaTeX. However, this package is not part of *Emacs Writing Studio* because Org has perfect LaTeX export capabilities, so you can take advantage of the lightweight Org markup. When you export a document, you can either export it to a LaTeX file or export it to PDF.

You don't need external software to export an Org file to LaTeX. To enable exporting Org files to PDF, you need to have LaTeX installed on your system. How you install LaTeX depends on your operating system. Your favourite search engine will point you in the right direction.

Keying `C-c C-e l p` creates and opens the PDF version of the current Org buffer and included files. Org converts the buffer to a `tex` file, after which the LaTeX software converts it to PDF (figure 8.1).

EWS customises the `ews-latex-pdf-process` to use the `pdflatex` program, part of all modern LaTeX installations. The configuration is optimised for creating PDF files and bibliographies.

Customise the preamble

The Org export function adds a standard preamble to the document content that defines the typography and layout. You have fine-grained control over how Org creates the preamble.

The default document class for Org export is `article`. This document class has wide margins, which can appear unusual to beginning LaTeX users. The margins are not too wide, but the paper is too large. The optimum length for a line of text is between 60 and 75 characters. LaTeX implements this standard, resulting in wide margins. However, you are not limited to these LaTeX defaults.

You can change the document class in the front matter of an Org file by setting the keywords below. This example calls the book class with A4 paper. These lines are exported to LaTeX as \documentclass[a4paper]{book}.

```
#+latex_class: book
#+latex_class_options: [a4paper]
```

To use a document class in Org, you must first define it in the init file. The standard available document classes `article`, `report` and `book` are available by default.

You can modify the LaTeX preamble in the front matter of an Org file by adding additional packages. The example below uses the `article` class with two columns. This setup also calls the geometry package and sets the paper size to A4 with 25 mm margins. The last line adds further preamble items, which, in this case, sets the font as Times New Roman.

```
#+latex_class: article
#+latex_class_options: [twocolumn]
#+latex_header: \usepackage[a4paper, margin=25mm]{geometry}
#+latex_header_extra: \usepackage{times}
```

When using linked documents (section 7.3), you only need to define the relevant packages in the source document. However, defining LaTeX configuration in included files could override the settings in the mother document, so use the skip option in your inclusion.

Using the front matter to define the LaTeX preamble would require repeating the same lines for every document you export. It would not be Emacs if you could not configure these settings to create a library of document preambles with a preset preamble. The org-latex-classes variable includes the preamble for the most commonly used document types. A LaTeX class in Org is a complete preamble added to exported files. You can define a library of classes for the documents you produce, such as dissertation, apa-paper, kluwer-book or whatever your publishing needs are. The EWS configuration includes the document class used for the paperback version of this book (ews). An in-depth discussion of this variable is outside the scope of this book. The Appendix discusses the EWS configuration in detail. Read the documentation of this variable with C-h v org-latex-classes.

Images and tables

Org converts images and tables to LaTeX floats. You can add specific attributes to these floats by using the #+attr_latex: keyword, as shown in the image example below:

```
#+caption: This is an example image caption.
#+attr_latex: :width 5cm :options angle=90 :placement h
[[directory/filename.png]]
```

Other size parameters are :height and :scale. The size parameter can be specified in centimetres (cm) or inches (in), as well as other size formats accepted by LaTeX. This parameter can also be expressed in relative dimensions, for example, 0.5\textwidth, which specifies half the width of the text column.

The :float parameter provides several options for placing an image or table:

- multicolumn: Span the image across multiple columns.

- wrap: Text to flow around the image on the right.

- `sideways`: For a new page with the image rotated ninety degrees.

Tables can be manipulated in the same way with a wide range of options. Please read the relevant section in the Org manual with `C-h g org <ret> g table latex`.

Citations

The last citation processor available in Org links directly to LaTeX, which provides three options:

- BibTeX only supports LaTeX's `\cite` and `\nocite` commands.

- NatBib allows more stylistic variants than LaTeX's standard citation command.

- BibLaTeX is an alternate bibliographic processor.

The example below demonstrates how to invoke the NatBib processor using the Harvard citation style as specified by the Wolkers-Kluwer publisher. The first part specifies the NatBib processor with the Kluwer bibliography and citation style.

```
#+cite_export: natbib kluwer
```

While the basic and CSL citation processors export fully formatted text strings, these three processors export LaTeX commands, such as `\cite{nietzsche_1883}`. This means you cannot use these processors when exporting to other formats, as the output will appear as LaTeX code. If you need to configure a manuscript for multiple formats, then the CSL processor is the ideal choice.

LaTeX snippets

You can write simple LaTeX commands directly into your org file. They will be exported as-is into the TeX file. For example. to define the start of the front and back matter of the document, use the \frontmatter and \backmatter LaTeX commands in your Org file at the appropriate locations.

This method works perfectly but is not ideal when exporting the file to multiple formats. You don't want these LaTeX commands littering your other outputs. Ideally, these commands should be included in a structure template. Press C-c C-, l to insert a source block. You can insert a source block for each output format using this method.

If you need to insert the same complex snippets repeatedly, consider using macros described in section 8.2 for LaTeX snippets.

Macros for multiple formats

If you export the same manuscript to multiple formats, then you can define a single macro that applies to these export formats. Multiple macro expansions are surrounded by double ampersand symbols (@@), followed by the export format and a colon, for example: @@latex:. The following example creates a macro to change text colour for HTML, LaTeX and ODT exports.

```
#+macro: hl @@html:<span style="color: $1;">$2</span>@@
        @@latex:\textcolor{$1}{$2}@@
        @@odt:<text:span text:style-name="$1">$2</text:span>@@
```

You deploy this macro like this {{{hl(red, This text is red.)}}}. When exporting this macro to HTML, the text will be displayed in red or the colour specified by the first parameter. When exporting to LaTeX, it will be printed in red using the xcolor package. The same macro can also be applied to ODT exports, but you must define a character style with the same name as $1 in your template file, in this case, "red".

8.7   Further study

This chapter only provides a cursory overview of the export possibilities of Org. For each format, additional configuration options are available. You can configure the export process of your manuscript at two levels:

1. Variable (all Org files)

2. Front matter (the exported file)

For example, the variable `org-export-with-tables` specifies whether the export includes tables (which is true by default). You can override the global setting for the exported file with `#+options |:nil`.

Org also provides a range of export formats not described in this chapter. You can export to Markdown or a plain text file. You can even export your file to Org mode. This option parses all citations and merges all included files into a single document. Additional packages exist for other export formats. These packages usually start with `ox`, such as ox-ePub discussed in section 8.5.

The Org manual discusses all functionality available for exporting, which you can find with `C-h R org <ret> g exporting`.

Chapter 9

Administration: Manage Your Projects

The core activity of an author is to research, write, edit and publish their work. But there is more to do. Writing also involves administrative tasks, such as meeting deadlines, managing projects, and maintaining an organised filing system. Emacs provides extensive functionality to undertake these tasks.

This chapter explains how to use Org mode to manage projects and action lists, loosely implementing the Getting Things Done (GTD) method. GTD is just one of a plethora of methods to manage a busy life. The beauty of Emacs is that you have the freedom to implement whatever method you prefer. The next two sections show how to manage files with the directory editor (Dired) and manage images with the Image-Dired package.

9.1 Getting Things Done

In our time-poor world, everybody wants to cram more stuff into their day. Judging by the abundant literature, you can become so productive that "getting things done" only takes a "four-hour work week" (Allen, 2005; Ferriss, 2011). We achieve these almost magical powers by learning from the "habits of highly effective people" who seem to "eat frogs" for breakfast (Covey, 1990; Tracy, 2016).

Methods to boost personal productivity are plentiful on the internet, and books with well-intentioned advice are readily available. The market is also brimming with software options to implement these systems, from established software giants like Microsoft's OneNote to agile mobile apps like Todoist.

All these methods boil down to three primary phases: setting a goal, defining the actions to achieve that goal, and undertaking these actions. These principles might sound simplistic, but they are the fundamental truth. Many published methods discuss different ways to manage these three steps effectively and efficiently.

The Org package not only enables you to write and publish prose, but it can also assist in managing actions and projects. Like any other Emacs package, it offers unlimited freedom to implement your preferred productivity method. This freedom empowers you to take control of your tasks and projects, implementing the method that best suits your circumstances.

This section demonstrates how to utilise Org to manage your projects and tasks, drawing inspiration from David Allen's *Getting Things Done* (GTD) method. David Allen describes iterative five steps to becoming more productive (Allen, 2005):

1. *Capture*: Empty your mind and write everything down.

2. *Clarify*: Determine what to do about your tasks.

3. *Organise* Place your tasks where they belong.

4. *Reflect*: Reflect on your progress.

5. *Engage*: Take action.

Capture: Empty your mind

One of the reasons we are often less productive than we like is that our minds are filled with irrelevant stuff. Creative and productive thoughts are suppressed when your brain is filled with thoughts about what you should do. Another problem with keeping ideas in your head is the risk that they will eventually fade into oblivion. I am sure you all recognise the experience of having the most beautiful idea when enjoying your morning shower. Still, half an hour later, you cannot recall your gem.

The first step to getting things done is surprisingly simple: empty your mind. This is not a Buddhist quest for enlightenment but a straightforward technique to help you focus. Open a new Org file and call it something like `todo.org`, or whatever you fancy. You can also use the Inbox as explained in section 6.2.

Write down everything floating around in your head for the next fifteen minutes. Dump the contents of your brain into this virgin Org file. Start every new idea with an asterisk so that they become headlines. Your list will contain a jumble of random things. From minor household tasks to big future projects you'd like to accomplish one day. Don't filter your thoughts; write them down.

Don't multitask! Instead, give this activity your undivided attention. Remember, multitasking is the enemy of productivity because our brains can only focus on one intellectual activity at a time. The fact that magicians can easily fool people illustrates why multitasking is a fool's errand (Prevos, 2013). Perhaps listen to music with the Emacs EMMS package to keep you focused.

Don't worry about when you'll need to do it or in what order it needs to be done; that is a concern for later. Ensure that your mind is empty by the time you complete your list. For most people, fifty actionable items, projects, and fuzzy goals are not uncommon. If you are overwhelmed, don't shoot the messenger, as the list reflects your life. You now have a long list of everything you need to complete.

```
* Mow the lawn
* Clean up the backyard
```

```
* Improve my job skills
* Learn how to use Emacs
* Write an ebook about ... (fill in your speciality)
* Empty your e-mail inbox
* Prepare presentation for the quarterly meeting next week
* And so on, and so on ...
```

Clarify: Describe what it means

Did you notice that most items on the list above require more effort than simply complet-ing a single action? In GTD-speak, these are projects. A project has a defined outcome and takes more than one action to complete. Other items on your list might be goals. A goal, such as learning a new language, is less defined as a project and is more aspirational than a project. Your list will contain tasks, projects, goals and vague ideas.

Your next task is to clarify what you captured. Firstly, you order the list in an ap-propriate hierarchy using the Alt and arrow keys. M-<up> and M-<down> will move a heading up or down, while M-<right> and M-<left> promotes or demotes your entry. With these four keystrokes, you can organise your list to create some order in the chaos that comes from your mind. So, in our example, the garden becomes a project with two tasks. You can add notes or link images and other documents below any heading to pro-vide context to the task.

```
* Gardening
** Clean up the backyard
    - Empty Shed
    - Rubbish tip
** Mow the lawn
```

Some items in your list could become part of a checklist to remind yourself of the required steps. Org can create checkbox items anywhere in your document by adding [ ] after a list indicator. Using M-S <Ret> after a tick box item creates a new list item with a tick box. Ticking and un-ticking any item is as simple as hitting `C-c C-c` (`org-toggle-checkbox`).

You can convert a plain list item to a checkbox item, or vice versa, with `C-u C-c C-c`. Two universal arguments add a horizontal line through the box to indicate that this item is no longer relevant (`C-u C-u C-c C-c`).

If you have a long list, consider including an indicator that shows your progress or lack thereof. You can add a so-called cookie. Add either `[/]` or `[0%]` in the line above the tick boxes, and Org records your progress the next time an item changes, as shown in the example below.

```
* Gardening
** Clean up the backyard [50%]
    - [X] Empty Shed
    - [ ] Rubbish tip
** Mow the lawn
```

Org lets you easily convert list items to headings and back again. The `C-c C-*` keyboard shortcut (`org-ctrl-c-star`) converts a paragraph to a heading. If the line contains a checkbox, it becomes a to-do item. Using `C-c C--` (`org-ctrl-c-minus`) converts a paragraph or a heading to a list item.

The problem with most to-do lists is that they can quickly become overwhelming. Most actions don't need to or can't progress immediately. The basic principle of the GTD approach is to have a manageable list of actions. Within this methodology, an action is either scheduled in your calendar, marked as the next action to be done as soon as possible, or delegated. The list of following actions forms your backlog of things you need to do. This method ensures that only a subset of activities is in your consciousness and you don't get overwhelmed by your inactivity, as action lists tend to be a promise to our future selves. Let's look at the last two options: next actions and delegation.

Org can associate each headline with a workflow status, indicated at the start of the headline, typically in all-caps, as shown below.

```
** TODO Mow the lawn
```

By default, there are only two states, TODO or DONE. However, more than these two is required to enhance your focus because there is no way to distinguish the importance of tasks. Some tasks depend on completing others or could be done in the future. You can set different keywords for each Org file in the front matter. The line below defines a workflow with five separate phases.

```
#+todo: TODO(t) NEXT(n) WAIT(w) | DONE(d) CANCELLED(c)
```

The first state implies that some action needs to be taken in the future (TODO). When a headline is a NEXT action, it should be done as soon as possible. Sometimes, an action cannot be undertaken because you are waiting for someone else or the task has been delegated (WAIT). The statuses after the vertical bar are a completed state, which, in this example, means either DONE or CANCELLED. You can, of course, adjust your task workflow to suit your needs. The keywords are commonly written in all capital letters, but this is optional.

Org cycles between the available states using the shift and left or right arrow keys. You can also change a state with `org-todo` (C-c C-t). When there are more than two options, this command shows a popup window. The letter between parenthesis is the keyboard shortcut for the popup menu.

Not all to-do items have to be undertaken as soon as possible. Emacs has a calendar, and Org can schedule tasks and set deadlines. Scheduling a task to a specific date commits your future self to the action on that date. A deadline indicates when a task needs to be completed due to external expectations.

To add a scheduled date, use C-c C-s when the cursor is on the relevant headline (`org-schedule`). Emacs will pop up a calendar that you can use to select a date. The shift and arrow buttons move the timestamp by day or week. The < and > keys move you a month in time. Press Enter when done, and the date will appear below the headline. You can add a deadline with the same method but with the C-c C-d keystroke (`org-deadline`). A scheduled task needs to be undertaken on a specific day, whereas a deadline is a task that must be completed by that day.

Timestamps use the ISO 8601 format: year, month, day. This format eliminates confusion between American formats and those of the rest of the world, making it easier to sort dates. Editing a timestamp is easy. Place your cursor on either the year, month, or date and use the arrow keys to move it up or down to modify the timestamp.

```
* TODO Complete Org-Mode article
SCHEDULED: <2021-05-08 Sat>
```

Tasks can also have recurring schedules or deadlines. For example, your weekly review. When you add +7d at the end of the date, Org recalculates the date every time you complete the task and resets the status to TODO. You can also use the letters w, m, and y to schedule a weekly, monthly, or yearly job.

In the example below, the seven days are recalculated every time you complete the task. So, whenever you complete this review, the new date will become 7 July, seven days after the original scheduled date.

```
* TODO Weekly review of inbox
SCHEDULED: <2024-06-30 Sun +7d>
```

The above method is acceptable if you complete your tasks near the scheduled date. For example, when completing the task after 7 July, the new target will be in the past. It is also possible to reschedule a task for a defined period after completion using a double plus sign. The example below adds increments of seven days to the scheduled date when the status of the action changes to DONE. For example, suppose we complete this task on 20 July. In that case, the new scheduled date will become Sunday, 21 July, retaining the weekly cadence. So, in this case, the new scheduled date will always be a Sunday.

```
* TODO Weekly review
SCHEDULED: <2024-06-30 Sun ++7d>
```

Adding a full stop and plus sign (.+) before the recurrence frequency moves the new scheduled date to seven days after the most recent completion. This type of recurrence is ideal when you want to perform an action every so many days, months, or years, regardless of when it was last completed.

```
* TODO Weekly review
SCHEDULED: <2024-06-30 Sun .+7d>
```

Only add a scheduled date if this is the time that you plan to take action. Try to avoid overloading your agenda with self-imposed scheduled tasks. You are better off setting a task as the next action and determining when to do it in your regular reviews. A deadline is only helpful if there is an external expectation that you must complete something by a specific date, such as getting travel insurance before your flight leaves.

Failing to meet a deadline can have consequences, so it may be helpful to be warned beforehand when one is approaching. The example below sets a deadline for Australia's upcoming total solar eclipse. I want to attend this event, so the -12m cookie ensures that this deadline is added to my diary a year before it occurs, allowing me to organise my trip to the Central Desert. More about the diary in section 9.1.

```
* Solar Eclipse Central Australia
SCHEDULED: <2028-07-22 Sat -12m>
```

More advanced schedules are available, but they require some basic Lisp code using the diary-float command. The example below schedules a task on every first Tuesday (day 2 of the week) of every month. The first parameter can be the number of the month or t for all months. The second parameter (2) indicates the day of the week, and the last parameter (1) is the number of days in the month. The week starts in Emacs on Sunday (day 0) and ends on Saturday (day 6).

```
* Monthly review
SCHEDULED: <%%(diary-float t 2 1)>
```

The key to a successful implementation of any productivity method is not to become your own abusive parent. Unless there are external deadlines, everything on my action list is optional. Putting the correct rubbish bin at the curb is not optional because I rely on the truck to pick it up. However, writing a new chapter for this book is optional because there is no external deadline. Use the capabilities of managing your life with Org wisely. Don't become enslaved to the list and lose self-esteem because you can't meet your own expectations.

Organise: Place it where it belongs

The previous two sections discussed establishing the starting point for an action list. You will need to review your system regularly to keep your focus on the relevant actions. A weekly review is a good habit, especially in dynamic environments.

The diagram in figure 9.1 shows a typical workflow for managing your digital life. Anything that comes to your attention is sent to the inbox as a fleeting note or new action. Your inbox is not only the Org capture file but also your email inbox, a physical inbox or whatever else. Reviewing each item, you ask yourself whether it can be done quickly; if so, do it. If it is an action that takes a bit more time, then add it to your to-do list (next action, scheduled or delegated), as described in the previous section.

Anything that does not require taking action or completed actions can be archived in your Denote system, as discussed in chapter 6, or straight to the digital trash.

Reflect: Monitor progress

The key to any productivity workflow is to regularly review your actions, priorities, and goals and actually take action on them. Your to-do list or multiple lists are structured in a logical manner. You can sort the various actions by date, type or tag. The agenda is the central tool in Org for ordering your list of registered actions.

The agenda is a time-based summary of the actions in your to-do file(s). You first need to add the relevant files to the agenda list. Add the file linked to the current buffer

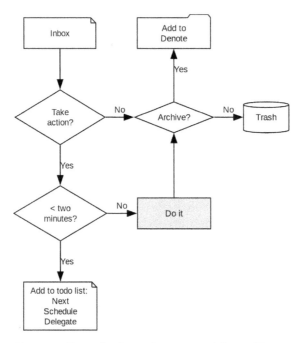

Figure 9.1: Example of a productivity workflow in Emacs.

to the agenda with `org-agenda-file-to-front` (`C-c [`). You can add multiple to-do files to your agenda list, for example, the inbox, a to-do file for your personal life, and one for your work. You remove a file from the agenda list with `org-remove-file` (`C-c ]`). Once your agenda files are on the list, you can jump to them quickly with `C-'` (`org-cycle-agenda-files`). This command cycles through the registered agenda files to provide quick access to them.

The agenda function in Org is highly versatile and configurable. When you evaluate the `org-agenda` function with `C-c a`, Org provides a menu with various entry points to your action lists.

The agenda for the current week (`C-c a a`) shows all actions scheduled for this period that have a deadline. This list also includes any overdue actions and deadlines within the warning period. You can navigate the agenda using the arrow keys, and pressing `Tab` or Ret takes you to an action, allowing you to edit it. The v button lets you generate a diary for the current day, week, fortnight, month, or year.

The menu also gives access to a list of all to-do items. You can filter this list by status to show, for example, only view the next items. Type the number displayed on top of the window and type r.

The Org agenda has extensive capabilities to finetune how your information is summarised. You can, for example, define your own menu items to show an agenda for private tasks and one for your work. The EWS configuration contains an example that shows your agenda for the next three days, any subsequent actions and a list of stuff you are waiting for. You access this construct with C-c a o, and it could look something like this:

```
3 days-agenda (W32):
Wednesday   7 August 2024
  TODO:       159 d. ago:  TODO Termite inspection
  TODO:       Scheduled:   TODO Inbox Zero
  TODO:       Sched.17x:   TODO Clean library
Thursday    8 August 2024
Friday      9 August 2024
  TODO:       Scheduled:   TODO Rubbish bin
```

However, constructing an agenda requires some Emacs Lisp coding skills, so it is outside the scope of this book. The Appendix explains how the EWS agenda is constructed. The Org manual has extensive documentation (C-h R org <Ret> g agenda views).

Engage: Take action

Emacs is a powerful multifunctional tool that cannot help you mow the lawn, go shopping, or complete any other tasks on your list. However, it's important to remember that no productivity system can do your tasks for you, no matter what the gurus promise. Yet, bringing order to your life is crucial to keep you focused on your goals.

Ticking a box or marking an action as done produces a satisfying dopamine hit. After a period of hard work, your to-do list will be filled with completed actions and projects. Org has some facilities for archiving these and decluttering old information.

The `org-archive-subtree` command (`C-c C-x C-s`) moves the content of the cursor subtree to another file. The default filename for the archive is the current file, appended with `_archive`. The archive command adds properties such as the archiving date and the original filename. You can customise the name of the archive by adding the `#+archive:` and the relevant filename as a keyword.

Learning more

The Org manual (`C-h R org`) provides further information about this major mode's project management capabilities, such as setting priorities and time clocking, which are not discussed in this book.

Bavarian Org guru Rainer König has developed a comprehensive series of YouTube videos that explain the use of Org mode for managing actions and projects in great detail. Ranier has also published a comprehensive course on Udemy, which provides more detail than the freely available videos (König, 2020).

9.2   Manage files

Working with Emacs means you will need to access, create, and manage files on your drives. Emacs comes shipped with Dired (pronounced *dir-ed*, from directory editor), a powerful file manager. Dired has an illustrious history. The first version of dired was a stand-alone program written circa 1974, so its origins lie even further back in time than Emacs.

This section explains the basic principles of using Dired and shows how to manage files to organise your hard drive. It also introduces the Image-Dired package, which helps you explore collections of images and photographs.

Opening directories and files

You activate the file manager with the `dired` function or the `C-x d` shortcut. After selecting the relevant directory in the minibuffer, Emacs creates a new buffer with the content of the specified directory. Another helpful function is `dired-jump` (`C-x C-j`), which opens Dired and jumps the cursor directly to the file linked to the current buffer.

The top line shows the current directory's path and the available disk space. Below that line, you find a list of all files and folders. EWS places all subdirectories at the top, followed by an alphabetically ordered list of files.

The first column in the Dired buffer shows the file type and permissions. The following two columns display the file size and the date it was last saved. The final column displays the file name. The example below shows the first lines of this book in the Dired buffer. Use the left parenthesis key (to remove the technical information and only show directories and file names.

```
/home/peter/documents/projects/ews/: (286 GiB available)
drwxrwxrwx 6 4.0K 2024-07-21 14:05 .
drwxrwxrwx 7 4.0K 2024-07-19 08:23 ..
drwxrwxrwx 2 4.0K 2024-07-17 06:33 images
-rw-r--r-- 1 5.3K 2024-07-20 19:51 00-emacs-writing-studio.org
-rw-r--r-- 1 3.7K 2024-07-20 08:51 00-i-foreword.org
-rw-r--r-- 1 2.5K 2024-05-04 16:47 00-ii-preface.org
-rw-r--r-- 1  24K 2024-07-20 20:04 01-why-emacs.org
```

You can navigate the content with the arrow keys or press j to jump to a specific file by entering part of its name in the minibuffer and selecting the one you like to visit. You open a file or a subdirectory with the Enter key. To open a file or directory in another window, press o. Using C-o opens the file in another window, but the cursor stays in the Dired window. The q button closes the Dired window but does not kill (remove) it.

Note that every time you open a directory, Emacs opens a new Dired buffer. After a while, you litter your Emacs session with unused Dired buffers. Pressing the a key instead of Enter opens a directory in the same buffer.

The default setting for Emacs shows hidden files, even though they are hidden for a reason. EWS provides some convenience by removing hidden files from view. Use the full stop (.) to toggle this behaviour and either view or conceal the hidden files.

You can open files with external software by pressing &, after which Dired will ask for the appropriate program name. You need to type the name of the executable file of the software you like to use, e.g. gimp.

Modifying directories and files

To copy a file, press the C button. Dired will ask for a new directory and name in the minibuffer. To move a file, you press R because moving a file is the same as renaming it with a new directory. You do not need to close a buffer before renaming an open file. Emacs will link the open buffer to the new filename. If you have two open Dired buffers in your frame, EWS copies and moves from the folder in the active window to the other Dired buffer.

It is sometimes helpful to copy the name of a file to the kill ring with the w key so you can use it to rename the file. So, to rename a file, copy the name with w, rename the file with R, paste the existing name with C-y and edit the name to your new version.

Select and deselect files for deletion with the d and u buttons. After you select the files you would like to delete, press x to execute the deletion. Press capital D if you want to remove a single file. Emacs will also ask you to close the appropriate buffer when you delete or trash a currently open file.

You can select multiple files to work on simultaneously by marking them. The m button marks a file, and the u removes the mark. The capital U removes all marks in the buffer. Using the t key reverses existing markings, which is helpful when you need to select everything except one or two files.

This method requires you to manually select each file. You can also use regular expressions to select files. Press % m to open the regular expression selection prompt. For example, ^2023.*_journal* selects all Denote files that start with the 2023 and have the `journal` file tag. Now press t to invert the selection and k to remove the selected files from view. This sequence is a valuable method for finding related files.

The `dired-narrow-regexp` function from the eponymous package by Matúš Goljer provides a more convenient method to narrow a list of files. This function prompts for a regular expression and displays only those files that match it. Pressing g clears the filter.

Another handy feature in Dired is the ability to search and replace regular expressions across a set of marked files. The first step is to mark the files you like to search in, either individually with m or by searching for a regular expression with %m, as described above. Use Q to start a `query-replace-regexp` session on the marked files. You can now search for a regular expression and replace it with a new string. The buffer now splits into three parts. Use the question mark to view all options.

File-naming conventions

When offices relied on paper archives, they adhered to strict rules for archiving documents. Misplacing a piece of paper in meters of shelves filled with files meant you would never find that document again. When office workers started using computers in the 1980s, all such rigour and process were abandoned. The computer's unlimited freedom resulted in chaos as there were no instructions on how to store files.

Office workers developed personal workflows and naming conventions for managing electronic files, leading to inconsistencies and lack of clarity. A typical directory might look something like this:

```
-rw-r--r-- 1 5.3K 1994-07-20 19:51 First draft EWS.org
-rw-r--r-- 1 3.7K 1994-07-20 08:51 EWS notes Jan 17 2023.org
-rw-r--r-- 1 2.5K 1994-05-04 16:47 Action list.org
-rw-r--r-- 1  24K 1994-07-20 20:04 FINAL paperback version.pdf
```

Such a naming convention may be insightful to the person who developed it, but memory fades, and these random filenames can become confusing over time. Handing over a folder like this to someone else will cause them lots of grief trying to figure out which is which. Any good project, therefore, needs a naming convention for files. Some rules of thumb for an excellent file-naming convention are:

- Add metadata to your filename, such as a chapter number, experiment identifier or date.

- Separate metadata elements with allowed punctuation.

- Start filenames with the element you want to sort your folder.

- Use only lowercase characters to avoid confusion.

Some file naming conventions include version identifiers, such as 'draft', 'edited', and 'final'. However, this practice is unnecessary when using a version control system (section 7.4), described in chapter 7. The Denote file naming convention is a perfect example of a best-practice naming convention, described in chapter 6.

Denote includes a minor mode that formats compliant filenames in the directory editor. Hence, it is easy to recognise the individual items of the note's metadata. The filenames not only provide metadata for the note itself, but they also serve as a heuristic to make it easy to find notes based on date, signatures, title, or keyword (Figure 9.2).

```
-rw-r--r--  1  15K 2023-05-20 10:09 20060103T195904--the-bystander-effect-in-helping-behaviour__ola_prevosnet_psy12_psychology.org |
-rw-r--r--  1  906 2022-08-27 13:08 20060105T173657--death-of-a-colleague__philosophy_prevosnet.org
-rw-r--r--  1 8.8K 2022-09-05 14:54 20060403T210804--goffman-and-marcuse-on-identity__ola_prevosnet_sgy230_sociology.org
-rw-r--r--  1 3.1K 2022-08-26 21:46 20060417T123727--existential-hot-air-balloon__philosophy_prevosnet.org
-rw-r--r--  1  14K 2023-05-15 19:46 20060427T092727--postmodernism-and-language-games__philosophy_prevosnet.org
-rw-r--r--  1 2.2K 2022-08-27 13:08 20060510T113929--reflections-on-life-after-death__prevosnet_religion.org
-rw-r--r--  1 2.6K 2023-12-14 18:45 20060518T054215--immanuel-kant-the-mystic__esoterica_philosophy_prevosnet.org
```

Figure 9.2: Extract of Denote files in Dired.

Because a Dired buffer is just another plain text buffer, you can edit the names of files directly with `dired-toggle-read-only`, bound to `C-x C-q`. This function allows you to directly edit file names in the buffer, which is convenient when you need to edit a list of files. To lock in the new file names, type `C-c C-c`.

Dired keyboard shortcuts

If your head buzzes with all the key bindings, table 9.1 lists the functionality described in this chapter. You can press the h key while in a Dired buffer to view all functionality and related keybindings.

Table 9.1: Dired key bindings.

Key	Function	Action
a	`dired-find-alternate-file`	Open folder in same buffer
C	`dired-do-copy`	Copy a file
J	`dired-goto-file`	Jump to the file linked to active buffer
g	`revert-buffer`	Refresh the dired buffer
m	`dired-mark`	Mark file under the cursor
% m	`dired-mark-files-regexp`	Mark by regular expression
o	`dired-find-file-other-window`	Open file in other window
C-o	`dired-display-file`	Display file in other window
q	`quit-window`	Close the buffer
R	`dired-do-rename`	Rename (move) a file
t	`dired-toggle-marks`	Inverse marked files
u	`dired-unmark`	Unmark file under the cursor
U	`dired-unmark-all-marks`	Unmark all files
&	`dired-do-async-shell-command`	Open file with other program
enter	`dired-find-file`	Open file

9.3 Viewing and manipulating images

Writing in plain text is marvellous, but as the well-worn cliché suggests, "an image is worth a thousand words". You have already seen that Org can embed images and export these to the desired format. Emacs also has some built in functionality to help you view and manage a collection of photographs.

Image mode is bundled with Emacs, but you might need external software for additional functionality. Emacs can display images without external software but cannot manipulate them. The ImageMagick software suite provides functionality for editing and manipulating images.

Image mode can display standard image formats out of the box. You can open an image file directly with `find-file` (`C-x C-f`) or through Dired. You can also open a linked image from within an Org file with `C-c C-o` (`org-open-at-point`) while the cursor is on the image.

Emacs automatically scales the image to snugly fit inside the window. A range of keyboard shortcuts are available to view photos. The n and p keys (next and previous) or the left and right arrow keys move through the pictures of the current directory, creating a slideshow. Image-mode also provides commands to change the display size of images, some of which are:

- `s o`: Show the image in its original size.

- `s w`: Fit the current image to the height and width of the window.

- `i +`: Increase the image size by 20%

- `i -`: Decrease the image size by 20%.

Furthermore, image mode can manipulate images:

- `i r`: Rotate the image by 90 degrees clockwise.

- `i h`: Flip the image horizontally.

- `i v`: Flip the image vertically.

- `i c`: Crop the image.

- `i x`: Censor a rectangle from the image, CIA style.

The crop and censor commands superimpose a rectangle on the image. Use the mouse to move and resize the frame. Type m to move the frame instead of resizing it, and type s to convert it to a square. When satisfied with the result, use Ret to crop or censor the image. You can exit the crop and cutting menu with q without changing the source file. Please note that these commands are only available if ImageMagick is installed.

When you're done watching images, use q to quit the image buffer or k to kill it altogether.

The Image-Dired package

Viewing images individually is helpful, but wouldn't it be nice to see thumbnails? The Image-Dired package provides a thumbnail buffer to view and maintain pictures from within a Dired buffer using thumbnails. Issue the `image-dired` command and select the directory you like to use (C-c w I). Emacs splits the screen and presents up to 1,000 thumbnails to explore your collection (figure 9.3). Emacs stores the thumbnails in the configuration directory for future reference and faster loading.

Figure 9.3: Viewing some travel photos in Emacs with image-dired.

The active image is marked with a flashing border around the thumbnail, and its filename is shown at the top of the thumbnail window. You can navigate the thumbnails with the arrow keys. The < and > keys take you to the start or end of the collection. You can remove a thumbnail, but not the file itself, from the preview buffer with C-d.

To view an image in another window, hit Ret on the selected thumbnail. You cycle through the marked images in your collection using the space and backspace keys (or the left and right arrow keys).

But why manually flick through your album if you can let Emacs do this? The S key starts a slideshow with each image shown for five seconds. You can customise the delay with the image-dired-slideshow-delay variable or drive the slideshow manually.

The main image display is in image mode, so all the actions described in the previous section apply. As usual, q quits the image or thumbnail window and k kills it altogether.

Pressing C-<Ret> opens the file in an external viewer or editor, such as GIMP. You can customise the image-dired-external-viewer variable to the name of your image editor. You open the external editor from within an Image-Dired viewer with C-<Ret>. Confusingly, when you are in a standard Dired buffer, this function is bound to C-t x. EWS uses C-<Ret> in both Dired and Image-Dired to open an image in your favourite external editor.

When inside a Dired buffer containing images, you can show the thumbnails by marking them with m and generate thumbnails with C-t C-t. If you don't mark any files, the program displays a thumbnail of the image under the cursor. The same shortcut also removes the thumbnails.

9.4 Learning more

The Dired package, including Image-Dired, is fully described in the Emacs manual. Type C-h r g dired. The Emacs manual also contains chapters about viewing images accessible with C-h r g image. The Image-Dired unfortunately has no manual.

Chapter *10*

Become an Emacs Ninja

Now that you have reached the end of this book, you know everything needed to research, write and publish a book, dissertation, or whatever else you want to share with the world with Emacs. Working your way through the *Emacs Writing Studio* (EWS) chapters, you have mastered the steepest part of the learning curve. However, after using Emacs for a while, you will undoubtedly want to fine-tune it to fit your needs. There are five stages towards becoming an Emacs ninja, the first of which you are taking right now:

1. Understand the basics

2. Modify the configuration

3. Create functions

4. Build a package

5. Help others

This final chapter puts you on a path to mastering Emacs by providing suggestions for deepening your knowledge.

10.1 Understand the basics

EWS covers most aspects of using Emacs as far as they relate to writing prose. However, this book is not a comprehensive manual of Emacs but an opinionated description of achieving a series of tasks. The text in this book is opinionated because it describes only one method to complete each objective.

The flexible nature of Emacs means that there is always more than one way to achieve the same outcome. This freedom is both a strength and a weakness, as it can create unnecessary debates and confusion over how to do something instead of just doing it. Donald Knuth, computer genius and original developer of LaTeX, once wrote that "premature optimisation is the root of all evil". And EWS reflects this principle by providing something that works.

If, after reading this book, you would like to know more or find out about different ways of doing things, then read other books such as *Learning GNU Emacs* by Debra Cameron, *Mastering Emacs* by Mickey Petersen or the built-in Emacs manual (Cameron, 2005; Petersen, 2022; Stallman, 2023).

Reading about Emacs is an excellent method for learning new things, but sometimes you like to see somebody use the system. YouTube is a great place to find informative channels that discuss Emacs, such as the highly recommended videos by Prot Stavrou and David Wilson's *System Crafters* channel. I have also published a series of videos demonstrating the capabilities of EWS.

10.2 Modify the configuration

Emacs Writing Studio offers a no-code solution by providing a thoroughly tested configuration and utilising a customisation front-end to configure Emacs. There will come a time when you would like to change some of the defaults directly inside the init file or add additional packages, which means you need to learn some Emacs Lisp.

So why would you want to configure Emacs by writing code instead of the modern graphical features provided by other programs? Commercial software provides graphical menus to define how it operates. For example, in figure 10.1, you might tick a box, select an item in a list, or enter a value in a text box to configure the program according to your wishes.

Figure 10.1. Typical graphical configuration screen.

The code below is equivalent to figure 10.1. This example determines whether Emacs shows a startup message when you first open it. The second line sets the initial scratch message. In this case, the parameter is a string of letters nested between quotation marks. The last line sets the cursor type to a bar. This variable has other predefined options, such as 'bar' or 'hollow'. It uses a single quotation mark before the text to prevent Emacs from confusing this option with a variable. Compare these lines with the image to reverse engineer the Elisp code.

```
(setq inhibit-startup-message t
      initial-scratch-message "Hello world"
      cursor-type 'bar)
```

Notice how the whole expression is surrounded by parenthesis, typical of programming in Lisp. These parentheses can confuse beginning users when nesting code multiple levels deep. As you get used to the syntax, parentheses will become helpful markers to help you understand the logic of your code.

While on the surface, the code-based method seems more complex than ticking and writing in boxes and picking a drop-down list, it is far more potent than a graphical interface. Once you learn how to write simple Emacs Lisp, you will realise that Emacs is, in reality, the most user-friendly system possible because of the power it gives you over your computer. Using Emacs Lisp is the epitome of user-friendliness. You decide how a computer behaves instead of some software company controlling your behaviour. But with this immense power comes great responsibility and a learning curve.

The easiest way to learn Lisp is to change your init file by copying the patterns from the EWS configuration. The Appendix explains the configuration and provides some guidance on modifying it. Many Emacs users freely share their configurations, and you should feel free to copy any parts of their code. Emacs is free software in the freedom sense of the word, so use this power and learn from fellow users.

One final tip: When you copy code from other Emacs users, don't add anything to your configuration until you understand precisely what it does. Read the documentation and try some alternative versions so you fully comprehend the code.

Modifying key sequences

Emacs ships with a range of predefined keyboard shortcuts for its core functionality and the built-in packages. Most external packages don't define key keyboard shortcuts to prevent conflicts with your configuration. The EWS configuration assigns shortcuts to the most common functions using the C-c w prefix. As explained in the Appendix, you can easily modify your keyboard shortcuts listed in the init file.

You can change the keyboard's behaviour at three levels: programmable keyboards, the operating system/window manager, and Emacs.

Some high-end keyboards are programmable, allowing you to define the output of each key. For example, you could map the right control key as the Hyperkey. At the second level, your operating system interprets the input from the keyboard. For instance, in Windows, s-E (Windows and E) opens the file explorer. You can erase this binding to make it available in Emacs. Each operating system has its own methods to change keyboard maps (keymaps). Some experienced Emacs users remap the Caps Lock key to act as the Control key, making it easier to use and preventing a repetitive strain injury known as 'Emacs Pinky'.

Last but not least, you can define keyboard sequences within Emacs itself. The example below binds the F5 key to toggle whitespace mode. This minor mode indicates whitespace in the current buffer with characters. The #' characters before the function name are a technical requirement to instruct Emacs not to evaluate this function but only to store its value. If you like to remove a keystroke, use nil as the function name.

```
(keymap-global-set "<f5>" #'whitespace-mode)
```

The previous example uses the global keymap, meaning the shortcut is available in all modes. You can also define a shortcut for a specific mode, which is only available when that mode is active. The example below sets the same shortcut but only applies when Org is active, so the F5 key can perform a different action in other modes.

```
(keymap-set org-mode-map "<f5>" #'whitespace-mode)
```

The secret to good keyboard shortcuts is to encode semantic information, so almost all EWS-specific shortcuts start with C-c w where the w stands for 'writing'. This approach does not always work because you will quickly run out of the most obvious letter.

Some people dislike the Emacs keyboard defaults because they require frequent use of the modifier keys. They suggest that repetitive use of these keys causes strain injury, the dreaded' Emacs pinky'. Several packages, such as Evil Mode and God Mode, exist within the Emacs ecosystem that change the default keybindings to a different model.

Additional or alternative packages

EWS includes many packages that enhance Emacs. There are, however, alternatives and enhancements that did not make it into EWS. One of the objectives of this configuration was to stay 'as close as humanly bearable' to the vanilla Emacs experience so new users could learn how to use Emacs rather than learning a specific configuration. This section mentions some packages additional or alternative packages in case you like to try something different.

EWS enhances the minibuffer completing mechanism with Vertico and associated packages. Some popular alternatives to this ecosystem are the Helm or Ivy completion frameworks. Both packages offer a diverse and comprehensive environment.

Embark is another package that can enhance your Emacs experience. Embark provides functionality similar to the right-click contextual menu in graphical software, accessible via a keyboard shortcut.

The built-in PDF viewer can be slow and lacks advanced features. The PDF-Tools package by Vedang Manerikar provides enhanced functionality, but it requires compiling source code to fully integrate it with Emacs.

The eBib package by Joost Kremers is a management tool for BibTeX files that add to the functionality of Citar. This package does not utilise the completion menu. Instead, it features a more traditional application interface, ideal for creating or editing bibliography files.

John Kitchin's Org-Ref package is part of his Scimax Emacs starter kit for scientists and engineers. This package includes advanced tools for managing bibliographies and cross-references in Org files and is worth checking out.

This is a brief overview of some alternative packages you could be using. Emacs offers a vast universe of package to undertake a broad range of tasks. The `list-packages` command provides a useful interface to the list of all available packages. You can explore this interface to find interesting software or update your existing system.

Is Emacs a productivity sink?

Configuring Emacs can be a daunting task that can take a lot of time and become a productivity drain due to its complexity. The freedom you enjoy in Emacs means that everybody has personal preferences. Emacs developers cannot cater to every personal preference, so they provide a skeleton system you must develop to suit your workflow. Emacs Lisp is like a box of Lego that you use to create toys. Working on your Emacs configuration is a lot of fun, but actually playing with them is even better.

It can be tempting to constantly fine-tune your configuration, but this can become a productivity sink. Wielding the power to create a bespoke Emacs system is a great temptation that can lead to fake productivity, which is one of the three forms of procrastination:

1. *Nihilistic procrastination*: Watching TV and playing computer games.

2. *Sophisticated procrastination*: Fake productivity, e.g. Emacs hacking, switching productivity tools, taking notes for volume instead of quality.

3. *Productive procrastination*: Daydreaming.

Tinkering with your Emacs configuration is not as bad as nihilistic procrastination, but it can become a form of fake productivity. The productivity gains from fine-tuning your Emacs to cut out a few keystrokes from your workflow can take more time than you will save with your new workflow over the rest of your lifetime. The act of writing is about much more than the number of words you can type into your buffer. Writing is as much a contemplative act as it is about keyboard efficiency.

10.3 Create functions

Suppose a computer is, in the words of Steve Jobs, a "bicycle for the mind". In that case, Emacs is the Hot Rod of the mind, providing ultimate computing freedom.

The third step in total computing freedom is writing bespoke functions to undertake tasks specific to your workflow. Most Emacs code exists because a user wants to achieve something that neither Emacs nor any existing package can do. The Emacs way is for you to develop your solution to the problem.

The code that runs Emacs is, for the most significant part, written as a collection of Elisp functions. The simplistic definition of a function is that it converts an input into an output. For example, every time you hit a letter on the keyboard in Emacs, the `self-insert` function turns the critical press into a character in the open buffer.

The code below shows the architecture of a simple Emacs function. When you run this command, Emacs will show a greeting in the echo area, extracting your name from the system.

```
(defun ews-greet-user ()
  "Display a greeting message in the minibuffer."
  (interactive)
  (message "Hello %s, Welcome to Emacs." user-full-name))
```

Now, let's break down how this function works:

- The function starts with the defun macro to define a new function. In this case, the name of the function is ews-greet-user. The function name starts with ews, following informal naming conventions that recommend starting function names with a group or package name. The parentheses at the end are empty, which means that this function has no input.

- The second line describes what the function does. Each function in the system has a documentation string, which you can read with C-h f. For interactive functions, the first line of these help files is also shown in the completion menu in the minibuffer when using M-x.

- The (interactive) line converts the function into a command. This means that you can call it using M-x ews-greet-user, or bind it to a key sequence.

- The last line displays the message in the echo area with the message function. In this case, the %s is replaced by the content of the user-full-name variable.

You can write this function in the scratch buffer to try it out. Then, you need to activate it by placing the cursor after the last closing parenthesis and using C-x C-e (eval-last-sexp). This action registers the function in memory, after which you can call it with M-x.

You could add this function to your init file to make it available every Emacs session. However, I doubt the usefulness of this example.

How you use functions is only limited by your imagination. EWS comes with a set of bespoke functions in the `ews.el` file that enhances some of the basic functionality. To see a list of all available EWS commands, use `M-x ^ews`. This sequence shows all commands in the minibuffer completion menu that start with (^) 'ews'.

10.4 Build a package

The next level of sophistication in Emacs is to share your bespoke functions with the world through a package. Most Emacs packages start with a user trying to solve a problem in their workflow and then deciding to share it with the world.

For example, my package Citar-Denote started with a desire to use Emacs for my bibliographic notes. I had no experience with Emacs coding, but I gave it a try anyway. I first published a rudimentary version of Citar-Denote. However, I was unable to figure out how to undertake specific tasks. As soon as I shared the code, other people quickly jumped in to assist, and soon, the Citar-Denote package became a fully functional tool for managing bibliographic notes.

10.5 Help others

The final step in becoming an Emacs ninja is helping other people on their journey. You can help fellow users through various online forums, such as Reddit, which has active Emacs communities.

This book began as a website where I shared my experiences with Emacs as an author. As the website gained popularity, I converted it to the book you are now reading.

The EWS project is my way of giving back to the Emacs community and also helping me better understand how the software works. Some cynics suggest that "those who can't do, teach". However, teaching any subject is the best way to systematise your knowledge and become better at it.

So, your task as an Emacs Ninja is to help others who are less advanced in their journey. Tell other authors about the freedom that Emacs gives you as a researcher, author, educator, or whatever else you do.

Appendix

This appendix presents and explains the *Emacs Writing Studio* (EWS) configuration. The configuration is annotated to explain the logic of the code and provides some options for enhancements or additional functionality. This configuration follows the following principles:

- Leverage functionality of the latest version of GNU Emacs

- Minimalist configuration

- Use standard keyboard shortcuts

- Centred around Org mode

- No configuration for writing code

This configuration is a starting point for your Emacs journey. Feel free to modify any part of the EWS initialisation file and study its effects. You can find the latest version of this configuration on GitHub:

```
https:://github.com/pprevos/emacs-writing-studio
```

This repository is not actively maintained. For beginning Emacs users, the configuration acts as a starting point to develop a configuration. More advanced users can copy ideas. The code will only be updated when there are bugs due to future changes in packages or Emacs itself.

Using EWS

The first part of the configuration sets the basic principles of the EWS configuration, such as package management, the user interface look and feel, the minibuffer completion system and basic settings to enable writing for humans.

Basic configuration

The first part of the configuration checks if the latest version of Emacs is running. EWS leverages some of the newest functionality, so you must install this version. Note that the expression or higher (`< emacs-major-version 29`) is in Polish notation. In Lisp, the operator is placed before the operands, unlike the more common infix notation, which places the operator between the operands, e.g. `emacs-major-version < 29`.

```
(when (< emacs-major-version 29)
  (error "Emacs Writing Studio requires version 29 or later"))
```

Emacs packages

Emacs users have developed and shared thousands of packages with the rest of the community. These packages are written in Emacs Lisp and extend its capabilities. This part of the configuration sets the essential elements to load and install packages from the MELPA archive (`melpa.org`).

```
(use-package package
  :config
```

```
(add-to-list 'package-archives
             '("melpa" . "https://melpa.org/packages/"))
(package-initialize))
```

This configuration implements John Wiegley's Use-Package. This package simplifies installing and configuring packages with a standardised and easy-to-read method. Software developers call such a tool 'syntactic sugar', which is syntax designed to make code easier to read or write, making the language "sweeter" for humans (Landin, 1964).

The Use-Package system consists of a set of statements between parenthesis, which is a macro. In its simplest form, it is something like (use-package <package-name>). The code can also contain one or more sections to set various options. The :custom section below sets three variables. These variables enact three protocols. Any missing package is automatically installed from its online source, and the source code is compiled to speed up Emacs. Thirdly, compilation warnings are kept to a minimum so as not to scare beginning users with log files.

```
(use-package use-package
  :custom
  (use-package-always-ensure t)
  (package-native-compile t)
  (warning-minimum-level :emergency))
```

To read the finer details of the Use-Package macro, read the manual with C-h R use-package.

Emacs Writing Studio convenience functions

EWS also provides a range of bespoke convenience functions for various aspects of the writing process. Ensure you download this file from the EWS repository.

```
(load-file (concat (file-name-as-directory user-emacs-directory)
                   "ews.el"))
```

The `ews-missing-executables` function checks if external software is available on your system. Emacs writes a message in the minibuffer if any of the recommended tools are missing. You can jump to the Messages buffer with C-h e to review the output. Emacs will function normally when this software is unavailable, but some features might not work.

The input for this function is a list, a series of strings between parenthesis that starts with a tick symbol: `'("this" "is" "a" "list")` The tick prevents Emacs from confusing the list of data with a function. In this function, some lists also contains other lists.

This function checks whether all these packages are available on your system. For software in a nested list, such as `("convert" "gm")`, only one of them has to be available, as these programs are alternatives for the same functionality.

```
(ews-missing-executables
 '(("gs" "mutool")
   "pdftotext"
   "soffice"
   "zip"
   "ddjvu"
   "curl"
   ("mpg321" "ogg123" "mplayer" "mpv" "vlc")
   ("grep" "ripgrep")
   ("convert" "gm")
   "dvipng"
   "latex"
   "hunspell"
   "git"))
```

Look and feel

EWS espouses a minimalist aesthetic to provide a distraction-free environment. These four lines of code disable the splash screen, toolbar, menu bar, and the scroll bar. The menu bar can be useful for beginners, and you can still access it with the F10 key. If you like to keep the tool, menu, and/or scroll bars, then either remove the relevant lines, change the -1 to a 1, or add two semicolons at the start of the relevant lines to convert them to comments.

```
(setq inhibit-splash-screen t)
(tool-bar-mode -1)
(menu-bar-mode -1)
(scroll-bar-mode -1)
```

Vanilla Emacs has the slightly paternalistic habit of requiring a single y or n answer, while on some occasions, it requires you to type yes or no, due to the perceived higher risk of typing the wrong answer. The setq function sets the use-short-answers variable to t. If you want to retain this behaviour, change the t to nil.

In Emacs Lisp, t means TRUE and nil is equivalent to FALSE. Emacs documentation often mentions setting a value to "non-nil", which is a double negative to suggest setting the variable to true.

```
(setq-default use-short-answers t)
```

The Scratch Buffer is by default set to Emacs Lisp mode. This is not so useful for authors, so we change this to Org mode and add a new default message.

```
(setq initial-major-mode 'org-mode
      initial-scratch-message (concat "#+title: Emacs Writing Studio\n"
                                      "#+subtitle: Scratch Buffer\n\n"
                                      "The text in this buffer is not saved"
                                      "when exiting Emacs!\n\n"))
```

The next two sections of code further improve the Emacs interface with two packages by Emacs guru Protesilaos Stavrou.

The spacious padding package creates space around windows, preventing crammed text on your screen. The :init section contains code Emacs evaluates when loading the package. In this case, it enables the Spacious Padding mode. The :custom section also sets the line spacing to a more generous value. You can read the manual for this mode with C-h R spacious.

This configuration also modifies the line-spacing variable to create some space between logical lines. This variable is not part of the Spacious Padding package.

```
(use-package spacious-padding
  :custom
  (line-spacing 3)
  (spacious-padding-mode 1))
```

The next package sets the Emacs theme. A theme is a set of configurations for fonts and colours. Themes are available in two types: light or dark background.

The Modus themes package is highly configurable. This Use-Package declaration contains a three sections. The :custom section customises variables used in the package. In this case, we instruct the package to use italic and bold fonts for emphasis and allow for fonts with fixed and variable pitch. The code also slightly increases the size of headings. You can toggle between a dark and a light version of this theme, and the last variable defines which to toggle between. EWS uses the tinted version of the themes, which you can modify.

The :custom section of the macro sets some variables to define fonts. This section also defines which themes are toggled when switching between light and dark themes with C-c w t t. The default is the tinted versions. If you want your configuration to default to the high-contrast versions or one of the two colour blindness-safe versions, customise the modus-themes-to-toggle variable. To see the possible options for the Modus themes, use the help file: C-h v modus-themes-collection.

The following section binds some keys to commands to toggle between dark and light or select any available modus themes. All EWS custom keybindings start with C-c w as the prefix key and C-c w t as the prefix key for the theme-related functions. You can obviously change these to suit your preferences. Read the Modus Themes package manual for details with C-h R modus.

The consult-theme command invoke the consult package to help you select between installed themes. To set a default theme, run the customize-themes command and select your preferred version. Click the button to store your chosen default in the custom.el file. As a bonus, this code also installs Port's Ef-Themes package, which is a wonderful collection of light and dark themes.

```
(use-package modus-themes
  :custom
  (modus-themes-italic-constructs t)
  (modus-themes-bold-constructs t)
  (modus-themes-mixed-fonts t)
  (modus-themes-to-toggle '(modus-operandi-tinted
                            modus-vivendi-tinted))
  :bind
  (("C-c w t t" . modus-themes-toggle)
   ("C-c w t m" . modus-themes-select)
   ("C-c w t s" . consult-theme)))

(use-package ef-themes)
```

The next section hooks the Variable Pitch mode to any Org buffer. This means that written prose is displayed in variable pitch, while metadata, code and other items are in fixed pitch. A hook is a construction in Emacs that associates modes with each other. In this case, variable pitch text is enabled for all text mode buffers.

```
(use-package mixed-pitch
  :hook
  (org-mode . mixed-pitch-mode))
```

This last code snippet in the look-and-feel section changes how Emacs automatically split windows to favour vertical splits over horizontal ones to improve readability. This section also installs the Balanced Windows package, which manages window sizes automatically. For example, when you have three open windows and you close one, the remaining windows each get half the screen.

```
(setq split-width-threshold 120
      split-height-threshold nil)

(use-package balanced-windows
  :config
  (balanced-windows-mode))
```

Minibuffer completion

EWS uses the Vertico-Orderless-Marginalia stack of minibuffer completion packages in their standard configuration. Chapter 4 explains how to use minibuffer completion.

```
(use-package vertico
  :init
  (vertico-mode)
  :custom
  (vertico-sort-function 'vertico-sort-history-alpha))

(use-package savehist
  :init
  (savehist-mode))

(use-package orderless
  :custom
  (completion-styles '(orderless basic))
  (completion-category-defaults nil)
  (completion-category-overrides
   '((file (styles partial-completion)))))

(use-package marginalia
  :init
  (marginalia-mode))
```

Keyboard shortcuts menu

The Which-Key package improves the discoverability of keyboard shortcuts with a popup in the minibuffer.

Due to the naming conventions in Emacs, most functions start with the package name, so some can be long. The problem is that the most interesting part of a function name is at the end of the string, so we don't want that to be hidden. This configuration widens the columns a bit to prevent truncated function names. This configuration also instructs Which-Key to order the list by function name rather than by key.

```
(use package which key
  :config
  (which-key-mode)
  :custom
  (which-key-max-description-length 40)
  (which-key-lighter nil)
  (which-key-sort-order 'which-key-description-order)
  :init
  (which-key-add-key-based-replacements
    "C-c w"   "Emacs Writing Studio"
    "C-c w b" "Bibliographic"
    "C-c w d" "Denote"
    "C-c w m" "Multimedia"
    "C-c w s" "Spelling and Grammar"
    "C-c w t" "Themes"
    "C-c w x" "Explore"))
```

Mouse use

This code snippet enables a contextual popup menu when clicking the right mouse button.

```
(when (display-graphic-p)
  (context-menu-mode))
```

Improved help functionality

Emacs is advertised as a "self-documenting text editor". While this is not entirely correct (if only computer code could document itself), every aspect of Emacs is documented within the source code.

Emacs has two levels of help. Firstly, there are the manuals for Emacs itself and some of the packages. Also each individual command and function contains documentation. The Helpful package by Wilfred Hughes adds contextual information to the built-in Emacs help. For example, when asking for documentation about a variable, the help file links to its customisation screen or the source code.

```
(use-package helpful
  :bind
  (("C-h f" . helpful-function)
   ("C-h x" . helpful-command)
   ("C-h k" . helpful-key)
   ("C-h v" . helpful-variable)))
```

Configure text modes

Emacs is principally designed for developing computer code, so it needs some modifications to enable writing text for humans. The config first ensures that Emacs does not try to install Text-Mode as a package, because it is built-in.

Secondly, we hook Visual Line Mode to Text Mode. Visual Line mode wraps long lines to the nearest word to fit in the current window, as is common in word processing software.

By default, Emacs does not replace text when you select a section and start typing, which is unusual behaviour when writing prose. The :init section enables a more common default so that selected text is deleted when typed over. The :custom section enables the page-up and page-down keys to scroll to the top or bottom of a buffer. This section also redefines the way Emacs defines a sentence (refer to section 7.3). The last variable saves any existing clipboard text into the kill ring for better operability between the operating system's clipboard and Emacs's kill ring.

```
(use-package text-mode
  :ensure
  nil
  :hook
  (text-mode . visual-line-mode)
  :init
  (delete-selection-mode t)
  :custom
  (sentence-end-double-space nil)
  (scroll-error-top-bottom t)
  (save-interprogram-paste-before-kill t))
```

Spellchecking

Writing without automated spell-checking would be quite annoying, even for the most experienced authors. The Flyspell package interfaces with the Hunspell software and the relevant dictionary to check spelling on the fly.

You must change the standard dictionary to your local variety by customising the `ews-hunspell-dictionaries` variable. EWS uses this particular variable because the dictionaries are set in two places to enable multilingual spelling. You can set multiple dictionaries for the same buffer. In my configuration I use `"en_AU,nl_NL"` so I can write in either the Australian variant of English or Dutch without having to change dictionaries. Section 4.6 explains how to use this package.

```
(use-package flyspell
  :custom
  (ispell-program-name "hunspell")
  (ispell-dictionary ews-hunspell-dictionaries)
  (flyspell-mark-duplications-flag nil) ;; Writegood mode does this
  (org-fold-core-style 'overlays) ;; Fix Org mode bug
```

```
:config
(ispell-set-spellchecker-params)
(ispell-hunspell-add-multi-dic ews-hunspell-dictionaries)
:hook
(text-mode . flyspell-mode)
:bind
(("C-c w s s" . ispell)
 ("C-;"       . flyspell-auto-correct-previous-word)))
```

Ricing Org mode

This part of the configuration sets a bunch of variables to improve the design of Org buffers. To learn what these variables do, use C-h v and enter the variable name.

Org has a plethora of variables to change its interface. You can add other variables or remove some to make Org look how you prefer. For example, to enable alphabetical lists and numerals, you must customise the org-list-allow-alphabetical variable to t. This adds a., A., a) and A) as additional options to number a list.

```
(use-package org
  :custom
  (org-startup-indented t)
  (org-hide-emphasis-markers t)
  (org-startup-with-inline-images t)
  (org-image-actual-width '(450))
  (org-pretty-entities t)
  (org-use-sub-superscripts "{}")
  (org-id-link-to-org-use-id t)
  (org-fold-catch-invisible-edits 'show))
```

The above code snippet hides emphasis markers from view for an uncluttered screen. Emphasis markers are the symbols used to indicate italics, bold and other font decorations, for example _italic_. Hiding the syntax of a plain text document is not ideal because it obfuscates essential information. The Org Appear package by Alice P. Hacker shows hidden markers in Org buffers when the cursor is used for an emphasised word, giving us the best of both worlds.

```
(use-package org-appear
  :hook
  (org-mode . org-appear-mode))
```

The Org Fragtog package is similar to Org Appear but for LaTeX snippets. It automatically toggles Org mode LaTeX fragment previews as the cursor enters and exits them. By default, the text is small and can become unreadable when changing between dark and light themes.

The `org-format-latex-options` variable controls the way Emacs presents fragments. This variable is a list with properties such as colours and size. The `plist-put` function lets you change options in the list. The foreground and background are set to take the same colour as your text. If you change from dark to light mode or vice versa, you should evaluate the `org-latex-preview` function (`C-c C-x C-l`) to change the preview images.

Automated LaTeX previews are disabled because they can delay loading a page and cause trouble when the user does not have LaTeX installed.

```
(use-package org-fragtog
  :after org
  :hook
  (org-mode . org-fragtog-mode)
  :custom
  (org-startup-with-latex-preview nil)
  (org-format-latex-options
   (plist-put org-format-latex-options :scale 2)
   (plist-put org-format-latex-options :foreground 'auto)
   (plist-put org-format-latex-options :background 'auto)))
```

The last package to modify Org buffers is Org Modern. However, most of the features have been switched off because it might be better for beginning users not to hide semantic symbols. You can experiment with changing these settings to change the look and feel of Org buffers.

```
(use-package org-modern
  :hook
  (org-mode . org-modern-mode)
  :custom
  (org-modern-table nil)
  (org-modern-keyword nil)
  (org-modern-timestamp nil)
  (org-modern-priority nil)
  (org-modern-checkbox nil)
  (org-modern-tag nil)
  (org-modern-block-name nil)
  (org-modern-keyword nil)
  (org-modern-footnote nil)
  (org-modern-internal-target nil)
  (org-modern-radio-target nil)
  (org-modern-statistics nil)
  (org-modern-progress nil))
```

Inspiration

Read e-books

The built-in Doc-View package can read various file formats with the assistance of external software. This configuration increases the resolution of the generated image file and raises the threshold for warning before opening large files to fifty MB (50×2^{20}). Section 5.1 explains how to use this package.

Reading PDF files requires the GhostScript or MuPDF package. When the Poppler package is available, you can convert a PDF to text for easier searching and copying. To view DjVu files, you need the DjVuLibre library to parse them.

```
(use-package doc-view
  :custom
  (doc-view-resolution 300)
  (large-file-warning-threshold (* 50 (expt 2 20))))
```

The Nov package by Vasilij Schneidermann provides valuable functionality for viewing ePub books inside Emacs. The init section ensures that any file with an epub extension is associated with this package. An ePub file is essentially a compressed website, so you will need the Zip program to enable reading these files. Refer to section 5.1 on how to read ePub files.

```
(use-package nov
  :init
  (add-to-list 'auto-mode-alist '("\\.epub\\'" . nov-mode)))
```

Emacs can read documents produced by standard office software. To achieve this, it converts these files to PDF with LibreOffice and presents them as such.

Bibliographies

These lines of code add two field types to BibTeX entries: keywords to help you order your literature and a link to a file so you can read any attachments in Emacs.

The `ews-register-bibtex` function assigns all files with the `.bib` extension in the directory stored in the `ews-bibliography-directory` variable to the list of global BibTeX files. You need to set this variable to the location where you store your bibliography. Section 5.2 explains creating and managing a bibliography. We use a special variable to ensure other variables have the same value.

```
(use-package bibtex
  :custom
  (bibtex-user-optional-fields
   '(("keywords" "Keywords to describe the entry" "")
     ("file"     "Relative or absolute path to attachments" "" )))
```

```
(bibtex-align-at-equal-sign t)
:config
(ews-bibtex-register)
:bind
(("C-c w b r" . ews-bibtex-register)))
```

The Biblio package enables you to extract literature from various databases.

```
(use-package biblio
  :bind
  (("C-c w b b" . ews-bibtex-biblio-lookup)))
```

Citar is the workhorse package for managing a bibliography and citations. It provides an interface between your text and the bibliography.

```
(use-package citar
  :defer t
  :custom
  (citar-bibliography ews-bibtex-files)
  :bind
  (("C-c w b o" . citar-open)))
```

Reading websites

The Elfeed package helps with reading RSS files, and the Elfeed-Org package lets you configure RSS feeds with an Org file. The EWS repository contains an example file. Read section 5.3 for more information on how to use this tool. Elfeed uses the cURL software to download feeds. If this software is unavailable, it will use a slower version built into Emacs.

```
(use-package elfeed
  :custom
  (elfeed-db-directory
    (expand-file-name "elfeed" user-emacs-directory))
```

```
  (elfeed-show-entry-switch 'display-buffer)
  :bind
  ("C-c w e" . elfeed))

(use-package elfeed-org
  :config
  (elfeed-org)
  :custom
  (rmh-elfeed-org-files
   (list (concat (file-name-as-directory (getenv "HOME"))
                 "elfeed.org")))))
```

The Org-Webtools package makes it easy to insert hyperlinks by converting the content of the kill ring to an Org hyperlink.

```
(use-package org-web-tools
  :bind
  (("C-c w w" . org-web-tools-insert-link-for-url)))
```

Playing multimedia files

The EMMS (Emacs MultiMedia System) package provides an interface to various multimedia players. You need one of these programs installed: mpg321, ogg123 (vorbis-tools), mplayer, mpv, or VLC.

```
(use-package emms
  :config
  (require 'emms-setup)
  (require 'emms-mpris)
  (emms-all)
  (emms-default-players)
  (emms-mpris-enable)
  :custom
  (emms-browser-covers #'emms-browser-cache-thumbnail-async)
  :bind
```

```
((("C-c w m b" . emms-browser)
  ("C-c w m e" . emms)
  ("C-c w m p" . emms-play-playlist )
  ("<XF86AudioPrev>" . emms-previous)
  ("<XF86AudioNext>" . emms-next)
  ("<XF86AudioPlay>" . emms-pause)))
```

Opening files with external software

The OpenWith package by Markus Trisk lets you open files in external software. Refer to sections 5.5 and 6.4 for further details.

```
(use-package openwith
  :config
  (openwith-mode t)
  :custom
  (openwith-associations nil))
```

Ideation

Org capture

The possibilities for capture templates are extensive and depend on your use cases. This configuration is only an example of the options. The Org documentation provides lots of detail (C-h R org <ret> capture). The default Org settings save your fleeting notes to a hidden file (~/.notes.org). Customise the org-default-notes-file variable.

```
(use-package org
  :bind
  ((("C-c c" . org-capture)
   ("C-c l" . org-store-link))
  :custom
  (org-capture-templates
```

```
'(("f" "Fleeting note"
   item
   (file+headline org-default-notes-file "Notes")
   "- %?")
  ("p" "Permanent note" plain
   (file denote-last-path)
   #'denote-org-capture
   :no-save t
   :immediate-finish nil
   :kill-buffer t
   :jump-to-captured t)
  ("t" "New task" entry
   (file+headline org-default-notes-file "Tasks")
   "* TODO %i%?"))))
```

Denote

Denote is a flexible note-taking and file management package. Refer to 6.4 or the extensive Denote manual with C-h R denote. At a minimum, you need to configure the denote-directory variable to indicate the location of your notes.

The EWS package includes a convenience function to improve how Denote displays links to attachments, linked to the denote-link-description-function.

```
(use-package denote
  :defer t
  :custom
  (denote-sort-keywords t)
  (denote-link-description-function #'ews-denote-link-description-title-case)
  (denote-rename-buffer-mode 1)
  :hook
  (dired-mode . denote-dired-mode)
  :custom-face
  (denote-faces-link ((t (:slant italic))))
  :bind
```

```
(("C-c w d b" . denote-find-backlink)
 ("C-c w d d" . denote-date)
 ("C-c w d l" . denote-find-link)
 ("C-c w d i" . denote-link-or-create)
 ("C-c w d k" . denote-rename-file-keywords)
 ("C-c w d n" . denote)
 ("C-c w d r" . denote-rename-file)
 ("C-c w d R" . denote-rename-file-using-front-matter)))
```

The Denote developers provide an ecosystem of packages that enhance functionality, two of which are enabled in EWS.

```
(use-package denote-journal)

(use-package denote-org
  :bind
  (("C-c w d h" . denote-org-link-to-heading)))

(use-package denote-sequence)
```

The Consult package provides some convenience functionality to make life in Emacs easier in many ways. The `consult-grep` function lets you search through files in the current directory. The search functionality requires access to the Grep software. The `consult-org-heading` command provides a table of contents of the Org mode file to quickly move around a large file.

Consult has a lot more functionality that replaces some base Emacs commands with more convenient version. Most of these have not been enabled to ensure we stay as close as possible to vanilla Emacs. The Consult documentation provides detailed descriptions of these enhanced commands.

```
(use-package consult
  :bind
  (("C-c w h" . consult-org-heading)
```

```
("C-c w g" . consult-grep))
:config
(add-to-list 'consult-preview-allowed-hooks 'visual-line-mode))
```

Consult Notes is a convenience package that builds on Consult. It provides access to Denote files and also lets you search through your notes.

```
(use-package consult-notes
  :custom
  (consult-notes-denote-display-keywords-indicator "_")
  :bind
  (("C-c w d f" . consult-notes)
   ("C-c w d g" . consult-notes-search-in-all-notes))
  :init
  (consult-notes-denote-mode))
```

The Citar-Denote package lets you create a many-to-many relationship between your Denote notes and items in your bibliography (section 6.4).

```
(use-package citar-denote
  :custom
  (citar-open-always-create-notes t)
  :init
  (citar-denote-mode)
  :bind
  (("C-c w b c" . citar-create-note)
   ("C-c w b n" . citar-denote-open-note)
   ("C-c w b x" . citar-denote-nocite)
   :map org-mode-map
   ("C-c w b k" . citar-denote-add-citekey)
   ("C-c w b K" . citar-denote-remove-citekey)
   ("C-c w b d" . citar-denote-dwim)
   ("C-c w b e" . citar-denote-open-reference-entry)))
```

The Denote-Explore package provides convenience functions to manage your collection of notes and attachments (section 6.6).

```
(use-package denote-explore
  :bind
  (;; Statistics
   ("C-c w x c" . denote-explore-count-notes)
   ("C-c w x C" . denote-explore-count-keywords)
   ("C-c w x b" . denote-explore-barchart-keywords)
   ("C-c w x e" . denote-explore-barchart-filetypes)
   ;; Random walks
   ("C-c w x r" . denote-explore-random-note)
   ("C-c w x l" . denote-explore-random-link)
   ("C-c w x k" . denote-explore-random-keyword)
   ("C-c w x x" . denote-explore-random-regex)
   ;; Denote Janitor
   ("C-c w x d" . denote-explore-identify-duplicate-notes)
   ("C-c w x z" . denote-explore-zero-keywords)
   ("C-c w x s" . denote-explore-single-keywords)
   ("C-c w x o" . denote-explore-sort-keywords)
   ("C-c w x w" . denote-explore-rename-keyword)
   ;; Visualise denote
   ("C-c w x n" . denote-explore-network)
   ("C-c w x v" . denote-explore-network-regenerate)
   ("C-c w x D" . denote-explore-barchart-degree)))
```

Production

Managing the writing process

The EWS repository provides some Org-related convenience files for inserting notes, drawers, and counting words. At this stage, the screenshot command is experimental.

```
(use-package org
  :bind
  (:map org-mode-map
        ("C-c w n" . ews-org-insert-notes-drawer)
```

```
("C-c w p" . ews-org-insert-screenshot)
("C-c w c" . ews-org-count-words)))
```

The Olivetti package removes distractions from the screen and converts your Emacs session to an electronic typewriter. The `ews-olivetti` function stores the screen configuration before you activate the distraction-free writing mode. When you disable Olivetti mode with this function then the original configuration is restored.

```
(use-package olivetti
  :demand t
  :bind
  (("C-c w o" . ews-olivetti)))
```

Vundo provides a graphical view of the various versions of the current buffer.

```
(use-package vundo
  :bind
  (("C-M-/" . vundo)))
```

Citations

This configuration sets the global bibliography equal to the `ews-bibtex-files` variable. To set this variable, configure the `ews-bibtex-directory` to register bibliography files and run the `ews-bibtex-register` function every time you add new bib-files.

```
(require 'oc-natbib)
(require 'oc-csl)

(setq org-cite-global-bibliography ews-bibtex-files
      org-cite-insert-processor 'citar
      org-cite-follow-processor 'citar
      org-cite-activate-processor 'citar)
```

Quality assurance

Emacs can hook into the dictionary server at dict.org, for definitions and a thesaurus. Refer to section 7.2 for details.

```
(use-package dictionary
  :custom
  (dictionary-server "dict.org")
  :bind
  (("C-c w s d" . dictionary-lookup-definition)))
```

The Writegood package helps to detect weasel words, passive writing, and repeated words. It also contains functions to estimate a text's complexity using the Flesch-Kincaid test.

```
(use-package writegood-mode
  :bind
  (("C-c w s r" . writegood-reading-ease))
  :hook
  (text-mode . writegood-mode))
```

The TitleCase package strives for the most accurate title-casing of sentences, lines, and regions of text in English prose. You can customise the titlecase-style variable

The EWS convenience function can do this for all headings in an Org file to ensure consistency (section 7.2).

```
(use-package titlecase
  :bind
  (("C-c w s t" . titlecase-dwim)
   ("C-c w s c" . ews-org-headings-titlecase)))
```

Abbreviations

Abbrev mode is a built-in program that helps you speed up your writing by defining abbreviations and common spelling mistakes and automatically replacing them with words, sentences, or complete paragraphs.

```
(add-hook 'text-mode-hook 'abbrev-mode)
```

The Lorem Ipsum generator can be helpful when designing a document's layout. This package inserts dummy Latin text into a buffer.

```
(use-package lorem-ipsum
  :custom
  (lorem-ipsum-list-bullet "- ") ;; Org mode bullets
  :init
  (setq lorem-ipsum-sentence-separator
        (if sentence-end-double-space "  " " "))
  :bind
  (("C-c w s i" . lorem-ipsum-insert-paragraphs)))
```

Version control

The built-in Ediff package compares different files and shows their differences. It also lets you decide how to merge the two versions, like a tracked-changes function in a Word processor. The `ediff` family of functions does not split its windows nicely by default, so these settings make the program more straightforward to use.

Advanced version control requires a Version Control System, such as Git.

```
(use-package ediff
  :ensure nil
  :custom
  (ediff-keep-variants nil)
  (ediff-split-window-function 'split-window-horizontally)
  (ediff-window-setup-function 'ediff-setup-windows-plain))
```

Other text in modes

Org is fantastic, but it is not the only text mode useful for authors. EWS installs both Markdown and Fountain. Refer to section 7.5 for details.

```
(use-package fountain-mode)
(use-package markdown-mode)
```

Publication

Basic settings

This snippet sets some basic export settings for org mode. You can either set these as variable to apply them to all files by default, or insert them as keywords in your front matter. The timestamp for exporting files is set to the European date format of day, month, and year. If you publish for American audiences, perhaps you like to modify the `org-export-date-timestamp-format` to "%B %e %Y". These letters stand for the full name of the month, the day number without leading zero, and the year in four digits. See the documentation of the `format-time-string` function for details on how to format dates in other methods. Read the Export Settings section in to Org manual for a detailed description of the possible configurations.

```
(use-package org
  :custom
  (org-export-with-drawers nil)
  (org-export-with-todo-keywords nil)
  (org-export-with-toc nil)
  (org-export-with-smart-quotes t)
  (org-export-date-timestamp-format "%e %B %Y"))
```

Epub

The ox-ePub package exports Org files to the most common e-book format. The `ox-org` code negates some issues with the table of contents (section 8.5).

```
(use-package ox-epub
  :demand t
  :init
  (require 'ox-org))
```

LaTeX

This configuration part defines the export process from Org to TeX to PDF. This setup also removes any temporary files created in the process. You will obviously need a working version of LaTeX with all relevant packages installed on your computer.

```
(use-package ox-latex
  :ensure nil
  :demand t
  :custom
  ;; Multiple LaTeX passes for bibliographies
  (org-latex-pdf-process
   '("pdflatex -interaction nonstopmode -output-directory %o %f"
     "bibtex %b"
     "pdflatex -shell-escape -interaction nonstopmode -output-directory %o %f"
     "pdflatex -shell-escape -interaction nonstopmode -output-directory %o %f"))
  ;; Clean temporary files after export
  (org-latex-logfiles-extensions
   (quote ("lof" "lot" "tex~" "aux" "idx" "log" "out"
           "toc" "nav" "snm" "vrb" "dvi" "fdb_latexmk"
           "blg" "brf" "fls" "entoc" "ps" "spl" "bbl"
           "tex" "bcf")))))
```

The next section defines the EWS document class, which is used to produce the paperback version of this book. The first part of the code defines the name used in the Org file, in this case #+latex_class: ews. The next par is the preamble in LaTeX code. Note that backslashes need to be escaped by using two of them. Org also adds standard packages, read the documentation for org-latex-classes for details on how to modify the standard inclusions. The last section defines how the heading levels in the Org file are translated to LaTeX commands. This code defines the first three Org heading levels.

```
(with-eval-after-load 'ox-latex
  (add-to-list
   'org-latex-classes
   '("ews"
     "\\documentclass[11pt, twoside, hidelinks]{memoir}
        \\setstocksize{9.25in}{7.5in}
        \\settrimmedsize{\\stockheight}{\\stockwidth}{*}
        \\setlrmarginsandblock{1.5in}{1in}{*}
        \\setulmarginsandblock{1in}{1.5in}{*}
        \\checkandfixthelayout
        \\layout
        \\setcounter{tocdepth}{0}
        \\renewcommand{\\baselinestretch}{1.25}
        \\setheadfoot{0.5in}{0.75in}
        \\setlength{\\footskip}{0.8in}
        \\chapterstyle{bianchi}
        \\setsecheadstyle{\\normalfont \\raggedright \\textbf}
        \\setsubsecheadstyle{\\normalfont \\raggedright \\emph}
        \\setsubsubsecheadstyle{\\normalfont\\centering}
        \\pagestyle{myheadings}
        \\usepackage[font={small, it}]{caption}
        \\usepackage{ccicons}
        \\usepackage{ebgaramond}
        \\usepackage[authoryear]{natbib}
        \\bibliographystyle{apalike}
        \\usepackage{svg}
\\hyphenation{mini-buffer}"
     ("\\chapter{%s}" . "\\chapter*{%s}")
     ("\\section{%s}" . "\\section*{%s}")
     ("\\subsection{%s}" . "\\subsection*{%s}")
     ("\\subsubsection{%s}" . "\\subsubsection*{%s}"))))
```

Administration

Getting Things Done

The Org configuration for managing actions and projects sets a custom agenda item that shows the agenda for the next three days, a list of to-do items marked NEXT, and a list of items marked WAIT.

The org-agenda-custom-commands variable provides a highly flexible system for crafting agenda views. You could, for example, build an agenda for your private actions and one for your work (section 9.1).

```
(use-package org
  :custom
  (org-agenda-custom-commands
   '(("e" "Agenda, next actions and waiting"
      ((agenda "" ((org-agenda-overriding-header "Next three days:")
                   (org-agenda-span 3)
                   (org-agenda-start-on-weekday nil)))
       (todo "NEXT" ((org-agenda-overriding-header "Next Actions:")))
       (todo "WAIT" ((org-agenda-overriding-header "Waiting:")))))))
  :bind
  (("C-c a" . org-agenda)))
```

Manage files

The Dired package is a convenient and powerful tool for organising your drives and accessing your information. Dired lists files and directories in alphabetical order. I prefer a different view, which shows directories on top and files below them. The variable called dired-listing-switches determines how files are displayed in a Dired buffer.

The dired-dwim-target variable instructs Emacs to guess a default target directory. This means that if a Dired buffer is displayed in another window, it uses that directory instead of this Dired buffer's current directory. This setting makes it easier to copy or move files between directories.

The `delete-by-moving-to-trash` variable moves deleted files to the wastebasket instead of vanishing them into thin air, so you are less likely to loose valuable work.

The last line in this part of the configuration enables opening new directories in the same buffer as the current one (using the a key), preventing littering your session with Dired buffers. The first time you use this, Emacs asks you to confirm whether you would like to use this option.

```
(use-package dired
  :ensure
  nil
  :commands
  (dired dired-jump)
  :custom
  (dired-listing-switches
   "-goah --group-directories-first --time-style=long-iso")
  (dired-dwim-target t)
  (delete-by-moving-to-trash t)
  :init
  (put 'dired-find-alternate-file 'disabled nil))
```

The default setting for Dired is to show hidden files, even though they are hidden for a reason. This configuration uses `dired-omit-mode` to remove these hidden files from view. You can toggle this behaviour with the full stop key.

```
(use-package dired
  :ensure nil
  :hook (dired-mode . dired-omit-mode)
  :bind (:map dired-mode-map
              ( "."     . dired-omit-mode))
  :custom (dired-omit-files "^\\.[a-zA-Z0-9]+"))
```

This next bit of configuration defines how Emacs manages automated backups. The default setting is that the system stores these files in the folder where the original files live, cluttering folders with copies of your stuff.

The setting below modifies the `backup-directory-alist` variable so that Emacs saves all backups (indicated by " . ") in the `bak` subdirectory of your init folder. Alternatively, you could instruct Emacs not to save backups by setting `make-backup-files` to `nil`. I prefer keeping backups as they have saved my bacon a few times.

This configuration also eliminates lock files, which are only useful when working in shared folders. Lock files prevent other users from opening a file when another user is already editing it, but create a lot of clutter when writing by yourself. Change this variable to `t` if you collaborate with others or maintain fles on multiple systems through a file-sharing service such as Nextcloud.

```
(setq-default backup-directory-alist
              '(("." . ,(expand-file-name "backups/" user-emacs-directory)))
              version-control t
              delete-old-versions t
              create-lockfiles nil)
```

Emacs saves a list of recent files using the `recentf` package. This package maintains a list of recently opened files and makes it easy to visit them. The recent files list is automatically saved across Emacs sessions. By default, the recent files mode stores the last twenty opened files, which you can change by adjusting the `recentf-max-saved-items` variable, which in EWS is fifty.

```
(use-package recentf
  :config
  (recentf-mode t)
  :custom
  (recentf-max-saved-items 50)
  :bind
  (("C-c w r" . recentf-open)))
```

This last file package enables you to set bookmarks for your favourite locations. The `bookmark-save-flag` is set to one, so the bookmarks file is saved every time you add a new one. The default value only saves it when you exit Emacs, which means you could lose bookmarks in the unlikely event of an Emacs or system crash.

```
(use-package bookmark
  :custom
  (bookmark-save-flag 1)
  :bind
  ("C-x r d" . bookmark-delete))
```

Viewing images

Emacs has two modes for viewing and managing images. The image viewer shows individual images, but you can also browse through a directory with the left and right arrow keys.

To enable image manipulation, you will need to install ImageMagic.

Using C-<ret> opens an image in the Dired buffer in your favourite editor. The `image-dired-external-viewer` variable defines the program you use to edit pictures, in my case GIMP, the GNU Image Manipulation Program.

```
(use-package emacs
  :custom
  (image-dired-external-viewer "gimp")
  :bind
  ((:map image-mode-map
         ("k" . image-kill-buffer)
         ("<right>" . image-next-file)
         ("<left>"  . image-previous-file))
   (:map dired-mode-map
         ("C-<return>" . image-dired-dired-display-external)))) 
```

The built-in Image-Dired package can generate thumbnails from within a Dired buffer and let you work on images from there.

```
(use-package image-dired
  :bind
  (("C-c w I" . image-dired))
  (:map image-dired-thumbnail-mode-map
        ("C-<right>" . image-dired-display-next)
        ("C-<left>"  . image-dired-display-previous)))
```

Customisations

You can access the `customise-variable` function with the C-c w v shortcut.

```
(keymap-global-set "C-c w v" 'customize-variable)
```

Any changes made by the Emacs customisation system in EWS are stored in `custom.el` instead of directly to the init file. This approach prevents the customisation system from modifying the initialisation file. The `custom.el` file is loaded when available. If variables are set in both the custom and the init files, the `custom.el` file takes preference.

```
(setq-default custom-file (expand-file-name
                           "custom.el"
                           user-emacs-directory))

(load custom-file :no-error-if-file-is-missing)
```

References

Ahrens, S. (2017). *How to Take Smart Notes: One Simple Technique to Boost Writing, Learning and Thinking: For Students, Academics and Nonfiction Book Writers*. North Charleston, SC: CreateSpace.

Allen, D. (2005). *Getting Things Done: The Art of Stress-Free Productivity*. London: Piatkus.

Berry, R. (1988). Common User Access. A consistent and usable human-computer interface for the SAA environments. *Ibm systems journal, 27*(3), 281–300. doi: 10.1147/sj.273.0281

Blevins, J. R. (2017). *Guide to Markdown Mode for Emacs*. LeanPub.

Bottiroli, S., Rosi, A., Russo, R., Vecchi, T., & Cavallini, E. (2014). The cognitive effects of listening to background music on older adults: Processing speed improves with upbeat music, while memory seems to benefit from both upbeat and downbeat music. *Frontiers in aging neuroscience, 6*. doi: 10.3389/fnagi.2014.00284

Cameron, D. (2005). *Learning GNU Emacs* (3rd ed). Sebastopol, CA: O'Reilly.

Clark, A., & Chalmers, D. (1998). The Extended Mind. *Analysis, 58*(1), 7–19. doi: 10.1093/analys/58.1.7

Covey, S. R. (1990). *The Seven Habits of Highly Effective People: Restoring the Character Ethic* (1st Fireside ed). New York: Fireside Book.

Even-Ezra, A. (2021). *Lines of Thought: Branching Diagrams and the Medieval Mind*. Chicago: The University of Chicago Press.

Ferriss, T. (2011). *The 4-Hour Work Week. Escape the 9-5, Live Anywhere and Join the New Rich*. London: Vermilion.

Forte, T. (2022). *Building a Second Brain: A Proven Method to Organise Your Digital Life and Unlock Your Creative Potential*. London: Profile Books Ltd.

Fox, J., & Tigchelaar, M. (2015). Creating an engineering academic formulas list. *Journal of Teaching English for Specific and Academic Purposes, 3*(2), 295–304.

Johnson, T. (2022). Emacs as a tool for modern science: The use of open source tools to improve scientific workflows. *Johnson Matthey Technology Review, 66*(2), 122–129. doi: 10.1595/205651322x16316969040478

Kadavy, D. (2021). *Digital Zettelkasten: Principles, Methods, & Examples*. Kindle Edition.

Kahn, C. H. (1997). *Plato and the Socratic Dialogue*. Cambridge University Press. doi: 10.1017/cbo9780511585579.013

Kelly, L. (2016). *The Memory Code: The Traditional Aboriginal Memory Technique that Unlocks the Secrets of Stonehenge, Easter Island and Ancient Monuments the World Over*. Allen & Unwin.

Khalili, A., & Auer, S. (2015). WYSIWYM — Integrated visualization, exploration and authoring of semantically enriched un-structured content. *Semantic Web, 6*(3), 259–275. doi: 10.3233/sw-140157

Kim, K., Erickson, A., Lambert, A., Bruder, G., & Welch, G. (2019). Effects of dark mode on visual fatigue and acuity in optical see-through head-mounted displays. *Symposium on Spatial User Interaction*. ACM. doi: 10.1145/3357251.3357584

Knuth, D. E. (1984). *The TeXbook*. Reading, Massachusetts: Addison-Wesley.

König, R. (2020). *Getting yourself organized with Org-mode. A supplement for the video course*. Udemy course.

Lamport, L. (1994). *LATEX: A document preparation system: User's guide and reference manual* (2nd ed). Reading, Mass: Addison-Wesley Pub. Co.

Landin, P. J. (1964). The mechanical evaluation of expressions. *The Computer Journal, 6*(4), 308–320. doi: 10.1093/comjnl/6.4.308

Lipovetsky, S. (2023). Readability indices structure and optimal features. *Axioms, 12*(5), 421. doi: 10.3390/axioms12050421

Monnier, S., & Sperber, M. (2020). Evolution of Emacs Lisp. *Proceedings of the ACM on Programming Languages, 4*(74), 1–55. doi: 10.1145/3386324

Mueller, P. A., & Oppenheimer, D. M. (2014). The pen is mightier than the keyboard: Advantages of longhand over laptop note taking. *Psychological Science, 25*(6), 1159–1168. doi: 10.1177/0956797614524581

Omanson, R., Miller, C. S., Young, E., & Schwantes, D. (2010). *Comparison of mouse and keyboard efficiency.* 600–404.

Petersen, M. (2022). *Mastering Emacs.*

Pohle, J., & Thiel, T. (2020). Digital sovereignty. *Internet Policy Review, 9*(4). doi: 10.14763/2020.4.1532

Prevos, P. (2013). *Perspectives on Magic: Scientific Views of Theatrical Magic.* Third Hemisphere.

Rayner, K., Slattery, T., Drieghe, D., & Liversedge, S. (2011). Eye movements and word skipping during reading: Effects of word length and predictability. *Journal of Experimental Psychology: Human Perception and Performance, 23*(2), 514–528.

Ryder, C. (2021). *The bullet journal method.* London: 4th Estate.

Stallman, R. (2023). *GNU Emacs Manual.* Free Software Foundation. Retrieved from `https://www.gnu.org/software/emacs/manual/emacs.html`

Stallman, R. M. (1981a). *Emacs manual for its users.* Retrieved from `http://hdl.handle.net/1721.1/6329`

Stallman, R. M. (1981b). EMACS the extensible, customizable self-documenting display editor. *Acm sigoa newsletter, 2*(1-2), 147–156. doi: 10.1145/1159890.806466

Stavrou, P. (2024). *Re: Advice regarding note-taking in emacs.* Retrieved from `https://protesilaos.com/`

Stephenson, N. (1999). *In the beginning . was the command line.* Avon Books.

Stickgold, R., Malia, A., Maguire, D., Roddenberry, D., & O'Connor, M. (2000). Replaying the game: Hypnagogic images in normals and amnesics. *Science*, *290*(5490), 350–353. doi: 10.1126/science.290.5490.350

Tesler, L. (2012). A personal history of modeless text editing and cut/copy-paste. *Interactions*, *19*(4), 70–75. doi: 10.1145/2212877.2212896

Tognazzini, B. (1992). *Tog on Interface*. Reading, Mass: Addison-Wesley.

Tognazzini, B. (1993). Principles, techniques, and ethics of stage magic and their application to human interface design. *Proceedings of the Interact '93 and CHI '93 Conference on Human Factors in Computing Systems*, 355–362. Amsterdam. doi: 10.1145/169059.169284

Tracy, B. (2016). *Eat That Frog! 21 Great Ways to Stop Procrastinating and Get More Done in Less Time*. London: Hodder.

Travis, B. E., & Waldt, D. C. (1995). Evolution of publishing systems. In *The SGML Implementation Guide* (pp. 21–36). Springer Berlin Heidelberg. doi: 10.1007/978-3-642-57860-1_2

Umejima, K., Ibaraki, T., Yamazaki, T., & Sakai, K. L. (2021). Paper notebooks vs. mobile devices: Brain activation differences during memory retrieval. *Frontiers in Behavioral Neuroscience*, *15*, 634158. doi: 10.3389/fnbeh.2021.634158

University of Chicago Press. (2017). *The Chicago Manual of Style* (Seventeenth edition). Chicago: The University of Chicago Press.

Watson, D. (2004). *Watson's Dictionary of Weasel Words, Contemporary Clichés, Cant & Management Jargon*. Milsons Point, N.S.W: Knopf.

www.ingramcontent.com/pod-product-compliance
Lightning Source LLC
Chambersburg PA
CBHW080358060326
40689CB00019B/4053